tear here

Ten Tips to Making the Most of Ta...

1. **Know your federal income tax bracket** by reviewin... card—and pay attention to state taxes, too. Some stat... interest and dividends.

2. **Buy municipal bonds issued in your state** if tax-free returns will put you ahead... the game—and if you live in a high-tax state. In most cases, these bonds will be free of both federal and state income tax.

3. **Buy individual bonds** with maturity dates tied to when you'll need the money. You're guaranteed the return of principal if you keep a bond to maturity, but you can make or lose money if you sell early.

4. **Buy shares of a national municipal bond fund** instead of a state-specific fund, if this will produce better after-tax returns. Stay short-term with funds for safety.

5. **Reinvest mutual fund dividends** to build your portfolio. But keep good records because dividends are taxed even if you don't take them in cash. You don't want to pay tax again on the same dividends when you sell your shares.

6. **Buy U.S. Treasury obligations** for absolute safety and partially tax-free returns—you pay federal income tax but no state income tax.

7. **Invest all you can in tax-deferred retirement accounts**, but pay attention to the complicated rules regarding withdrawals from these accounts, or you'll shoot yourself right in the tax trap foot.

8. **Check out the tax savings in college savings plans** if you have kids and grandkids.

9. **Check out the tax savings in owning your home**, and take advantage of mortgage interest and property tax deductions as well as tax breaks for job-related moving expenses and capital gains exclusions when you sell.

10. **Make gifts today and write a will for tomorrow**, and you can save big on taxes while you live. You'll also win the tax avoidance game when you die.

Equivalent Tax-Free and Taxable Yields

Tax Rates	4%	5%	6%	7%	8%
15%	4.71%	5.88%	7.06%	8.24%	9.41%
28%	5.56%	6.94%	8.33%	9.72%	11.11%
31%	5.80%	7.25%	8.70%	10.14%	11.59%
36%	6.25%	7.81%	9.38%	10.94%	12.50%
39.6%	6.62%	8.28%	9.93%	11.59%	13.25%

The higher your tax bracket, the more you'll gain from tax-free investing. In the 15 percent tax bracket, a 5 percent tax-free return is worth 5.88 percent in a taxable investment; paying a 15 percent tax leaves you with just about 5 percent. In the 39.6 percent bracket, however, a 5 percent tax-free return is the equivalent of earning 8.28 percent in a taxable investment.

alpha books

Tax Brackets and Rates for the 2000 Tax Year

Taxable Income (Married, Filing Jointly, and Surviving Spouses)	Tax Rate	Taxable Income (Single Taxpayers)
$0 to $43,850	15%	$0 to $26,250
$43,851 to $105,950	28%	$26,251 to $63,550
$105,951 to $161,450	31%	$63,551 to $132,600
$161,451 to $288,350	36%	$132,601 to $288,350
$288,351 and over	39.6%	$288,351 and over

Average Itemized Deductions

Adjusted Gross Income	Medical Expenses	Taxes	Interest	Contributions
$25,000–$30,000	$4,772	$2,312	$5,468	$1,577
$30,001–$35,000	$4,685	$2,615	$5,753	$1,607
$35,001–$40,000	$4,019	$2,861	$5,835	$1,562
$40,001–$45,000	$3,724	$3,155	$6,197	$1,562
$45,001–$50,000	$5,003	$3,420	$6,359	$1,744
$50,001–$55,000	$3,445	$3,762	$6,563	$1,810
$55,001–$60,000	$5,698	$4,052	$6,829	$1,851
$60,001–$75,000	$5,261	$4,664	$6,987	$1,982
$75,001–$100,000	$7,319	$6,114	$8,371	$2,491
$100,001–$200,000	$13,429	$9,459	$11,268	$3,620
$200,001–$500,000	$24,221	$20,493	$18,479	$8,002

These average deductions are for the 1997 tax year, the most recent available. Use them as guidelines, not as gospel; your own deductions must be documented.

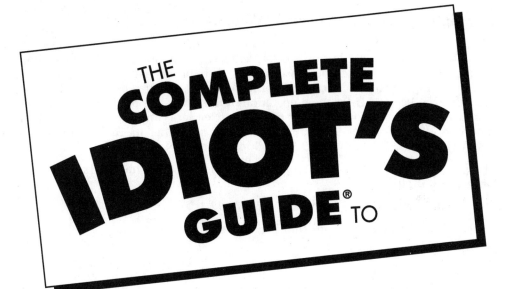

THE

COMPLETE IDIOT'S GUIDE® TO

Tax-Free Investing

by Grace W. Weinstein

alpha books

Macmillan USA, Inc.
201 West 103rd Street
Indianapolis, IN 46290

A Pearson Education Company

Copyright © 2000 by Grace W. Weinstein

All rights reserved. No part of this book shall be reproduced, stored in a retrieval system, or transmitted by any means, electronic, mechanical, photocopying, recording, or otherwise, without written permission from the publisher. No patent liability is assumed with respect to the use of the information contained herein. Although every precaution has been taken in the preparation of this book, the publisher and author assume no responsibility for errors or omissions. Neither is any liability assumed for damages resulting from the use of information contained herein. For information, address Alpha Books, 201 West 103rd Street, Indianapolis, IN 46290.

THE COMPLETE IDIOT'S GUIDE TO and Design are registered trademarks of Macmillan USA, Inc.

International Standard Book Number: 0-02-863892-1

Library of Congress Catalog Card Number: Available upon request.

02 01 00   8 7 6 5 4 3 2 1

Interpretation of the printing code: The rightmost number of the first series of numbers is the year of the book's printing; the rightmost number of the second series of numbers is the number of the book's printing. For example, a printing code of 00–1 shows that the first printing occurred in 2000.

Printed in the United States of America

Note: This publication contains the opinions and ideas of its author. It is intended to provide helpful and informative material on the subject matter covered. It is sold with the understanding that the author and publisher are not engaged in rendering professional services in the book. If the reader requires personal assistance or advice, a competent professional should be consulted.

The author and publisher specifically disclaim any responsibility for any liability, loss, or risk, personal or otherwise, which is incurred as a consequence, directly or indirectly, of the use and application of any of the contents of this book.

Publisher
Marie Butler-Knight

Product Manager
Phil Kitchel

Managing Editor
Cari Luna

Acquisitions Editor
Randy Ladenheim-Gil

Development Editor
Nancy D. Warner

Production Editor
Billy Fields

Copy Editor
Krista Hansing

Illustrator
Jody P. Schaeffer

Cover Designers
Mike Freeland
Kevin Spear

Book Designers
Scott Cook and Amy Adams of DesignLab

Indexer
Deborah Hittel

Layout/Proofreading
Svetlana Dominguez
Timothy Osborn
Wendy Ott

Contents at a Glance

Appendixes

Contents

Foreword

Don't believe the book title! This book's not for idiots. However, if you have a sense of humor and want to improve your financial life, but have minimal knowledge about tax-free investing, this is the book for you. Read on, and I'll tell you why.

I've been a financial planning practitioner for almost 20 years. During that time, I've had occasion to read far more than my share about personal financial planning. For the most part, I could have saved my time by shoving the material straight into the trash. Only occasionally do I come across a writer who conveys useful information. It's really rare to find one who conveys the information *and* is easy to read. When that happens, I make a note of the author and keep my eye out for subsequent articles or books. That's how I first met Grace Weinstein. I don't remember the subject of the first story of hers that I read, but I do remember being so impressed that I copied it for my partners and added her name to the top of my "look out for" list. Since my original discovery of Grace's work, I've had the privilege of reading many subsequent articles and books. I've never been disappointed.

When I was asked whether I would consider writing the foreword to Grace's new book, *The Complete Idiot's Guide to Tax-Free Investing*, I was not only complimented, but I was thrilled with the opportunity to alert others to her wonderful ability to simply and pleasantly convey important personal investment planning knowledge. Now that I've seen the actual text, I can tell you that it's a must for anyone interested in tax-free investing.

This book is chockfull of the necessary details you'll need to keep more money in your pocket and give Uncle Sam less. Starting right off with a detailed list of the income you can exclude from the tax troll, it continues with easily understood, solid tax-free investment advice. Some of the recommendations may seem contrary to common sense ("... you may sometimes do better in taxable investments than in tax-free"; "Owning six mutual funds doesn't mean that your portfolio is diversified"; and "... sell winners and invest in losers"). Other recommendations are adamant ("Whether your 401(k) at work or an Individual Retirement Account ... retirement plans are a must for every investor"). All the recommendations are worth heeding. They are on par with what I would expect from a highly paid and experienced financial planner. And there's more! *The Complete Idiot's Guide to Tax-Free Investing* doesn't just provide terrific advice, but it's also peppered with money-saving tax tips and useful warnings about potential tax traps. If you simply page through and pick up a few ideas from the series of "tips" and "traps," your pocketbook will be well rewarded. Bottom line, this book is written for real people. Buy it and read it; you'll not only enjoy it, but you'll also profit.

Harold Evensky, CFP, is a principal of Evensky, Brown & Katz in Coral Gables, Florida. Mr. Evensky received his Bachelor's and Master's degrees from Cornell

University. He is Chair of the International CFP Council and past Chair of the CFP Board of Governors, the Board of Appeals, and the CFP Board of Examiners. He has served on the national board of the International Association for Financial Planning and the Charles Schwab Institutional Advisory Council. He is a contributing writer for *Financial Planning Magazine* and Chair of the Editorial Advisory Board of the *Asia Financial Planning Journal,* and has served on the Editorial Advisory Board of the *Journal of Financial Planning.*

Mr. Evensky is an internationally recognized speaker on investment and financial planning issues. In addition, he has written for and is quoted frequently in the national press. He is the author of *Wealth Management,* published by McGraw/Hill, and *Sitting Duck Software,* published by PIE Technologies.

Introduction

This book may be called *The Complete Idiot's Guide to Tax-Free Investing*, but it takes a smart person like you to want to shelter hard-earned dollars from the tax collector.

You already know some ways to hold on to your money. I'm sure you put every dollar you can into tax-deferred retirement plans, as an example, and think about taxes when you invest. But thinking about taxes and knowing what to do to keep them under control can be two different things.

This book covers the whole range of tax-saving strategies. Of course, it delves into tax-free investing in a big way. But there's more—so much more, from handling your mortgage, to putting your kids through college, to thinking ahead to retirement and estate planning.

I'll give you the big picture in each of these areas, along with lots of tidbits that can make you a confident and tax-savvy investor. For instance, did you know that:

➤ Taking money out of a tax-sheltered retirement plan just one day early can cost big tax penalties?

➤ A vacation home can produce tax savings?

➤ Your kids can be great tax shelters—but you may not want to put college savings in their names?

➤ Sometimes a taxable investment gives a better return than a tax-free investment?

➤ You can save big tax bucks by giving money away during life instead of leaving it in your will?

Read on, and save money!

What You'll Learn in This Book

The Complete Idiot's Guide to Tax-Free Investing is divided into six parts.

Part 1, "More for You, Less for Uncle Sam," gives you the down-and-dirty on taxes—how federal tax rates are applied, the impact of state taxes, and a rundown of taxable, tax-deferred, and taxable investments. You'll learn how to look at investment opportunities in light of your own tax situation, and whether tax-free or taxable investments make the most sense for you.

Part 2, "Shelter Equals Shelter," describes the tax advantages of owning your own home—from mortgage interest and property tax deductions to the ins and outs of home offices, from home renovations to home equity loans and reverse mortgages. It describes what happens when you sell your house and covers the tax ramifications when that sale is due to a job change, divorce, or death. It also explores the tax consequences of owning a vacation home, whether you use the home yourself or turn it into rental property.

Part 3, "Kids Cost, Kids Save," deals with those bundles of joy, and sometimes dismay—your kids. You'll find information on tax deductions and tax credits related to children, and you'll get an in-depth discussion of the many tax-advantaged ways to save for their college education. One chapter in this section is especially for grandparents who want to give the grandchildren a head start in life.

Part 4, "Buying Futures," focuses on retirement planning. You'll find chapters on 401(k) plans, employer-funded traditional pension plans, Individual Retirement Accounts, retirement plans for the self-employed, and annuities. And don't miss this one—a chapter on holding on to your gains by being tax-smart when you start to take the money out.

Part 5, "Put Your Money to Work," is the one you've been waiting for, the section that covers investments. This section gives details on money market mutual funds, tax-free (and sometimes taxable) municipal bonds, Treasury obligations, mutual funds, and alternative investments—I call them "blue plate specials"—such as real estate investment trusts, closed-end mutual funds, unit investment trusts, and limited partnerships. Important: Don't skip the chapter on the tax consequences of all these investment vehicles—this is where you'll learn what you'll owe in taxes while you invest and when you sell.

Part 6, "End Game," deals with the unpleasant but tax-vital subjects of life insurance, estate planning, and wills. If you want to hold on to your tax gains and preserve them for your loved ones, these chapters are essential reading.

At the end, you'll find an appendix with resources for additional information and an appendix with a glossary.

Extras

For your reading pleasure, *The Complete Idiot's Guide to Tax-Free Investing* contains a variety of boxed sidebars. They'll all add to your knowledge in some way, but they do it differently. Here's the rundown:

Tax Traps

These point out pitfalls along the way to tax savings and tell you how to avoid them.

Tax Tips

These offer tidbits of advice, geared to specific points.

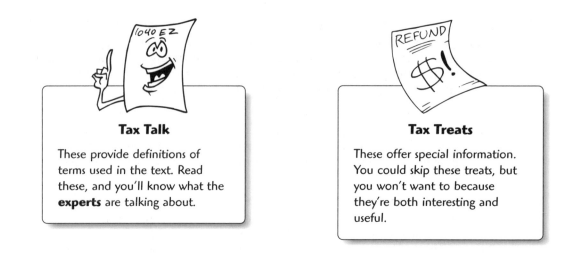

Tax Talk

These provide definitions of terms used in the text. Read these, and you'll know what the **experts** are talking about.

Tax Treats

These offer special information. You could skip these treats, but you won't want to because they're both interesting and useful.

Acknowledgments

No book is ever a solo effort. I'd like to thank the many people and organizations, too many to name, whose expertise was made available to me. Special thanks go to:

Richard Mayer and Janice Chapman, partners in Positive Financial Advisors, for reviewing Chapters 16 (Jan) and 23 (Rich); Daniel Pederson of The Savings Bond Informer, for reviewing Chapter 7; and Mary Dale Walters of CCH Incorporated, for putting the tax wisdom of CCH and its analysts at my disposal.

In addition, every word of *The Complete Idiot's Guide to Tax-Free Investing* was read— no, scrutinized—by our technical editor, Ed Slott. Ed is a Certified Public Accountant and a tax expert in Rockville Centre, New York, but he is also one of the most knowledgeable people in the United States on the subject of tax-deferred retirement plans. His newsletter, "Ed Slott's IRA Advisor," is an encyclopedia of information about the ins and outs of retirement plans. To Ed, my heartfelt thanks.

Special Thanks to the Technical Reviewer

The Complete Idiot's Guide to Tax-Free Investing was reviewed by an expert who double-checked the accuracy of what you'll learn here, to help us ensure that this book gives you everything you need to know about investments that will save money in taxes. Special thanks are extended to Ed Slott.

Trademarks

All terms mentioned in this book that are known to be or are suspected of being trademarks or service marks have been appropriately capitalized. Alpha Books and Macmillan USA, Inc., cannot attest to the accuracy of this information. Use of a term in this book should not be regarded as affecting the validity of any trademark or service mark.

Part 1

More for You, Less for Uncle Sam

"There's nothing certain but death and taxes" is a familiar saying and one that's oh so true. We can't do much about death, and we can't eliminate taxes, but we can take steps to minimize the taxes we must pay.

These chapters introduce a basic understanding of our tax structure, followed by a closer look at investments that are taxable, tax-sheltered, and tax-free. When you finish this part of The Complete Idiot's Guide to Tax-Free Investing, *you'll have a much better idea of which investments make the most sense for you, in your tax bracket, and you'll be ready to learn about the specific tax-saving strategies in succeeding chapters.*

Chapter 1

The Toll Taxes Take

> ## In This Chapter
>
> ➤ Realizing that you can't escape taxes but that you can try to keep them to a minimum
>
> ➤ Finding that some income isn't taxable at all
>
> ➤ Using deductions and credits to slash your tax burden
>
> ➤ Learning that an audit needn't be terrifying if you're prepared

Before you can embark on tax-sheltered investing, you have to understand how taxes work. It ain't easy, as the saying goes, because the U.S. tax structure is very complicated—so complicated that an explanation of the tax code by one respected tax publisher grew from 400 pages in 1913, when the income tax became a federal institution, to 42,560 pages in 1997!

Most of those pages, of course, don't apply to the ordinary doings of most ordinary folk. In this chapter, we'll tackle the highlights of tax law as they do apply.

"I Owe My Soul to the Company Store"

For 137 years, the United States did without a permanent income tax. There were a couple of brief attempts—one to finance the Civil War, and another in 1894 that was shot down by the Supreme Court in 1895—but the income tax didn't become a permanent part of our lives until 1913. At that, it took an amendment to the U.S. Constitution, the 16th amendment, to legalize the concept.

Tax Tips

When do all of your earnings belong to you? Not until May 3, in the year 2000, the latest "Tax Freedom Day" ever calculated by the Tax Foundation in its yearly roundup of how much of the year Americans work for the tax collector. In 1913, the year the federal income tax was enacted, Tax Freedom Day would have arrived on January 30.

The Tariff Act of 1913 imposed an annual tax of 1 percent on individuals with a net income above $3,000—a lot more money in 1913 than it is today, especially because a $1,000 exemption was allowed for a husband or wife (but not both). The law itself took 16 pages; its interpretation ran to 400 pages.

Since then, the tax code has been amended, revised, and reformed repeatedly, to the point where some political candidates suggest throwing the whole thing out and starting over again. Meanwhile, we must deal with what we have.

Graduating with Honors

The federal income tax is a graduated tax, with rates rising from 15 percent to a maximum of 39.6 percent. The federal income tax is also an instrument of social policy, offering tax breaks to encourage home ownership, education, investment, and retirement planning. You can take advantage of these special tax breaks—described throughout this book—to reduce your tax burden.

New York hotel magnate Leona Helmsley may have echoed popular opinion when she reportedly said, "Only the little people pay income tax." Many people believe that the rich exploit tax breaks that the rest of us can't reach. But Mark Luscombe, federal tax analyst for CCH Incorporated, claims that "people with incomes between $30,000 and $100,000 probably have the greatest ability to take advantage of the various breaks in the tax code." Those breaks include tax-qualified retirement plans, childcare credits, deductible college loan interest, and tax-free employer-paid health insurance, many of which are unavailable to people with incomes over a specified level.

Being Bracketed

Currently there are five income tax brackets, but the qualifying incomes change each year. Married couples filing jointly are in the 15 percent bracket for income earned in the year 2000 (tax returns due in 2001) with taxable income up to $43,850. For single taxpayers, the 15 percent bracket is on income up to $26,250. At the other end of the scale, both married and single taxpayers are in the 39.6 percent bracket at income exceeding $288,350. The following table shows the tax brackets for 2000.

Tax Brackets in the Year 2000

Taxable Income (Married, Filing Jointly, and Surviving Spouses)	Tax Rate	Taxable Income (Single Taxpayers)
$0–$43,850	15%	$0–$26,250
$43,851–$105,950	28%	$26,251–$63,550
$105,951–$161,450	31%	$63,551–$132,600
$161,451–$288,350	36%	$132,601–$288,350
$288,351 and over	39.6%	$288,351 and over

Source: CCH Incorporated

But taxable income is not the same thing as all the income you earn. Here's where there are opportunities to cut your tax bill.

What's Taxable, What's Not

Your gross income consists of every item of income from every source—including the cash from your last tag sale—unless that income is specifically excluded in the tax law. Gross income includes wages, salary, tips, business receipts, interest and dividends, royalties, annuities, pensions, and so on.

To figure your taxable income, gross income is reduced by *exclusions* and by *deductions,* and the resulting tax liability may further be reduced by *credits*. Each of these will be explained in the sections to follow.

Exclusions

Some income is excluded from tax right from the start. For example, you do not have to count these items:

➤ Distributions from Education IRAs used for qualified educational expenses (see Chapter 8, "Education Tax Breaks").

➤ Distributions from Roth IRAs that have been in effect for five years, when the owner is past age 59½ (see Chapter 12, "On Your Own [IRA] Account").

Tax Talk

Exclusions are items not subject to tax; many need not even be listed on your tax return.
Deductions reduce the amount of taxable income. The actual saving from a deduction depends on your tax bracket; if you are in the 28 percent tax bracket, you save 28 cents on every dollar spent on a deductible item.
Credits are a direct reduction of the tax owed; a dollar credit is a dollar saved.

➤ Gifts and inheritances, although income from both is taxable (see Chapter 24, "You Can't Take It with You").

➤ Interest on municipal bonds (see Chapter 17, "Muni Madness").

➤ Life insurance death benefits (see Chapter 23, "Your Money for Your Life").

➤ Scholarships and fellowships made to degree candidates.

➤ Disability insurance benefits, if you paid the premiums. Benefits based on employer-paid premiums are taxable to the recipient.

➤ Proceeds of damage awards for physical injury.

➤ Up to $500,000 from the profit on the sale of a home for married couples filing jointly, up to $250,000 for a single taxpayer (see Chapter 4, "Territorial Imperatives").

Deductions

Every taxpayer is entitled to a standard deduction. For tax returns filed in 2001 for the 2000 tax year, the standard deduction is $7,350 for married couples filing jointly, and $4,400 for single taxpayers. These deductions are increased for taxpayers who are over age 65 or are blind—by $850 for married taxpayers and by $1,050 for single taxpayers.

If your deductions add up to more than the standard deduction, you should itemize your deductions on Schedule A of Form 1040.

Itemized deductions include the following:

➤ Interest on a home mortgage and on home equity loans.

➤ Charitable contributions.

➤ State and local income taxes.

➤ Real estate and property taxes.

➤ Medical expenses in excess of 7.5 percent of adjusted gross income.

➤ Casualty and theft losses in excess of 10 percent of adjusted gross income plus $100.

➤ Miscellaneous itemized deductions exceeding 2 percent of adjusted gross income. This category includes tax preparation fees, investment expenses, safe-deposit box fees, union dues, and unreimbursed employee business expenses.

Deductions mean more to middle-income taxpayers because they phase out as you earn more. For the 2000 tax year, taxpayers must reduce itemized deductions by 3 percent of adjusted gross income in excess of $128,950—except that medical expenses and casualty losses are not included in the phaseout, and deductions subject to phaseout cannot be reduced by more than 80 percent.

It's important to keep good records substantiating your deductions. The IRS releases information about average deductions in various income categories. The information is fun reading, but don't take it to mean that you can claim the same deductions. The following table shows the average itemized deductions for 1997; because the IRS is always a couple of years behind in releasing the information, this is the most recent information available at this writing.

Average Itemized Deductions, 1997

Adjusted Gross Income	Medical Expenses	Taxes	Interest	Contributions
$25,000–$30,000	$4,772	$2,312	$5,468	$1,577
$30,001–$35,000	$4,685	$2,615	$5,753	$1,607
$35,001–$40,000	$4,019	$2,861	$5,835	$1,562
$40,001–$45,000	$3,724	$3,155	$6,197	$1,562
$45,001–$50,000	$5,003	$3,420	$6,359	$1,744
$50,001–$55,000	$3,445	$3,762	$6,563	$1,810
$55,001–$60,000	$5,698	$4,052	$6,829	$1,851
$60,001–$75,000	$5,261	$4,664	$6,987	$1,982
$75,001–$100,000	$7,319	$6,114	$8,371	$2,491
$100,001–$200,000	$13,429	$9,459	$11,268	$3,620
$200,001–$500,000	$24,221	$20,493	$18,479	$8,002

Source: CCH Incorporated

Credits

Tax credits are dollar-for-dollar reductions in the amount of tax you owe, and are therefore more valuable than tax deductions.

Tax credits include education credits (see Chapter 8), the child and dependent care credit, a credit for the elderly and disabled, adoption credits, and the child credit instituted in 1998 for each child under age 17. All have specific income qualifications and income phaseout levels.

Other investment-related credits may be claimed for developing low-income housing, rehabilitating historic structures, using solar energy, and so on. Chapter 21, "Blue Plate Specials," suggests some ways to use investment tax credits.

Off the Top

Other items are not deductions or credits (even though they're sometimes called above-the-line deductions), but they serve to reduce your *adjusted gross income* or *AGI*. These special items reduce the amount of income on which tax is calculated.

Tax Talk

Adjusted gross income (AGI) is total income, minus adjustments for such things as contributions to Individual Retirement Accounts, and is the income used to figure federal income tax.

Above-the-line deductions pack a double whammy because, by reducing your adjusted gross income, they may increase your eligibility for additional tax benefits. As an example, you can take full advantage of tax credits for higher education expenses (see Chapter 8) only while your adjusted gross income is under $80,000; these credits are gone altogether at AGI of $100,000. In another example, income of more than $100,000 means that you can't roll a traditional IRA into the tax-friendly Roth IRA (see Chapter 12).

So, it's a brilliant tax move to reduce your adjusted gross income as much as possible. One way to do this is by shifting income into another year. The self-employed have the most opportunity to make this move, but employed folks sometimes can shift bonuses or, as described in Chapter 19, "Uncle Sam Treasures You," interest from Treasury bills.

Another strategy is to take as many above-the-line deductions as you can. Items that come off the top of your income are contributions to qualified retirement plans (IRAs, Keoghs, SIMPLE plans, and so on), job-related moving expenses, a portion of health insurance premiums for the self-employed, and alimony payments.

Two Things Certain: Death and Taxes

Death and taxes may both be sure things, but it's possible to plan to minimize the financial consequences attached to both. Solid estate planning, discussed in Chapters 24 and 25, "You Must Be Willing," can minimize the cost of death. Good tax planning—and the tax-sheltered investing discussed throughout this book—can cut your tax bill.

You can keep your taxes down, but you still have to file a tax return. The annual federal income tax return is usually due on April 15 every year; if April 15 falls on a weekend, tax returns are due on the next business day.

Tax Traps

The "marriage penalty" hits hardest on two-income couples earning comparable salaries because combining the two incomes often moves couples into a higher tax bracket. If you're planning to get married late in the year, putting off the wedding date into the following year could save some money—if only for the one year. Couples who are already married can figure their taxes both as a married couple filing jointly and as married filing separately. While most folks come out ahead by filing jointly, a couple with one partner who has incurred heavy deductible medical expenses might do better by filing separately. Run the numbers both ways to see.

Form by Form

There are three major federal income tax forms and hundreds of subsidiary forms and schedules. The three major forms are these:

➤ 1040EZ

➤ 1040A

➤ 1040

You can file the 1040EZ if you are under age 65, your taxable income is under $50,000, you have no dependents, and you didn't earn more than $400 in taxable interest.

The 1040A is for those folks who have taxable income under $50,000 but who also have dividends, interest, deductible IRA contributions, and/or deductible interest on student loans.

If you have any other deductions or credits, you have to use the long form, Form 1040. For all you folks seeking tax-sheltered income—that's why you're reading this book—the 1040 offers the most opportunities to minimize taxes.

You may have to attach one or more schedules to the 1040:

➤ Schedule A is where you list deductions, including mortgage interest, medical expenses, state and local income taxes, and property taxes.

➤ Use Schedule B if you have investment income in excess of $400; list all the interest and dividends from bank accounts, stocks, bonds, and mutual funds.

➤ Use Schedule C if you earn any income from self-employment as a sole proprietor rather than a corporation.

➤ Schedule D is for reporting capital gains and losses if you sold assets during the year (see Chapter 22, "There's No Free Lunch"). Filling out forms has gotten a bit easier, however, because you no longer have to complete Schedule D for mutual fund capital gains distributions if you didn't sell any shares.

Putting Off Tax Day

If you can't get your federal income tax return in on time, you may obtain an automatic four-month extension by filing Form 4868. But the extension is not permission to postpone paying taxes. Along with Form 4868, you must send a check for the tax you think you will owe when you complete your return. When the final figures are in, you'll owe interest on any unpaid tax from April 15 until the date you file. If you've underestimated your tax bill by more than 10 percent, you'll face penalties as well.

Form 4868 gives you an extension to August 15. If you're really up against it, it's possible to secure an additional extension to October 15. This one isn't automatic, however; you must file Form 2688 along with a detailed explanation of why you should be given an extension.

Sometimes the less you earn, the more likely you are to be audited. The following audit odds are from 1997 federal income tax returns, the most recent available at this writing.

Individual Tax Returns by Income	Percentage Audited
Up to $25,000	
Form 1040A	1.44%
Other forms	1.21%
$25,001–$50,000	0.70%
$50,001–$100,000	0.77%
$100,001 and over	2.27%

Self-Employed Individuals Filing Schedule C	Percentage Audited
Up to $25,000	3.19%
$25,001–$100,000	2.57%
$100,001 and over	4.13%

Source: CCH Incorporated

Audit Blues

Few words strike more terror into a taxpayer's heart than the one simple word: *audit*. In fact, the new consumer-friendly IRS is conducting fewer audits than ever before. And, more to the point, if you report accurately and keep documentation to back up your tax returns, you have little to fear if your return is examined.

For most taxpayers, the most likely communication from the IRS is a letter asking for more information or supporting documents. Because arithmetic errors are a common reason for an IRS letter, you can forestall many such communications by doing your math and checking it twice.

You should also be sure to include Social Security numbers for every dependent, including an ex-spouse receiving alimony and children receiving child support payments. And be extra careful about matching your reported income to the W-2 forms for wages and 1099 forms reporting dividends, interest, mutual fund gains, pension distributions, and so on. These forms are given to the government as well as to you. If the numbers don't match, your return could be flagged for an audit.

Audit Ins and Outs

True audits—beyond simple written requests for more information—take one of two forms. Either you are summoned to appear in an IRS office or the IRS comes to you.

For most people, an audit takes the form of a summons to appear in an IRS office to review one or more items on the tax return. Some words to the wise here: Bring the records related to the specific items, but don't bring anything else; you don't want to open up new areas for questioning. And don't make small talk. A casual remark about a recent vacation could spur IRS interest in your sources of income.

Tax Traps

Watch that W-4. It may be tough to estimate just how much you should have withheld from your wages, especially if you're part of a two-income couple. But having too much withheld isn't the answer either. When you let Uncle Sam take more of your money than necessary, you're extending an interest-free loan. Why should the government have the free use of your money when you could be earning interest on it instead? Contrary to what some people think, tax refunds aren't a good idea unless you're absolutely incapable of saving any other way.

You may bring your accountant or attorney along to an audit or—and this is a better idea—send him or her in your place. Tax professionals are used to dealing with the IRS and are more likely to keep the discussion on track.

A field audit is conducted at your home or place of business, or sometimes at your accountant's office. This type of audit is more serious and is more likely to dig into more details of your financial affairs.

Most audits don't lead to additional tax. Often there is no action at all. Sometimes the taxpayer actually receives a refund. In any case, the worst outcome of an audit is additional taxes due, with interest and possibly penalties. Unless you are guilty of fraud, as in deliberate underreporting of income, you won't go to jail.

Taxpayer Rights

In 1998, the IRS was directed to be more consumer-friendly, and taxpayers received specific new rights under the law, including these:

➤ Protection for "innocent spouses" has been expanded so that divorced individuals may be able to avoid being held liable for taxes owed by their former spouses.

➤ Auditors are no longer supposed to ask random questions about how much you spent for your house or on your daughter's wedding, in an effort to see if you're spending more than you're reporting as income. So-called "lifestyle" audits will be conducted only when there is a reasonable likelihood that income has been underreported.

➤ The burden of proof in Tax Court is now on the IRS—although this means that taxpayers must maintain fully documented tax records and cooperate with the IRS in an audit.

➤ The IRS may not seize a taxpayer's home for unpaid taxes under $5,000. Even when the tax liability is more substantial, home or business assets cannot be seized before all other payment options are exhausted.

Records to Keep

Some tax-related documents should be kept indefinitely; others can be thrown away after a few years. Here's what's what when it comes to record keeping.

Papers to keep for at least three years after filing your tax return—until April 2005 for the tax return filed in 2002 for 2001—include documents substantiating the following:

➤ Medical expenses

➤ Charitable contributions

➤ Mortgage interest

➤ Property taxes

➤ Casualty and theft losses

➤ Home office expenses

➤ Unreimbursed employee business expenses

Records to keep (almost) forever include these:

➤ Records on a home purchase and home improvements.

➤ Records on Individual Retirement Accounts and other tax-sheltered retirement plans.

➤ Purchase and sales receipts on securities, artwork, rare coins, and other assets that might generate a capital gain or loss.

➤ Tax returns for prior years. You don't absolutely need them for more than a few years, but tax returns are a valuable record of your financial life.

For more information, see IRS Publication 552, "Record Keeping for Individuals." It's available online at www.irs.ustreas.gov and by telephone at 1-800-829-3676.

States Have Taxes, Too

Most states tax income, but there are still seven states with no broad-based personal income tax: Alaska, Florida, Nevada, South Dakota, Texas, Washington, and Wyoming. New Hampshire and Tennessee tax interest and dividends, but not income from other sources.

Tax Treats

If you run a small business, you can glean valuable audit-prevention know-how from the IRS' Market Segment Specialization Program. To make its auditors more knowledgeable about the operations of specific small businesses, from bed-and-breakfasts to attorneys, the IRS has prepared guides telling auditors what to look for. Most of these guides are available on the Internet, at www.irs.gov. At the site, click on "Tax Info for Business."

But there are two key pieces of information here:

➤ First, most states that have an income tax automatically fall into step with the federal government, but some do not. If specific legislation is required in your state to mirror federal tax breaks, you need to find out. As an example, married taxpayers filing jointly can exclude $500,000 from profit on the sale of a home from federal income tax; the exclusion may or may not be available in every state.

➤ Secondly, no income tax is not the same thing as no tax at all. States levy a variety of taxes, including sales taxes and taxes on personal property, which can more than make up for not having an income tax.

According to the Tax Foundation, the average per-person tax burden in the United States in 1999—including every conceivable kind of tax, from income to property to

Social Security to excise taxes—was $10,298. On average, the American taxpayer paid 35.7 percent of income in taxes.

But there's a huge variation. The states with the highest per capita tax burden in 1999 were Connecticut ($16,139), New Jersey ($13,785), and New York ($13,420). The states with the lowest per capita tax burden were West Virginia ($6,801), Mississippi ($6,925), and Montana ($7,199).

Put another way, as I mentioned earlier, the national Tax Freedom Day was May 3 in 2000. The average resident of the United States worked until May 3 just to pay taxes. But the Tax Foundation notes that the residents of Connecticut and New York had to work until May 22 to pay their federal and state taxes.

The Least You Need to Know

➤ Middle-income taxpayers reap some special benefits under our graduated federal income tax system.

➤ There are five federal tax brackets, with tax rates ranging from 15 percent to 39.6 percent.

➤ You can minimize your tax bill by taking advantage of exclusions, deductions, and credits.

➤ Fewer taxpayers are being audited these days.

➤ Tax planning must include state taxes as well as federal.

Chapter 2

Pay Now,
Pay Later,
Pay Not at All

In This Chapter

➤ Keeping a mix of assets in your investment portfolio helps to minimize risk

➤ Understanding the differences among investments that are taxable, tax-deferred, or tax-free

➤ Knowing your tax bracket tells you whether tax-free investments or taxable investments make the most sense

➤ Realizing that tax deferral is always a good thing, in every tax bracket

The investment world has blossomed in recent years with an almost unbelievable variety of investment vehicles. Most are taxable; some are not. Some may be taxable under some circumstances, tax-free in others. Some are tax-deferred so that you pay tax later instead of right away.

Many folks want tax-free investments above all else. That's probably why you're reading this book. But you can't think about tax-free investments until you understand the whole range of investments—and, more important, until you understand your own goals, time horizon, and attitude toward risk. This chapter will help you decide when tax-free investments are right for you.

The Investment Universe

There are three basic types of investment—conveniently pigeonholed as growth, income, and cash equivalents—and an almost infinite variety of investment vehicles within the three categories.

Most investments are fully taxable. Earnings along the way are taxed as ordinary income. Profits are taxed as *capital gains*. Losses—yes, they do happen—can be written off against gains, as described in Chapter 22, "There's No Free Lunch."

Your primary interest may lie in sheltering investments from the long arm of the tax collector. But you still need to understand the broad investment universe in order to decide which investments are best for you. Believe it or not, even if it goes against the grain, you may sometimes do better in taxable investments than in tax-free.

Tax Talk

Capital gain is an increase in value, calculated as the difference between the cost basis—how much you pay for an asset, including commissions—and the selling price. Conversely, a **capital loss** describes a loss in the value of an investment.

Tax Talk

Equities are another name for common stock, so-called because buying shares makes you a part owner of the corporation.

Investing for Growth

Think growth, think *equities*. When you buy shares of common stock, you are buying equities because share ownership gives you an equity position in the corporation. As a part owner—admittedly, a very small part—you prosper when the company does well, and you suffer when the company does poorly.

Growth may be obtained in relatively safe investments and in riskier ones, along a range from blue chip stocks to speculative new issues. In mutual funds, a similar range runs from balanced or growth-and-income funds, seeking stability in a mixture of stocks and bonds, to aggressive growth and *sector funds*. There's usually some income along the way, in the form of dividends from individually owned shares and interest from mutual fund shares, but income is generally lower when opportunities for capital appreciation are greater.

This is the relationship between risk and reward. The less risk you take by opting for income and low volatility, the lower your potential returns. The more risk you are willing to take by forgoing income and accepting volatility, the greater the potential reward. That's not guaranteed reward, mind you—there are no guarantees in investing—but potential reward.

As the stock market went wild in the sustained bull market of the 1990s, it became hard for some investors—and some portfolio managers—to remember that what goes up generally comes down. But economic cycles haven't yet been repealed, and it's reasonable to expect periodic stock market corrections. A *correction* is when the prices of stocks or bonds reverse direction; the term is typically applied to downward movement after a period of rising prices. Nevertheless, over time, investments in common stock have outdistanced any other investment.

According to data compiled by Ibbotson Associates, an investment research firm in Chicago, common stock had a compound annual return from 1926 through the end of 1999, including reinvested dividends, of 11.4 percent. U.S. intermediate-term government bonds returned just 5.3 percent during the same period, while inflation averaged 3 percent.

The wild growth of the late 1990s was concentrated in technology and especially in so-called dot.com stocks, as Internet-related offerings proliferated. Because many of these stocks saw their shares multiplying in value while the company was still losing money, there was considerable fear that the stock market was a bubble about to burst.

But dot.com companies are only one small part of the stock market, and there are still many other investment vehicles to consider. Here are a few points to ponder as you build your portfolio:

Tax Talk

Sector funds are mutual funds focusing on securities issued by companies in a specific area of concentration. The area may be an industry, as in the healthcare sector, or it may be geographic, as in the Pacific Basin. Because sector funds are concentrated, they are more volatile than many other mutual funds.

Tax Talk

Large cap means companies with multimillion or billion dollar capitalization and **small cap** refers to companies with a smaller financial base.

➤ *Large cap* companies are the giants of the corporate world, while *small cap* companies tend to be smaller start-up ventures.

➤ International investing can be achieved through buying shares of a U.S. company with extensive overseas operations, or through buying shares of an *international* or *global* mutual fund.

➤ Index funds mirror the performance of a stock market index. The Dow Jones Industrial Average is an index of 30 large industrial companies, but the Standard & Poor's 500 is more widely used because it reports on the broader base of 500 companies. The Russell 2000 is an index of small companies.

➤ Value funds seek undervalued companies expected to turn around. Growth funds look for companies with sustained growth.

Tax Talk

An **international** fund includes stock issued by companies all over the world, except the United States. A **global** fund can add U.S. stocks to the investment mix and therefore might be less volatile.

Tax Traps

Investing in tax-free bonds doesn't mean that you can forget about taxes altogether. The income from municipal bonds issued by your state is generally tax-free, but you'll still owe capital gains tax if you make a profit when you sell or redeem the bond. So, you still have to keep track of the purchase cost and sales price.

Investing for Income

While returns on most growth investments are fully taxable, income investing can be taxable or tax-free.

Income investing usually takes the form of investing in bonds and bond mutual funds. Corporate bonds are taxable. Municipal bonds are free from federal tax and, if issued in your state, are generally tax-free. Municipal bonds are discussed in Chapter 17, "Muni Madness," and Chapter 18, "Making the Most of Bonds." Bond funds are covered in Chapter 20, "Ganging Up with Mutual Funds."

U.S. Treasury notes and bonds are a hybrid, subject to federal income tax but not state and local income tax. As such, they can be a good bet for residents of high-tax states. Treasuries are described in detail in Chapter 19, "Uncle Sam Treasures You."

Substitutes for Cash

Every investor needs cash. Readily available liquid assets can help you cope with such emergencies as a job layoff or a roof replacement. Having liquid assets on hand also means that you can take advantage of investment opportunities.

But cash doesn't really mean cash. No one should keep thousands of greenbacks on hand. Instead, you want what the investment world calls cash equivalents. Cash equivalents are anything you can readily convert to cash with no loss of principal.

Cash equivalents include these:

➤ Checking and savings accounts

➤ Certificates of deposit

➤ Money market mutual funds

➤ U.S. Treasury bills

You may want a bank checking account for convenience in paying bills, but the rest of your liquid assets should be in instruments that pay a better return. This includes short-term certificates of deposit, money market mutual funds (discussed in Chapter 16, "Everyone into the [Money Market] Pool"), and U.S. Treasury bills (described in Chapter 19). *Yields* vary more than you might think, as shown in the following table.

Average Interest Rates in Early May 2000

Money market deposit accounts at banks	3.73%
Six-month certificates of deposit	5.62%
Money market mutual funds	5.45%
Three-month Treasury bills	5.78%
Six-month Treasury bills	5.93%

Interest earned on bank accounts and certificates of deposit is fully taxable at ordinary income tax rates. Money market mutual funds may be taxable or tax-free; tax-free money market funds may be national or state-specific. Choose your money market mutual fund by your tax bracket; see "When It Pays to Pay" later in this chapter.

Interest on T-bills is paid in the form of a discount on the purchase price but is taxable when the bill matures. Like other U.S. Treasury obligations, interest on T-bills is subject to federal income tax but not state income tax.

Allocating Your Assets

Investing isn't an either/or proposition. You don't decide whether to buy stocks *or* bonds. Instead, as a wise investor, you diversify holdings among various types of investment vehicles. You hold both stocks and bonds, and several types of each. Or, you invest through mutual funds, which diversify for you.

Tax Tips

T-bills let you postpone the tax bite. If you buy a six-month bill in July, the interest becomes taxable in January—but you don't have to pay the tax until you file your tax return the following year. You get the interest in July 2001, as an example, in the form of a discount on the purchase price. But you don't actually pay the tax on that interest until April 2003 when you file your tax return for 2002, the year in which the bill matures.

The general idea is that if you don't put all your eggs in one basket, they won't be scrambled when the basket falls. Baskets do fall. Markets go down as well as up. But different investments react to economic circumstances in different ways. Holding a variety of investments is one of the best ways to minimize risk.

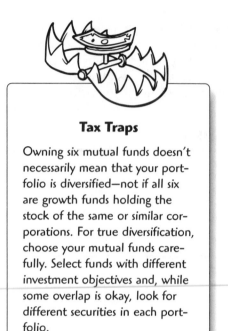

Tax Traps

Owning six mutual funds doesn't necessarily mean that your portfolio is diversified—not if all six are growth funds holding the stock of the same or similar corporations. For true diversification, choose your mutual funds carefully. Select funds with different investment objectives and, while some overlap is okay, look for different securities in each portfolio.

In fact, an academic study a few years back found that more than 90 percent of investment success can be traced to the mix of investments rather than to the choice of any specific investment vehicles. While this study has been challenged, it is clear that a mix of investments minimizes volatility over the long term. Over one 10-year period, an investor who put 60 percent in stocks, 30 percent in intermediate-term Treasury bonds, and 10 percent in short-term Treasury bills came out way ahead of an all-Treasury portfolio and not that far behind the much riskier all-stock portfolio.

Achieving a mix of investments doesn't mean randomly buying one from column A and another from column B. Instead, you should consciously allocate your assets, deciding on the specific proportions of your assets to invest for growth and for income. A simple allocation, as an example, might be half-and-half growth and income. A more complex allocation might look something like the following table.

Asset Allocation Suggestion for Early Retirement

Growth funds	45%
Balanced funds	15%
Growth-and-income funds	15%
Income funds	15%
Money market mutual funds	10%

Once you've established an appropriate allocation, you need to rebalance your allocation periodically to keep it on target. When stocks do particularly well, as they have in recent years, you may find that the 60 percent of your portfolio that you allocated to stocks has become 75 percent. That's the time to sell some stock, take the profits, and invest the money in a portion of your portfolio that hasn't done as well.

Does it seem counterintuitive to sell winners and invest in losers? It's really not. Just think of the classic investment advice to "buy low and sell high." The only way to do that is to take some profits and plow them back into another part of your portfolio. Remember, too, that profits on paper are not real profits until you take them. If you let your portfolio become unbalanced, you will lose diversification—and you may be in for an unpleasant shock when the market turns down.

Meanwhile, exactly how much you'll want in each category as you set your initial allocation depends in part on your investment time horizon and in part on your tolerance for risk.

Your Time Horizon

You shouldn't invest in stocks unless you have a long time before you will need the money. As I've said before, share prices can go down as well as up.

If you need your money next year, to buy a house or pay college tuition or whatever, you might have to sell securities when prices are down. The place for this short-term money is in one of the cash equivalents discussed in the section "Substitutes for Cash" earlier in this chapter.

On the other hand, if you're investing to pay for college for a child who is currently age 5, or to fund retirement for yourself when you are age 50, you have plenty of time to ride market ups and downs. The long-term investor, in fact, can view market downturns as buying opportunities.

Tolerating Risk

How much you'll invest for growth and how much for income depends in part on your time horizon and your specific investment objectives, but it also depends on how you feel about risk.

Remember, though, that there is more than one kind of risk. While you don't want to invest in anything that will leave you sleepless at night, you also have to recognize that being completely "safe" means that you will inevitably lose ground to inflation. Conservative income-oriented investments do not earn enough to keep the purchasing power of your dollars intact over time. Even at the moderate 3 percent rate of inflation we've had in recent years, a car that costs $20,000 today will cost more than $36,000 in 20 years. In order to afford that car, you need an adequate return on your investments.

Potential investment rewards go hand in hand with risk. Take this quiz to get a handle on how you react to risk and to see what it means for your investments.

1. In planning for my retirement, in 15 years, I keep my money in:
   a. Certificates of deposit and money market mutual funds
   b. A mix of stock and bond funds
   c. Stocks and stock funds
2. I know that higher returns can help beat inflation, but they also involve more risk. When it comes to inflation, risk, and return:
   a. I'll be okay if my investments keep pace with inflation.
   b. Moderate risk is okay if it helps me keep a little ahead of inflation.
   c. I'll accept more risk if it may help me outpace inflation.

3. If my bond fund does poorly, I'll switch to another investment:

   a. Right away

   b. Within one to two years

   c. After more than two years

4. If within two months of investing in the stock market my stock fund loses 15 percent of its value, I will:

   a. Sell my shares so I can sleep at night

   b. Hold my shares; it might come back

   c. Buy more shares to average my cost

5. A stock you own has doubled in price, and your broker wants you to buy more. You:

   a. Sell all your shares

   b. Sell half your holdings to lock in some profits

   c. Buy more

If all of your answers are "A," you're conservative—and you're likely to lose serious ground to inflation. If you consistently chose "C," you're an aggressive investor with a high tolerance for risk. In between? That's a good place to be. Keep up the good work, with a diversified portfolio of stocks for growth and bonds for income.

Tax-Sheltered Investments

There's a whole category of investments that are not tax-free but that are tax-sheltered. Generally, this means that taxes are deferred for a time. Without the drag of taxes, these investments grow enormously—usually by far more than enough to offset the taxes that must eventually be paid.

The following table shows the huge advantage that can be gained by deferring taxes. It is based on investing $5,000 a year in a tax-sheltered retirement account such as a 401(k) plan. At an average return of 10 percent, including reinvested dividends and capital appreciation, this is how much you'll have over time, assuming that no withdrawals are made and that you are in a 31 percent federal income tax bracket.

Time	Invested Amount	Taxable Account	Tax-Deferred Account
10 years	$ 50,000	$ 88,481	$ 134,284
15 years	$ 75,000	$166,231	$ 280,505
20 years	$100,000	$285,760	$ 463,786
25 years	$125,000	$469,475	$ 791,172
30 years	$150,000	$751,900	$1,318,431

Source: The Vanguard Group

Among the tax-sheltered investments you may want to consider are retirement plans, annuities, and U.S. government savings bonds.

Retirement Plans

Whether you have a 401(k) at work or an Individual Retirement Account that you fund on your own, tax-sheltered retirement plans are a must for every investor. These plans and their tax advantages are discussed at length in Chapters 10 through 14.

Although there are variations from plan to plan, most contributions to tax-qualified retirement plans come off the top of pretax income. Earnings accumulate free of taxes. And everything that eventually comes out of the plan is subject to income tax at ordinary tax rates. You get no benefit from lower capital gains rates within a tax-sheltered retirement plan.

The important thing to remember is that a retirement plan is not itself an investment vehicle. It is a container for investment vehicles you choose. You can put stock or a stock fund within a retirement plan, and you can put bonds or a bond fund. But it does not make any sense to put a tax-advantaged investment such as a municipal bond or an annuity within a tax-sheltered retirement plan. You can't derive a double tax benefit from the same investment.

Annuities and EE-Bonds

Annuities are like private retirement plans. Contributions are not deductible, but earnings compound tax-deferred. Annuities are discussed in Chapter 15, "The Ins and Outs of Annuities." For now, you'll want to remember that a qualified retirement plan should always be fully funded before you turn to an annuity. Annuities have some of the same drawbacks as qualified plans like 401(k) plans—for example, you can't take money out early or you will face a tax penalty—but they don't have all of the same advantages.

U.S. government savings bonds—Uncle Sam's familiar EE-bonds—are readily available at banks and through payroll deduction at many employers. Like annuities, they are bought with after-tax dollars, but earnings compound tax-free until the bonds are re-deemed. At that point, tax must be paid—unless the bonds qualify for tax exemption because they are used for tuition and meet the requirements described in Chapter 7, "Uncle Sam's IOUs."

When It Pays to Pay

There are two guidelines for every investor to follow: Take full advantage of tax-sheltered retirement plans, and diversify your investments. As you develop an asset allocation strategy, though, consider all your investments—both inside and outside retirement plans—as a whole pie to be divided.

Every investor can benefit from tax-sheltered investments, but not every investor should be in tax-free investments. Whether or not you should buy municipal bonds or bond funds depends on your tax bracket. Lots of folks in the 15 percent tax bracket are so blinded by the gleam of tax-free returns that they invest in munis when they would come out ahead with taxable bonds. But you're smart. You'll pay attention to your tax bracket before you decide whether to invest tax-free.

Let's say that you can earn 4 percent on a tax-free bond and 6 percent on a taxable bond. As the following table shows, you would have to be in the 36 percent tax bracket before the tax-free bond makes sense for you.

Tax-Free Yield	Equivalent Taxable Yield at Federal Tax Rate				
	15%	28%	31%	36%	39.6%
4.00%	4.71%	5.56%	5.80%	6.25%	6.62%
4.50%	5.29%	6.25%	6.52%	7.03%	7.45%
5.00%	5.88%	6.94%	7.25%	7.81%	8.28%
5.50%	6.47%	7.64%	7.97%	8.59%	9.11%
6.00%	7.06%	8.33%	8.70%	9.38%	9.93%

The Pros Have It

Still puzzled about whether tax-free or taxable investments are best for you? Consult a professional adviser, an accountant, or a financial planner to help you out. These advisers can help you with year-round tax and financial planning. They also can help you when tax time rolls around.

You can probably fill out your own income tax return if your financial affairs are relatively uncomplicated. Once you begin sheltering money from taxes, however—especially if you are investing in tax-free or tax-deferred vehicles—professional help may be a good idea. A knowledgeable pro may be able to save you more in taxes than you could do on your own.

Tax laws are a moving target. According to tax publishers CCH Incorporated, there have been more than 8,100 changes to the tax code since 1986, including 900 changes between 1998 and the beginning of 2000. You want someone who is up to date with current law and who has access to current-year computer software.

You also want someone who is available for year-round planning, and who can represent you in an audit. Tax professionals allowed to represent clients at an audit include certified public accountants, enrolled agents, and tax attorneys.

Start by asking friends and other professional advisers for referrals. Interview two or three candidates and ask these questions:

➤ What is your training and experience, and how do you keep up with changes in tax law? Laws and regulations change with numbing frequency. It's vitally important to use a tax professional who keeps up to date.

➤ Do you handle clients like me, in a comparable income range and with similar tax concerns? (Similar experience is important. If you run a small business, you want a tax professional familiar with your type of business. If you invest in limited partnerships to generate tax credits, you want experience here, too.)

➤ Are you aggressive in interpreting tax law? (There are gray areas in the tax code, and some tax preparers will push the limits more than others. But you should be comfortable with the stance taken by your advisers when it comes to things such as claiming deductions that may be questioned.)

Tax Tips

You may pay someone to prepare your tax returns, but you are still responsible for their accuracy. The IRS will charge you—not your tax adviser—any additional tax, interest, or penalties it decides are due. So review your completed return carefully, and raise any questions with your tax adviser before you sign it and send it in.

Online Tax Help

Getting answers to tax questions can help you prepare your own tax return or save time—and therefore money—when working with a professional adviser.

Some of the best resources (in addition to the books listed in Appendix A, "Resources") can be found online. Useful Web sites include these:

➤ **www.irs.gov** (the Internal Revenue Service Web site) offers tax forms, publications, news, and official regulations.

➤ **www.taxsites.com/state.html** can lead you to your state and local taxing authority.

➤ **www.taxweb.com** offers links to a range of tax resources.

➤ **www.nolo.com/encyclopedia/** is run by Nolo Press, a publisher of self-help law books, and offers information on tax problems.

Just take any online tax advice with a grain of salt. Some information is out-of-date but still posted; other information may be just plain inaccurate. Remember, the IRS isn't even responsible for its own advice. In the end, the tax code governs, and you are responsible for information on your return.

Tax Software

If you're computer-savvy, you'll find that tax preparation software can help you turn a jumbled pile of receipts and check stubs into a neat, tidy, and arithmetically correct tax return. Software also has the advantage of automatically transferring data from one line on the tax form to another, and of feeding information from federal income tax return to a state return so that you have to enter it only once.

If your tax return is at all complicated, though, it may still be a good idea to have a tax professional review the completed return. Your work won't be wasted—it will cost you a lot less to have your return prepared if you've used software to organize the information instead of showing up at your accountant's office with your receipts in a shoebox.

The IRS is also encouraging electronic filing, touting increased accuracy and quicker refunds. Right now, about one in four tax returns is filed electronically either online or through Telefile, the IRS' telephone filing system by touch-tone telephone. The goal is to have at least 80 percent of all individual returns filed electronically by 2007.

If you file online, through one of the popular software programs or through your tax preparer, you can pay any amount owed either by direct debit from your bank account or by charging it on American Express, MasterCard, or Discover Card (right now Visa is not participating). If you choose to charge, the IRS won't impose a fee, but the charge card or credit card issuer may charge as much as 2 percent.

Tax Tips

Two of the top software programs are TurboTax for Windows and MacInTax Deluxe, both from Intuit (at 1-800-224-0991 or www.intuit.com/turbotax), and TaxCut for Windows and Macintosh, from Block Financial Corporation (at 1-800-235-4060 or www.taxcut.com).

The Least You Need to Know

➤ The investment universe consists of stocks, bonds, and cash equivalents.

➤ Investing in bonds offers the choice of taxable or tax-free income.

➤ Diversifying your investments lets you minimize risk.

➤ Both your time horizon and your tolerance for risk play a role in the investments you choose.

➤ A tax professional can help you with tax planning and tax filing.

Part 2
Shelter Equals Shelter

Your home may be one of your best investments—and one of your best tax shelters as well. But you have to know the rules of the game, or you'll lose out.

The chapters in this part describe the tax breaks that go along with home ownership and the tax consequences of moving, divorcing, and dying.

Read on, and you'll learn the ins and outs of mortgages, reverse mortgages, and home equity loans. You'll also learn about vacation homes—and the tax implications of enjoying a vacation hideaway yourself or using it as a rental property.

Chapter 3

The Roof Over Your Head

In This Chapter

➤ Owning a house: one of the best tax shelters

➤ Working at home generates additional tax deductions

➤ Making well-chosen home renovations add value

➤ Tapping into the dollars locked in your home

Uncle Sam seems to love homeowners—not because he made so many of them, but because he offers so many tax breaks to property owners. You can shelter dollars from income taxes by deducting many of the costs of buying, owning, and improving a home. You can enjoy tax-free appreciation while you own your home. And you can reap tax benefits by tapping that appreciation and using some of the dollars locked into your home's value.

"Home" in this context means your *principal residence,* whether that residence is a house, a condominium unit, a motor home, or a sailboat.

You have to understand the tax benefits—and claim them—or they will be wasted. You shouldn't buy a house because it's a tax shelter. You buy one as a home for you and your family. But you might as well enjoy the tax benefits while you enjoy your home. In this chapter, I'll tell you how to make the best use of the tax advantages Uncle Sam so generously bestows on homeowners.

Your Hidden Wealth

Despite occasional declines in home values, the prices of houses have marked a steady upward trend over the decades. The average price of a new house in the United States in 1979 was $71,800. By midyear 1999, the average price of a new house was $186,000. If you bought that average house in 1979 and still owned it in 1999, you would have added to your *net worth* by $114,200. Better yet, that additional value is yours, all yours; it won't be taxed until you sell the house. It may not be taxed at all.

House prices keep going up. Look at these average prices on new and existing homes from 1978 to 1998.

Year	New Homes	Existing Homes	Year	New Homes	Existing Homes
1978	$62,500	$55,500	1989	$148,800	$118,100
1979	$71,800	$64,200	1990	$149,800	$118,600
1980	$76,400	$72,800	1991	$147,200	$128,400
1981	$83,000	$78,300	1992	$144,100	$130,900
1982	$83,900	$80,500	1993	$147,700	$133,500
1983	$89,800	$83,100	1994	$154,400	$136,700
1984	$97,600	$86,000	1995	$158,700	$139,000
1985	$100,800	$90,800	1996	$166,500	$141,800
1986	$111,900	$98,500	1997	$176,200	$150,500
1987	$127,200	$106,300	1998	$181,800	$159,100
1988	$138,300	$112,800			

Source: National Association of Home Builders

We're not talking peanuts here. According to the National Association of Home Builders, home ownership accounts for close to half of the nation's total net worth—far more than any other investments, including retirement accounts, stock and mutual fund shares, bank accounts, and saving bonds.

Naturally enough, not every home appreciates in the same way. Where you live makes a big difference. If you're in the market to buy a house, in fact, sticking with an area of solid job growth is the best way to ensure the continuing value of your house. *Smart Money* magazine reported in mid-1999 that new jobs were fueling housing booms in cities from Louisville, Kentucky, to Austin, Texas. Before you buy, check out the job market, especially if you're considering a long-distance move.

Wherever you live, though, your home is a tax shelter. Many expenses associated with home ownership are sheltered from federal income taxes. If your state or city have income taxes, the same expenses may be deductible on these tax returns as well.

Uncle Sam Shares the Costs

Tax policy is often social policy. The powers-that-be in Washington believe that homeowners are stable citizens, so the tax code confers tax benefits to encourage people to buy homes.

Here's a handy-dandy list of home-related tax deductions:

➤ Mortgage interest

➤ Closing costs

➤ Property taxes

➤ Interest on a home equity loan or line of credit

➤ Casualty losses

Each of these items can create a tax shelter for your hard-earned dollars.

Mortgage Interest

This is the biggy. If you remember the "good old days," before the Tax Reform Act of 1986, interest on every kind of loan was deductible. No more. The interest on mortgage loans is almost the only type of interest that now qualifies as a deduction on your federal income tax. (If your state has an income tax, it's most likely deductible there as well.) Of course, a mortgage probably represents the biggest chunk of money you'll ever borrow, so this is a good thing.

The interest on a mortgage loan of up to $1 million is deductible. For most people, this ceiling is high enough—although it is a combined limit applied to both first and second homes.

Mortgage payments are made up of both principal and interest. In the early years of a mortgage loan, most of the money goes toward interest. This gives you larger deductions. In the later years, as the mortgage is gradually paid off, more of the money will go toward principal and your deductions will be smaller.

Bear in mind that the value of a tax *deduction* is directly related to your tax bracket and, therefore, to

Tax Tips

There's a big difference between tax **deductions** and tax **credits** (see Chapter 1, "The Toll Taxes Take"). Tax deductions reduce taxable income, with savings related to your tax bracket. In the 28 percent federal tax bracket, a $100 deduction saves you $28 in taxes. Tax credits, as dollar-for-dollar write-offs against the amount of income tax you owe, are more valuable: A $100 credit saves you $100. Tax savings for homeowners take the form of deductions.

how much you earn. If you are in the 31 percent tax bracket, you save 31 cents on every dollar you pay in mortgage interest. If you're in the 15 percent bracket, you save just 15 cents on every dollar.

But you get the full benefit of the deduction only if you itemize deductions on your income tax return in the first place. And you'll itemize your deductions only if they exceed the standard deduction. At this writing, the standard deduction for a married couple filing jointly is $7,350.

So, you'll reap the full tax benefits of home ownership only if all your other itemizable deductions (state and local taxes, charitable contributions, and so on) combined equal at least as much as the standard deduction. Deductions related to home ownership may push you over the top and make it possible to file an itemized return, but only the deductions in excess of the standard amount represent the added benefit of buying and owning a house.

Closing Costs

The day you actually take title to your new home is also the day you write a seemingly endless number of checks. Some of those checks will be for tax-deductible items:

➤ Any portion of the year's real estate taxes that you pay at closing.

➤ Interest on the mortgage until the day of closing.

➤ Points charged by a lender in association with the mortgage. Each point usually represents 1 percent of the mortgage loan.

These items are deductible on the federal income tax return you file for the year of the purchase. There is one exception: Points on refinanced mortgage loans must be deducted over the life of the mortgage. A recent Internal Revenue Service ruling presented this option for purchasers as well as those who are refinancing a mortgage: If it will help your tax picture, points may be amortized over the life of the loan.

Other closing costs—including attorney's fees, real estate commissions, title costs, and the like—are not immediately deductible but can be added to the *cost basis* of your home. When you eventually sell the house, any potential taxable capital gain will be lower because of these costs.

Still other closing costs—including homeowner's insurance premiums, utility costs, and the like—are purely out-of-pocket expenses and don't yield any tax benefits.

Other Deductible Items

Several other items are deductible on your federal income tax return and, in most cases, on state and local income tax returns as well. This list includes the following:

➤ Real estate and personal property taxes, whether you pay them directly or as part of your monthly mortgage payments.

➤ Interest on a home equity loan or line of credit up to $100,000, no matter what you use the money for. This is a combined limit applied to both first and second (vacation) homes.

➤ Casualty and theft losses that exceed 10 percent of adjusted gross income.

A casualty loss stems from a catastrophe such as a hurricane or earthquake that severely damages your home. A theft loss could result from a break-in and the theft of considerable amounts of property.

You may deduct the amount of the damage or theft loss in excess of 10 percent of adjusted gross income minus $100 plus any insurance reimbursement. Homeowners along the Atlantic coast who suffered the floods spawned by Hurricane Floyd in September 1999 may have found some small relief in claiming a tax deduction for the casualty loss. Flood damage is not covered by standard homeowner's insurance policies, and few people carried separate flood insurance. A casualty deduction was almost the only financial relief available.

Tax Talk

Cost basis (also called **tax basis**) is the original purchase price of your home, used to determine the taxability of any profit when the home is sold. The cost basis may be increased by certain closing costs and by home improvements. It may be decreased by factors such as gain postponed from the sale of a previous home (discussed in Chapter 4, "Territorial Imperatives").

Work Makes Strange Bedfellows

Lots of people are eager to get away from the stress of Monday-through-Friday commuting by setting up a business at home. You may be even more eager to join the growing ranks of work-at-home men and women when you realize the additional tax benefits.

If you set up an office in your spare bedroom, whether you work there part-time or full-time, you can add a list of deductions to your federal (and probably state as well) income tax returns.

But be careful. You must follow the rules. If you don't, you could find yourself in big trouble with the Internal Revenue Service. And, while the IRS is trying to cultivate a new, friendly image, no one really wants the hassle of being audited.

Some folks say that a home office deduction is like waving a red flag in front of the IRS, provoking an audit. That may or may not be so. But if you're entitled to a home office deduction and can back up your deduction with documentation, you should

Tax Tips

Use Form 8829 to document your deductions. Attach it to your federal tax return to supplement the Schedule C that reports income and outgo. On Form 8829, you report the square footage of your office and the percentage of your home this represents. This percentage governs the indirect expenditures that you can deduct for maintaining your office, as described in the accompanying paragraphs.

Tax Tips

If you're a salaried employee working at home, you can't deduct home office expenses unless you are at home for the convenience of your employer. Even then, because you're not self-employed and don't file a Schedule C, your home office expenses are reported on Schedule A, where they are subject to the 2 percent floor on miscellaneous itemized deductions.

claim the deduction. There's no point in throwing money away that's rightfully yours.

The most important rule is this: The space you use for your office at home must be used exclusively as your principal place of business. Don't watch television in the same room, let your kids play video games, or put up a visiting relative on the pull-out couch. If you do, you'll disqualify the home office deduction.

You don't have to use an entire room to meet this rule—a blessing for apartment-dwellers, who may not have an extra room to spare. But you do have to clearly separate your place of business from any other purpose. Put up a partition, use a bookcase, or place masking tape on the floor to mark your space, and you'll be okay.

One restriction has recently been eliminated. You no longer have to spend most of your time in your home office in order to claim a tax deduction. This is a boon to traveling sales representatives, computer consultants, interior designers—in short, anyone who must spend considerable time outside the home office, whether on the road, visiting clients, or for any other business reason. As long as the office is your principal place of business and is used exclusively for that purpose, you are allowed to claim a deduction.

Home office deductions come in two flavors, direct and indirect. Direct expenditures, such as painting your office or buying a desk chair, are deductible in full. So are the direct costs of running your business: postage, stationery, filing supplies, and the like. The cost of long-distance and local telephone calls are also completely deductible, with the exception that the basic charge for the first phone line in your home may not be deducted. If you install a separate phone line for your office, you won't have to keep a log of every deductible call you make.

Indirect expenditures, such as the money you spend on roof repair, homeowner's insurance, and utilities, are deductible in the proportion applicable to your office. That's where Form 8829, with its square-footage count for your office as a proportion of your home, comes in. But be careful when it comes to utilities;

unless you run an electricity-intensive business, your office is not likely to consume its proportional share of the household's electric bill.

Feathering Your Nest

There are two nice things about home improvements: Not only do they make your home a more pleasant place to live, but they can also yield financial rewards. Well-chosen improvements can enhance the value of your house when it's time to sell and move on. To add icing to the cake, the cost of the improvements adds to the cost basis of your house and may reduce the eventual tax bite when you sell the house for more than you paid for it.

So, if the past summer made you think you've lived long enough without central air-conditioning, or if a growing family makes you yearn for a family room where children (or grandchildren) can play without wrecking the living room, take the plunge. Join the legion of homeowners who, as a group, spend upward of $126 billion a year on remodeling projects.

Which improvements are the most cost-effective when it comes to making back the money when you sell your house? *Remodeling Magazine,* a trade journal, reports that the three projects that return most of their cost are a minor kitchen upgrade (returning 81 percent of the cost as a national average), an added bathroom (72 percent), and a bathroom remodel (77 percent). But there are great regional variations, and a local real estate agent can give you an idea of the difference that a new kitchen, as an example, might make in the selling price of your house.

If you want to make your money back, consider upgrading your house to new-house standards for your neighborhood. In most areas, that means at

Tax Traps

Don't expect tax benefits from painting your house or fixing the gutters; these expenses are classified as repairs or ordinary maintenance. Home improvements, on the other hand, are defined by the Internal Revenue Service as things that add to the value of your home, considerably prolong its useful life, or adapt it to new uses. Items that can be classified as improvements range from installing an attic fan to adding a bathroom.

least three bedrooms and two bathrooms. It may also mean a family room or study. So-called "personal preference items"—an outdoor hot tub, a greenhouse, and a swimming pool, for example—may delight your family but may make your house more difficult to sell.

How much of the cost will you get back when you sell your house? There are no guarantees, but *Remodeling Magazine* reports these added values, as a national average, if the house is sold within a year. Keep the house longer, and returns are generally even better.

Improvement	Return on Investment
Minor kitchen remodel	81%
Bathroom addition	72%
Bathroom remodel	71%
Family room addition	71%
Major kitchen remodel	70%
Master suite	68%
Attic bedroom	65%
Two-story addition	62%
Replacement siding	60%
Replacement windows	56%
Deck addition	54%
Home office	50%

Source: Reprinted with permission from the November 1999 issue of Remodeling Magazine ©
Hanley-Wood, LLC

Tapping the Wealth

The money tied up in your home is money in the bank. The untaxed appreciation—
the added value that your home builds over the years, which is not taxed until you
sell the house (if at all)—can come in very handy if you're pinched for cash. What's
more, tapping that *equity* can yield additional tax benefits.

Tax Talk

Equity is the part of your home
that you actually own—and the
part you can borrow against—
because you've paid for it in full.
You don't own the entire value
of your home as long as you
carry a mortgage. Until the
mortgage is paid off, the mortgage lender is a co-owner.

For most people, the increase in home value over the
years of ownership will never be taxed. Under federal
law as it now stands, single taxpayers may exclude
$250,000 in profit on the sale of a home from capital
gains tax while married couples filing jointly may exclude $500,000. This sounds like—and is—a lot.
However, if you moved several times over the years,
each time rolling the profits on one home into the
next (as the prior law permitted), you could be taxed
on the accumulated profits when you sell your current
home. More detail on the tax implications of selling
your home is in Chapter 4.

Meanwhile, before you're even thinking about selling
your home, you can tap the equity. You'll remember
the point made earlier in this chapter, that just about
the only loan interest that is still deductible from your
federal income tax is the interest on a loan secured by

your home. Generally, that means a mortgage loan. But other types of equity-based loans can yield tax benefits as well.

There are two types of equity-based loans: The first is a home equity loan or line of credit. The second, most appropriate for house-rich, cash-poor older folks, is a reverse mortgage.

Loans and Lines of Credit

Home equity loans and home equity lines of credit are actively promoted by banks and other lenders. If you have a good credit record, you probably receive mailings and cold calls several times a week. The mailings are proof positive that these products are moneymakers for lenders. But they also can be helpful for you, if wisely used. Both loans and lines of credit tap the equity in your home. Here are some of the main differences between them:

➤ A *home equity loan* is basically a second mortgage; it's given to the borrower as a lump sum and is repaid on a specified schedule over the life of the loan. The interest rate is generally fixed at the time of the loan.

➤ A *home equity line of credit* is more like the revolving credit you're familiar with from credit cards. You are preapproved for a maximum loan, but you can take the money as you need it—sometimes with a special "credit card," but most often in the form of checks drawn on the account. The interest—paid only on the amount you've borrowed, not the maximum you can borrow—is generally variable and is pegged to the *prime rate*.

Home equity loans and lines of credit have become very popular for two reasons: First, because your house backs the loan, the interest rate is typically several percentage points less than on an unsecured personal or home improvement loan. Second, the interest on loans of up to $100,000 is deductible. But be careful. Tapping the equity means that your home is on the line; if you can't repay the loan, you could lose your home.

Don't use your house as collateral for a loan unless you know you can repay the loan. And don't borrow against your house for frivolous purposes such as a vacation that will be long forgotten by the time the loan is repaid. Good reasons to borrow might include paying for home improvements (to enhance the value of your home as well as its livability) and financing a college education.

Tax Talk

The **prime rate** is the base rate that banks extend to their best customers in setting interest rates on commercial loans. The interest rate on many consumer loans, including automobile loans and home equity line of credit, is tied to the prime rate.

How much you can borrow, with either a loan or a line of credit, depends on several factors:

➤ The amount of equity in your home, defined as the difference between the home's current value and the amount you still owe on your first mortgage

➤ Your credit rating

➤ The amount a lender is willing to lend, which varies from 65 percent to 125 percent of equity

You read that right. While the typical home equity loan or line of credit is for 70 percent to 80 percent of equity, some lenders cap loans below 70 percent and others will lend more than the house is worth. If you have a good credit rating and the amount of equity you have in your home is $100,000, as an example, you might be able to obtain a home equity loan or line of credit for anywhere from $65,000 to $125,000. Do some comparison shopping among lenders to see what is available.

Just because a loan is available for more than the amount of your equity, however, doesn't mean you should leap at the opportunity. First, the interest rate will be considerably higher than it will be on a more modest loan. Second, the interest on any amount exceeding the value of the home is not deductible. And, last, you could wind up owing more than your house is worth.

Tax Tips

Home equity loans and lines of credit resemble mortgages in many ways. Before you sign on the dotted line, you should find out the interest rate and how it can change. Ask about closing costs, including points, and inquire about fees. Ask if there are prepayment penalties if you decide to pay a loan early. Finally, be sure to comparison-shop for the best deal.

Applying for a home equity loan or line of credit is very much like applying for a mortgage. Once you decide how much you want to borrow and have done some comparison-shopping on rates and fees among lenders, you will need to do the following:

1. File an application with the lender you select.

2. Arrange to have the house appraised. Most lenders will want to use their own appraisers to perform this task.

3. Provide the lender with your most recent property tax statement, a balance-due statement from your mortgage lender showing how much of your original mortgage you have left to pay, and proof of homeowner's insurance.

If everything checks out, you can proceed with the loan. Keep in mind that any points and closing costs you pay to secure a home equity loan or line of credit must be deducted over the life of the loan and not in the first year, as you can do with your original mortgage.

Reverse Mortgages

For older people living on limited incomes and wanting to remain in their own familiar homes, a reverse mortgage can be a lifesaver.

As the name implies, a reverse mortgage is the opposite of a regular mortgage. Instead of borrowing money and building equity as you repay the principal and interest each month, you borrow money against existing equity in your home. But the real distinguishing factor is that the loan does not have to be repaid until the borrower dies or makes a permanent move. (A short stay in a hospital or nursing home will not necessitate repayment.)

To obtain a reverse mortgage, you must meet certain criteria:

➤ You must be at least age 62.

➤ You must own your home, and it must be your principal residence.

➤ If you have an outstanding mortgage, you must either pay it off before obtaining the reverse mortgage or—as most borrowers do—use part of the proceeds of the reverse mortgage to repay the original loan.

Because you are not obligated to repay the loan out of current income, income typically doesn't count. Instead, lenders look at your age, the current value of your home, and current interest rates. The largest loans go to the oldest borrowers because their life expectancy is shorter, and repayment can be expected fairly soon. In fact, it may not pay to apply for a reverse mortgage until you (or your parents, if they need the cash from their equity) are at least 70 or 75.

Closing costs and fees can be as steep as—and sometimes steeper than—they are on a regular mortgage, although they can be rolled into the amount of the loan. Costs are high because the lender is taking a big risk. No money is repaid on the loan until the borrower moves out or dies; no one knows whether that will be in 2 years or 20 years.

If you do apply for a reverse mortgage, you can choose between receiving the cash as a lump sum or in regular monthly payments. As a big plus, you (or your heirs) can never owe more than the value of the home at the time the loan is repaid. If the house is sold to repay the loan, the lender typically cannot collect more than the net proceeds from the sale.

Tax Traps

Don't pay a commission for advice on a reverse mortgage. Free counseling is available from the Department of Housing and Urban Development. For a state-by-state list of government-approved counseling agencies, go online to www.reverse.org and click on Sources. If your state isn't listed, call HUD at 1-800-569-4287 or 1-800-217-6970 or online at www.hudhcc.org.

Consider the following advantages before applying for a reverse mortgage:

➤ You have the ability to convert an asset to cash.

➤ No payments are due on the loan as long as you live in the house.

➤ Repayment can never exceed the value of the home or the proceeds when it is sold.

➤ Proceeds from the loan are not taxable.

Consider the following disadvantages before applying for a reverse mortgage:

➤ Fees are high and are not refundable.

➤ The loan uses some or all of your home equity, leaving less for your heirs.

➤ If the loan carries a variable interest rate, rising rates may decrease monthly payments.

Reverse mortgages are complicated and can be burdened with hard-to-understand fees and expenses. To get a handle on the total cost of any loan you're considering, visit the Web site run by the nonprofit National Center for Home Equity Conversion, at www.reverse.org.

The Least You Need to Know

➤ The interest on mortgage loans is the only interest that is still fully deductible for most folks.

➤ Working at home can yield a tax bonus in the form of more deductions.

➤ Improving your home can boost resale value and save on eventual taxes by increasing the cost basis.

➤ Home equity can be tapped via a home equity loan, a line of credit, or a reverse mortgage.

Territorial Imperatives

You may love your house and want to stay in it forever. But the truth is that most people do move. Perhaps it's a step up from a starter house. Maybe it's a job-related transfer or the quest for a new job. Sometimes it's a move to an apartment or a smaller house late in life when the children are grown and a big house becomes a burden to maintain.

Whatever the reason, you'll probably move at least once in your adult life. When you do, you can reap rewards from the tax laws. But—surprise!—these laws can be complicated. Here's the lowdown on what you need to know.

Sharing the Wealth

Some assets come with built-in tax deferral. You don't pay any tax on your profits in a hot stock until you sell the stock. And you don't have to pay any tax on the increased value of your home until you sell the property. In fact, thanks to recently enacted federal laws, you may never have to pay tax on any profit you earn by selling your house.

Until the Taxpayer Relief Act of 1997 was passed by Congress and signed into law by the president, there were just two ways to minimize the federal tax bill due on the sale of a primary residence.

You could postpone tax on the sale of one home if you purchased another home within two years of the sale, if both the old and the new house were your primary residence, and if the cost of the new house was at least as much as the sales price of the old house.

The tax could be deferred indefinitely, from one move to the next, as long as you followed the rules each time. Eventually, of course—perhaps when you downsized to smaller quarters late in life—the piper would probably have to be paid. But the other pre-1997 way to minimize taxes might have meant no taxes at all.

That rule went like this: If you (or one of you, for married taxpayers filing jointly) were age 55 or over at the time of the sale, you could exclude from taxes a maximum of $125,000 of the profit on the sale. The home had to have been used as your principal residence for at least three of the five years preceding the date of the sale.

In addition, the over-55 tax break was a once-in-a-lifetime deal. If a married couple used the exclusion, then one died, and the other remarried and wanted to use the exclusion with the second spouse, it was no deal. Many a second marriage was postponed until the sale of a house (by the partner who never used the tax break before) could be consummated.

The Taxpayer Relief Act of 1997 has made a dramatic difference, greatly simplifying the whole complicated tax picture on the sale of a principal residence. The applicable provisions went into effect on May 7, 1997. This was—and still is—a critical date for many homeowners.

Tax Treats

Under the old rules, you needed to keep track of tax-related household expenditures for all the years you lived in the house, plus at least three years after you filed a federal income tax return for the year of the sale. That's because some closing costs and most home improvements (as described in Chapter 3, "The Roof Over Your Head") could increase the cost basis of your home. An increase in cost basis brings a corresponding decrease in the profit and in the tax on that profit. Don't be too quick to dump those records, or to stop keeping track of current expenditures. You may need the documentation if your profit tops the excluded amount or if—it's been known to happen—the law is changed.

Moving On

The new law replaces both the deferral of tax on the buying of a new principal residence and the exclusion for taxpayers over age 55. In their place, the law states simply that there is no federal tax on amounts up to $250,000 in profit on the sale of a home for single taxpayers and up to $500,000 for married taxpayers filing jointly.

Of course, it isn't quite that simple. You still have to comply with some rules. You also still have to cope with the fallout from prior deferrals of tax if you sold a house and rolled over the profits into a new house before May 7, 1997.

The rules limit the tax exclusion to one sale every two years, without counting any sales before May 7, 1997. They require that you owned and occupied the residence as a principal residence for a total of at least two of the five years before the sale. The tax exclusion applies only to a principal residence, not to second (or third or more) homes.

But tax laws were made to have exceptions, and there is an exception to the two-year occupancy rule. If you must move because of ill health or because of a change in the location of your job, you can exclude the amount of the gain in proportion to the time you actually were in residence.

If this sounds like gobbledygook, it certainly started out to be. The IRS was initially interpreting the law strictly so that the portion of gain excludable from tax was related to the amount of profit.

Here's a simple example: You live in a house for one year, and then your boss strongly suggests that you move. You dutifully sell the house, making a $100,000 profit. According to the original IRS interpretation, $50,000 of this profit could have been excluded from tax because you lived in the house for one half of the two-year residency requirement. The result: At the capital gains tax rate of 20 percent, you owe Uncle Sam $10,000.

Congress corrected this misimpression on the part of the IRS in its 1998 tax legislation. Now, under the same set of circumstances, half of the

Tax Tips

Own a vacation home? Even though the tax break applies only to a primary residence, it's possible to double-dip. First, sell your principal residence (after, of course, meeting the residency rule). Then move into your vacation home. After living there for at least two years, you can sell the second house and reap the same tax benefits as if it had always been your primary residence.

Tax Traps

Sell your house at a loss? Too bad. While any profit on the sale of a house is potentially taxable, a loss is not deductible. (Losses on investments, on the other hand—whether real estate or securities—can count against gains in calculating taxes that may be due.)

maximum exclusion (not half of the profit) is allowed because you lived in the house half the required time before you moved for an approved reason. In this example, the result is no tax at all. The $100,000 profit is less than half of the $250,000 gain allowed a single taxpayer tax-free and, of course, far less than the $500,000 allowed a married couple.

Once and Again

While most people will never owe any tax on the sale of a home under the new laws, it can happen. And you don't have to be selling a multimillion-dollar property to face a hefty tax bill. It's even possible that you could sell a house at a loss and still owe tax. That's all because you've followed a typically American path and moved several times during the course of your adult life.

Let's say you started your home-buying odyssey in 1969, buying a starter house for $22,000. You sold the house in 1974 for $52,000 and bought a new larger home for $64,000. Under the laws in effect until 1997, you didn't have to pay any tax on the $30,000 in profit because you put all the money into your new, more expensive house.

You continued this progression, moving up every few years until, in 1998, you purchased a house worth $875,000. Now you've retired, the kids are long since grown and gone, and you're ready to sell and move to smaller quarters. In the hot California real estate market, you've been offered a round million dollars for the house. That's a profit of $125,000. Not bad, in just a couple of years. And, under the new law, you think, it should be completely tax-free. It isn't.

Under prior law, you couldn't roll over profits unless the new house was worth at least as much as the one you sold. Under prior law, therefore, the most profit you could have excluded from tax was the $125,000 allowed to people over age 55. That's the amount of your profit in this case, so you're home free—even without the benefit of the new law and its higher exclusions.

In fact, you sit there with accumulated profit (the sum of all the rollovers) of $650,000. Because the maximum amount excludable from tax for a married couple is $500,000, you owe tax on the remaining $150,000. At the 20 percent capital gains rate, that's a $30,000 tax bill. If you're single, it's worse. All you can exclude as a single taxpayer is $250,000. So, you owe tax on $400,000; at 20 percent, that's $80,000.

Tax Tips

Need help? Call the Internal Revenue Service, at 1–800–829–3676, and request a copy of IRS Publication No. 523. It contains worksheets for calculating the cost of your house for tax purposes. The information is also available online, at www.irs.gov.

None of this should matter to the next generation. Assuming that the tax law doesn't change (always a risky assumption), all that your children and grandchildren will have to do is live in each house they own for at least two years. Then, as long as the profit is less than $250,000 or $500,000 (depending on whether they are single or married at the time of the sale), no taxes will be due.

When a House Is Not a Home

Selling a house in which you've maintained a home office is a more complicated situation. In fact, here's where a home office can come back to haunt you—or, at least, cause you to pay more tax than you anticipated on the sale of your house.

When you sell a house that contains an office, you're actually selling two pieces of property: a residence and a business. Not surprisingly, the rules are different. The tax breaks that apply to your principal residence do not apply to the business portion of your property.

When you sell, therefore, you will owe capital gains tax on the portion of the house you've claimed as an office. If you've been using 25 percent of the square footage for your business, then 25 percent of the profit will be subject to tax. If you make a $100,000 profit, then $25,000 will be taxable. At the 20 percent capital gains rate, you will owe $5,000.

In addition, because you've been claiming a deduction for *depreciation* each year on the office portion of your house, you will owe tax on the accumulated depreciation at the special rate of 25 percent. If your depreciation totals $6,000 over the years, you will owe an additional $1,500.

You can't get around the tax on depreciation claimed since May 7, 1997, the date the new law went into effect. However, you can bypass the capital gains tax on the business portion of your home—if you're able to plan in advance. Because the law requires that you own and occupy a principal residence for two years out of the last five in order to claim the $250,000/$500,000 exclusion from tax, stop taking home office deductions at least two years before you sell. Doing this will convert your entire house back into a home and make any profit on the sale eligible for the exclusion.

New Job, New Home

If you move because you're changing jobs, you can reap some additional tax benefits. The rules aren't as liberal as they used to be, in terms of deducting most of the costs of a job search, but it's still possible to gain some tax advantage if you must pay the cost of a job-related move out of your own pocket.

The deductions may be claimed whether you had to move because of a change in location of an existing job or moved voluntarily because you started a new job. They also may be claimed by anyone taking a first full-time job or someone returning to full-time work after a lengthy period of unemployment.

Tax Treats

Tax benefits for job-related moves are still called deductions, but they're really better than deductions. That's because, unless you itemize deductions—and most taxpayers don't, taking the standard deduction instead—deductions don't do much good. These costs are actually considered adjustments to income and can lower your tax bill whether or not you file an itemized return.

To claim job-related deductions, you must meet tests of both time and distance.

The time test is clear-cut. You generally can deduct only eligible expenses incurred within one year of starting the new job. If your family stays behind for 18 months because you couldn't sell your former home, you're out of luck in terms of claiming job-related moving costs. However, the accounting firm of Ernst & Young points out in *The Ernst & Young Tax Guide 1999* that delaying the move for 18 months so that your teenage son or daughter could finish high school is okay.

The distance test is a bit more complicated. You pass the test if your new place of work is at least 50 miles farther from your old home than your previous job location was from that same home. You read that right; the location of your new home is irrelevant.

An example should help. Let's say that you used to live 3 miles from your place of work. That same house is 38 miles from your new place of work. You don't pass the test because the new job is not at least 50 miles farther from your former residence than your last job. Presumably, you could still tolerate the commute. However, if your new job is 58 miles from your former residence, you can "pass Go and collect the $200." You can take job-related moving deductions.

There is one more stipulation: You must be employed full-time for at least 39 weeks during the year immediately following the move. If you're self-employed, the time test is more stringent: You must work full-time for at least 39 weeks during the first 12 months and a total of at least 78 weeks of the two years following the move.

The weeks of work do not have to be for the same employer. And, if you start out as self-employed, it doesn't mean that you must remain self-employed. But you must be working for the designated number of weeks in the new location.

If you meet the rules, you may deduct two significant expenses: The cost of moving your household goods and travel to your new home, including lodging but not meals. Forget about pre-move house-hunting expenses and temporary living expenses; these used to be deductible but no longer are.

The cost of moving household goods includes packing and shipping costs, including the cost of moving belongings from another location. If your newly minted college graduate will be joining you at your new location, for example, you can include the cost of moving her possessions from a dormitory or off-campus apartment to your new home.

Expenses must be reasonable. The IRS doesn't insist that you use the least-expensive moving company, but it will rule out deductions for travel that include some extra days for sightseeing.

At the End of the Road

Tax benefits don't necessarily end when you sell your home—or even when you die. But the rules can get complicated when divorce or death leads to the sale of a home.

The exclusion from taxes of $250,000 per single taxpayer and $500,000 per married couple still applies. But there are special wrinkles to the calculation when property is sold in connection with a divorce, is inherited by a surviving spouse, or is sold following the death of the owner.

Splitting Up Is Hard to Do

The family home is typically one of the two most valuable assets you own. (In case you're wondering, a retirement plan is the other.)

So, don't act hastily if you and your formerly ever-loving spouse are severing the ties that bind. Give careful thought to who gets the house and who gets other assets.

You have emotional consequences to consider, particularly if you both want your children to remain in the family home. But don't casually trade a house worth $200,000, for example, for securities worth $200,000. Assets of comparable value may carry very different tax consequences. The key element is the cost basis of each asset, what it cost at the time of purchase compared to its current market value.

Tax Tips

The number of weeks you must work to qualify for job-related moving expenses can straddle a calendar year—and even go beyond the date you file your tax return for the year of the move. Go ahead and claim the deduction if you expect to meet the test. If your expectations aren't met, you can either file an amended income tax return for the year in question or report the moving expense deduction as income on your next tax return.

When you transfer property to your about-to-be-ex-spouse, you also transfer the cost basis of that property. That means that your ex-spouse eventually will have to pay tax on the entire appreciation, from your date of purchase to his or her date of sale.

Tax Traps

No immediate tax consequences are evident when you're divvying up property acquired during marriage; one spouse can transfer property to the other without reporting any gain. Don't let this tax-free transfer blind you to the fact that taxes must eventually be paid on the entire appreciated value from date of purchase by whichever partner owns the asset at the date of sale.

Let's say that you transfer $200,000 worth of securities with a cost basis of $160,000; the unrealized capital gain is $40,000. If you transfer a $200,000 house with a cost basis of $100,000, the unrealized capital gain is $100,000. (Unrealized gains are paper gains. Gain isn't "realized"—or taxed—until the asset is sold.)

At the 20 percent capital gains rate, a sale of the securities would produce a current tax bill of $8,000, while a sale of the house would produce a hypothetical tax bill of $20,000. Because a single taxpayer can exclude up to $250,000 in gain on the sale of a home, there is no actual tax bill in this particular example. But tax could be due if the gain exceeds the exclusion, and this should be considered in dividing appreciated assets in divorce. One of you could come out ahead, and the other could lose out if securities and a house are treated as equivalent assets for purposes of the divorce settlement.

There's something else to consider: when to sell the old homestead. If the first rule of real estate is location, location, location, then the first rule in a divorce is timing, timing, timing.

Tax Treats

Contemplating remarriage? Do you each own a house? If you sell the houses you own individually, you each get a tax exclusion of $250,000, even if you are now married and filing jointly. If you sell one house and move into the other, and then wait two years to fulfill the residency requirement, you can relish a tax exclusion of $250,000 on the first sale and $500,000 on the second.

If you sell your house before the divorce is final, you're entitled, as a married couple filing jointly, to the full $500,000 tax exclusion. If you wait until you're officially divorced, the now-single owner selling the house can exclude only $250,000 of profit from taxes. If a house has appreciated in value over the years—and if you've rolled the profit from previous sales into the current house—the resulting tax bill could be painful.

Two Things Are Certain: Death and Taxes

You don't escape taxes by dying, but you do minimize their impact. Thanks to a welcome provision in the U.S. Tax Code, inherited property benefits from a *step-up in basis*. That is, its value for tax purposes is its value on the date of death instead of at the date of purchase. This can mean significant tax savings on highly appreciated property, whether that property is securities, an art collection, or a house.

Remember the house we talked about earlier? The one you purchased in 1969 for $22,000 that is now worth a cool million dollars? Sell it and, even with the new exclusion, you'll owe megabucks in taxes. But go to your heavenly reward, and your heirs won't owe a penny. Their cost basis will become the market value at the date of your death, even if that market value of $1 million vastly exceeds the original cost basis.

But most married couples own the family home together. What happens when the house is jointly owned and one owner dies? The survivor automatically becomes the sole owner of the property, with half of its value receiving the step-up in basis.

This has several tax-related implications. The first fact that probably springs to mind is that you won't owe as much tax if you sell the family homestead. Your tax bill will be based on the difference between the price you get for your house and the combination of your half of the original cost basis and the stepped-up value of your spouse's half.

To take a simple example, imagine that you and your spouse have lived in the same house for decades. You bought it for $100,000, but a rising real estate market has brought its value to $750,000. Ignoring any improvements you probably made over the years, and anything else that would affect the cost basis, you would have a profit of $650,000 if you sold. With the $500,000 exclusion for married couples, you would owe tax of $30,000—that's 20 percent of the $150,000 difference between your profit and the exclusion.

If one of you dies, however, the picture changes. The cost basis is now made up of two parts. Your

Tax Talk

Basis (cost basis or tax basis) is the cost of acquiring an asset, used to calculate gain or loss when the asset is sold. Inherited assets receive a **step-up in basis;** their cost basis is their value on the date of the owner's death.

half is $50,000, representing half of the original cost basis. Because your spouse's half of the tax liability evaporates at the date of his death, his share of the cost basis is $375,000 (half of the market value of the house at the date of death). The total is $425,000, bringing the profit on the sale down to $325,000.

Now you have a problem. While most advisers strongly suggest that a surviving spouse should stay put, without making any major change for at least a year, holding on to the family home may dent your wallet. The situation won't affect most people, but it could be an issue if you own a house that has become considerably more valuable or if you have accumulated gains from a lifetime of moves.

The tax law permits you to file a joint income tax return for the year in which your spouse dies. Selling the house within that year entitles you to the $500,000 exclusion for married couples. If you wait the recommended year, however, all you get is the $250,000 exclusion for a single taxpayer. In this example, $75,000 would be subject to tax at a cost of $15,000.

For some people, good emotional advice may have to give way to financial practicality. But be sure to consult competent advisers before you decide what to do.

The Least You Need to Know

➤ Under current law, single taxpayers may exclude $250,000 of profit on the sale of a home from taxes. Married couples filing jointly get the first $500,000 of profit tax-free.

➤ Deferral of tax on earlier home sales will be counted toward the tax-free amount.

➤ Converting a home office back to a home at least two years before selling your house will ease the tax bite.

➤ Moving yourself and your household goods may be deductible if your move is job-related.

➤ Get professional advice before selling a house following divorce or death.

Chapter 5

By the Sea, by the Sea

In This Chapter

- Finding that vacation homes come in all price ranges
- Discovering that mortgage interest and property taxes on second homes are tax-deductible
- Renting out your vacation home may yield additional tax breaks
- Understanding that vacation homes are to enjoy—and not expecting a profit—or a tax break—when you sell

A lakeside cabin, a cottage by the shore, a condominium on a Caribbean island .... Vacation paradise means different things to different people. Wherever your personal paradise may be located, owning a second home can be a source of great pleasure. If you play your cards right, it can also yield some tax breaks.

This chapter introduces second homes, in all their variety, and describes the tax implications of owning, renting, and selling.

A Dream Come True

The economy has been good, baby boomers are aging and affluent, and all signs point to a surging market in second homes.

Although some people like to fly south for vacations and don't think twice about buying property far away, the most popular vacation spots are within a two- to three-hour drive of home. Being within manageable driving distance lets you enjoy weekends year-round as well as extended stays.

Recent developments make second-home ownership better than ever:

➤ Money that was formerly tied up by a tax code imposing capital gains taxes on the sale of a primary home has been freed by new tax laws that exclude up to $250,000 of gain for a single taxpayer and $500,000 for a married couple filing jointly. Now "empty nesters" can trade down to a smaller primary residence when the family has grown and put the profits into a vacation home.

➤ Mortgage lenders in many parts of the country used to charge higher interest rates for second homes. Many have stopped doing so, putting rates on par with mortgages on primary residences. However, you may still be required to make a hefty down payment. Where you can buy a permanent residence with as little as 5 percent down, you'll probably have to come up with at least 10 percent and possibly 20 percent of the purchase price on a vacation home.

➤ Homeowner's insurance on second homes typically costs more than on primary residences because second homes often are vacant for long periods. Unoccupied homes are considered more vulnerable to break-ins and theft. Some insurers are now lowering premiums, but you'll have to shop around.

Location, Location, Location

Where you buy your second home is just as important as where you choose to make your permanent home. As real estate professionals say, location is everything.

Tax Tips

A vacation home doesn't have to be a house. Under the tax rules, mobile homes qualify. So do boats. But the "home" must have sleeping space, a toilet, and cooking facilities.

First, think about your purpose. A cottage that will be used strictly for holiday weekends and a couple of weeks in the summer is one thing. A cabin intended for vacation use now and a retirement residence later is something else. And a vacation home that will be rented out much of the time is in a category all its own.

In every one of these scenarios, you'll want vacation amenities. Depending on personal preference, these might include access to water for swimming and boating, trails for hiking and/or cross-country skiing, and nearby entertainment in the form of theater, concerts, and movies.

If you plan to retire to your vacation hideaway, however, you'll want to be sure that it meets your needs year-round and not just on a seasonal basis. You may find that an ideal summer spot, bustling with activities, falls dormant in the winter months. You may discover that the 10-mile jaunt to the nearest full-size grocery store, tolerable in spring and fall, is a chore when the roads are clogged with either tourists or snow. And you definitely need to check out local healthcare facilities for competence and convenience.

If you're looking at a vacation home as rental property, you need both resort amenities plus conveniences. You'll want to consider buying a larger home than you might otherwise want, within easy driving distance of a metropolitan area, and furnishing it so that it will attract renters. You may prefer to do without a TV when you want to "get away from it all," but tenants will want a TV and a VCR as well.

Tax Tips

When you're adding up the costs involved with owning a vacation home, don't forget garbage service—or the need to make regular trips to the town recycling center, if there is no pickup. Think about snow plowing in the North, flood insurance near the coasts, and higher homeowner's insurance premiums if you're miles from the fire department.

Be prepared for extra costs. Insurance premiums probably will be higher if you have a transient population of renters. You also may need a cleaning service between tenants, and you may want to pay a real estate broker or management company to locate and screen renters. Some of these costs, as described later, are tax-deductible on rental property.

Sharing Space and Time

You may not want the responsibility of owning and maintaining your own individual vacation home. What's more, you may not want to spend all your vacations in one location.

Time-sharing, also called "interval vacations" or "club memberships," may provide an answer.

Time-sharing means buying a vacation home piecemeal, typically for a week or two each year. The concept fell into disrepute from a combination of hardball sales tactics and developer failures, but it is coming back into its own with the entry of respected hotel names into the field.

More than two million Americans now own fractional interests in vacation homes.

According to the American Resort Development Association, the industry trade association, the average two-bedroom time-share unit costs about $10,000 for one week per year. Maintenance costs an average of an additional $360 a year. Some large units in fancy ski resorts, however, can cost three or four times as much.

Tax Tips

For more information on time-sharing, go online to www.arda.org or call the American Resort Development Association at 1-202-371-6700. Ask for the booklet "A Consumer Guide to Vacation Ownership."

Tax Traps

Before you sign up for a time-share, find out what happens if the developer has financial problems. The Federal Trade Commission suggests checking to see if your contract includes two specific clauses. A "nondisturbance provision" should ensure that you'll continue to have use of your unit in the event of default and any third-party claims against the developer or management company. A "nonperformance protection clause" should allow you to keep your ownership rights even if a third party is required to buy out your contract.

What are you actually buying? In some cases, buyers receive a deed conveying the use of a specific condo at a specific time every year forever. In others, often termed right-to-use or club membership, you get the right to use a unit—any unit—for a certain number of years.

Most consumers buy time-share units outright or finance them with consumer credit. However, if you have a deed and own the property as a second home, you may be able to deduct the interest on a mortgage. In right-to-use time shares, in which you don't actually own the unit, mortgage interest is not deductible.

Your own time-share unit may be nice—it may even be in a lavish resort setting—but what many buyers like most about time-sharing is the ability to exchange their own unit for another unit in another location. If you want to swap, be sure that the unit you buy is in a resort that participates in an exchange arrangement. Buy a unit with at least two bedrooms in a popular season. Don't expect anyone to offer you a week in Hawaii's high season in exchange for your midwinter week on Maryland's Eastern Shore.

And don't expect a time-share unit to be a rewarding investment. It's really not an investment at all, but should be compared to the cost of hotel or rental vacations. In fact, because units are usually extraordinarily difficult to unload, you may do a lot better buying a resale unit from an eager seller instead of buying a new unit from a developer.

Whether you buy a new unit or a resale, cover your bases before you buy:

➤ Check out the developer. Is the company financially stable and the facility well managed?

➤ Read all the documents. Be sure that you understand whether you are buying deeded property or a right-to-use plan, a fixed week each year or a floating week within a given season.

➤ Have the documents reviewed by a financial adviser, or, at the very least, take them home to read at your leisure. Don't let yourself be pressured to buy.

➤ Find out if the resort belongs to an exchange network such as Resort Condominiums International or Interval International. What is the exchange policy? What fees will you pay to participate in an exchange?

Going In Together

Some folks bypass formal time-sharing arrangements and simply join forces with relatives or friends to purchase and share vacation property. In terms of taxes, there's no problem. If four of you own the house and make equal payments, four of you can each deduct one-fourth of mortgage interest and property tax payments.

This can work well, but it's important to put the agreement in writing and to anticipate potential problems. Consider these factors:

➤ How costs will be split. Will all names be on the mortgage? Will you set up a reserve fund for unanticipated expenses, or will you meet them as they arise?

➤ How use of the property will be allocated. If you're in ski country, there are just so many weeks a year for good skiing; who gets dibs on the best weeks? Ditto at a north-country lake in the summer.

➤ How decisions will be made—and disputes will be resolved—about renovations and improvements.

➤ Whether to rent the property to others when it is not being used by one of the co-owners.

➤ What procedure will be followed when one co-owner wants to sell.

Where the Grass Is Greener

Perhaps you've heard tales of vacation homes abroad, where costs are low and the sun always shines. The idea may be particularly attractive if you can spend several months at a time in your home away from home.

The more time you spend, however, the more likely you are to run into tax hurdles. Consider these points, for example:

➤ If you stay overseas more than six months, you may be taxed as a resident while still paying income tax to the United States. Check this one out before you go. The United States has tax treaties with many, but not all, countries. The treaties generally preclude double taxation.

➤ Some countries have more onerous capital gains taxes.

➤ In some countries, you'll have to pay a sales tax when you buy property and a transfer tax when you sell.

➤ If you're retired, you can receive your Social Security retirement checks anywhere in the world. But you can't use Medicare to cover healthcare—it applies outside the United States only in limited emergency situations.

Tax Talk

Points, often charged on a mortgage as an origination fee and a way to increase yield for the lender, are deductible by the borrower because they are considered prepaid mortgage interest. Each point represents 1 percent of the mortgage loan amount. If you take a mortgage loan of $70,000 with one point, you actually receive $69,300.

Tax Tips

You can switch the tax treatment of your Shangri-La from year to year. Use it yourself one year, rent it out the next, and then combine personal use and rentals the third year—it's all okay, in any sequence. Just claim the appropriate treatment on your income tax return when you file for the year, and you're all set.

Don't skimp on good advice if you're considering a second home in another country. Use a local attorney, preferably one fluent in both English and the native language.

Permutations and Combinations

The tax rules that apply to second homes depend on how you use the place. The rules are simple when you use your home yourself and don't rent it out.

Mortgage interest is deductible on first and second homes for loans totaling up to $1 million. In addition, interest on home equity loans of up to $100,000 is deductible. Note that this applies to two homes only. If you're lucky enough to own more than two homes—or unlucky enough, given the chore of remembering which house needs what—mortgage interest on the third and any additional properties is not deductible.

Every once in a while, the powers that be in Washington toss around the idea of eliminating the mortgage interest deduction on second homes. So far, the deduction remains intact.

If you take a mortgage with *points* on your vacation hideaway, the points are deductible over the life of the loan. On a primary residence, they may be deducted in the first year.

Property taxes are also deductible on a second home, as on a first.

One special rule yields a special tax break: If you rent out the house for less than 15 days a year, the rental income is not taxable, and you don't even have to declare it on your income tax return. You also can't claim any deductions for the cost associated with renting the property, but they probably are so minor that you should come out ahead.

Every once in a while, someone suggests repealing this tax break and taxing rental income even if it's only for a few days a year. President Clinton made this suggestion in February 2000. So far it hasn't happened, and Congressional sentiment seems strongly opposed.

The tax treatment of vacation property becomes more complicated when it's a rental or mixed-use property.

Strangers in the House

If you rent out your vacation house for 15 or more days a year but use it no more than 14 days—or 10 percent of the number of days it was rented, whichever is greater—it is considered a rental property. If you rent it for a total of 200 days during the year, as an example, it will qualify as a rental property unless you use it yourself for more than 20 days.

Once your vacation home is classified as a rental property, you may deduct what you spend on utilities, maintenance, repairs, insurance, rental costs (such as advertising for prospective tenants), and *depreciation,* in addition to mortgage interest and property taxes.

If you buy a vacation property as an investment and plan to rent it out most of the time, then you should look at it as a business and evaluate its financial merits as you would any other investment.

But don't count on clearing megabucks in profit. The appeal of rental property can be a sometime thing, depending on what's "hot" in a given year. Many owners are happy to break even during the years of ownership, hoping for profit when they sell. Profit at sale can be ephemeral, too, although a tax loss may ease some of the pain. (Tax treatment at sale is discussed later in this chapter in the "Moving On" section.)

Tax losses for property owners aren't what they used to be before the Tax Reform Act of 1986 changed the rules, resulting in a significant loss of value for investment real estate throughout the United States. Today, spending more than you take in qualifies as a fully deductible loss only if your

Tax Tips

Any day that you spend working substantially full-time repairing and maintaining your property is not counted as a day of personal use. In fact, the IRS comes right out and says (in Publication 17, "The Tax Guide for Individuals") that family members can use the property for recreational purposes while you're working, and the day still won't be counted as a personal day.

Tax Talk

Depreciation is a method of allocating the cost of a property—and spreading the deductions for that cost—over its useful life. For rental residential real estate, you subtract the cost of the land and then depreciate the cost of the building over 27.5 years.

adjusted gross income is less than $100,000. Even then, you can't deduct a loss of more than $25,000. Such *passive losses* phase out altogether at an adjusted gross income of $150,000.

At higher incomes, you can write off passive losses only against income from other passive investments—such as another rental property or a limited partnership, described in Chapter 21, "Blue Plate Specials." Or, you can carry them over from year to year until you sell the property, and then use them to reduce your gain or increase your loss on the sale. Then again, you could forget about renting and use your vacation home for personal vacations.

This and That

So-called mixed-use property, partly personal vacation residence and partly rental property, is the most complicated of all in tax terms.

If you rent out the house for more than 15 days a year and use it yourself for more than the 14 days or 10 percent of the rental days described previously, you must report the rental income on your income tax return. You also must allocate expenses between personal and business use, depending on the proportion of use for each purpose.

Tax Talk

Passive losses are from activities in which taxpayers don't actively participate. In tax law, they are differentiated from investment income, wages, and income from an active trade or business. Losses from rental real estate are classified as passive losses except for professionals who spend at least half their time managing the property.

Tax Traps

If you're trying to stay within the business property rules by keeping personal use within the limits, don't rent your property to a relative or friend unless you charge fair market value. If you give family or friends a break on rental costs, the IRS will consider the time they spend your personal use—which may knock you out of the running for some deductions. In one Tax Court case, though, a taxpayer was allowed to discount the fair rental value in exchange for the renters (in this case, the owner's parents) taking such good care of the property that fees to an outside manager were unnecessary.

Here's a simple example, mathematically speaking: If you rent out the house half of the total number of days the house is in use during the year—not the total number of days in the calendar year—you can deduct 50 percent of the insurance, utilities, maintenance, rental costs, and depreciation as business expenses. Attach Schedule E to your federal income tax return to report rental income and expenses.

Expenses on the rental portion may be deducted only up to the amount of actual rental income for the year. Excess expenses may be carried forward to subsequent tax years. You can't apply a tax loss to other income.

Before you decide to buy a vacation home as rental property, ask yourself these questions:

➤ How desirable is the area for renters?

➤ Will rental income be predictable?

➤ Are operating expenses likely to remain stable?

➤ Can you carry the cost of the property if rentals don't meet expectations?

Making It Permanent

Many people look at second homes as trial retirement homes. If you think that your vacation cottage may eventually be a year-round residence, however, you have to look at in a different light.

A totally rural hideaway may be delightful for weekend getaways, but it may be an inappropriate location for year-round living—initially because it may be too isolated in the off-season and, eventually, as you get older, because it's just too isolated altogether.

If you're buying with an eye to eventual year-round living, check out the availability of everything from year-round entertainment options—some areas hop in the summer and cool down considerably in the winter—to good medical care.

Taxing Times

If your weekend cottage will eventually become your retirement home, think taxes when you buy. Look at these factors:

Tax Traps

Mortgage interest on mixed-use property must be reported on different tax return schedules, based on the proportion of personal and business use. The mortgage interest on the business segment is reported on Schedule E, while the mortgage interest allocated to personal use is reported on Schedule A of Form 1040.

➤ **Income taxes**—Some states, including Florida and Nevada, don't tax income.

➤ **Other taxes**—New Hampshire taxes dividends and interest. New York taxes the transfer of real estate.

➤ **Property taxes**—Look beyond the raw numbers to the tax rate and the frequency of reassessment.

➤ **Sales taxes**—Some states exempt food, clothing, and prescription drugs; some tax everything.

Tax Treats

Will you be moving from a high-tax state to a low-tax or no-tax state in retirement? If so, you have one less thing to worry about. Federal law now prohibits states from taxing the retirement income of former residents. If you earned your pension in New York, as an example, you can move to Florida knowing that New York can't come after you for state income tax on that pension.

Double Trouble

Will buying a vacation home in another state produce tax trouble? It might.

If you use a second home in another state only occasionally, the only tax problem may be the eventual cost and delay of probate proceedings in both states. This can be avoided by married couples owning the property jointly and single owners (including widowed owners) placing the house in a revocable living trust.

But if you divide the year between two residences in two different states, you may face undreamed-of tax complications. It is actually possible to be classified as a legal resident of two states simultaneously and to have two states claiming income tax.

This doesn't happen to many people. If you spend more than six months in one of the states, you are normally considered a resident of that state for income tax purposes. But if you are in a high tax bracket and want to convince skeptical state taxing authorities in your home state that you have changed your legal residence, take these steps:

➤ Shift your legal identity—in the form of driver's license, automobile registration, and voter registration—to the new state.

➤ Establish new civic, social, and religious connections. If you want to maintain memberships in your old community, make them nonresident memberships.

➤ File tax returns from your new address.

➤ Consider drafting a new will, using your new address; this step may not be necessary, but it could buttress your position if it comes to an audit.

Most important: Use your head. If you're claiming Florida as your legal residence, don't hang on to a rent-stabilized apartment in Manhattan or claim residency to avoid the New York City garage parking tax. If you do, New York could come after you—and probably will—for current income taxes or chase your estate for estate taxes.

Moving On

Vacation homes have been best bought to enjoy, not for investment potential. This may be changing. The National Association of Realtors notes that the median age of vacation homeowners is 52 and that the bulge of the Baby Boom generation is moving into their 50s. In addition, because many of the most desirable locations are already developed, there is some upward pressure on prices. So, it's possible, although you can't count on it, that you'll make a profit when you sell.

To improve the investment potential, think about moving on before moving in. In other words, buy a home with features that can maximize resale value. Three bedrooms are better than two, and two bathrooms are better than one. A fireplace is a plus, and so is a deck.

When you sell a vacation home, the tax treatment of the gain (or loss) goes back to whether you used the property yourself or rented it out. There is no capital gains exclusion when you sell a second home used for personal pleasure. Every penny of profit is taxable, although at lower capital gains rates if you've owned the property more than a year. You also can't write off a loss, just as you can't on a primary residence, if you happen to sell the house for less than you paid for it.

Different rules apply if the house was a mixed-use property, rented out more than 15 days and personally used more than 14 days or 10 percent of the rental days. Now you have to treat the sale as the sale of two different properties. That means allocating the initial cost of the house, its selling price, and any selling expenses between the personal and rental segments as if there were two separate transactions. Profit on both transactions is taxable, but loss may be claimed only on the rental portion. Here's another place where you need good tax advice.

Tax Treats

Want tax-free profit when selling your vacation home? Sell your primary home, move in to the vacation place, and live there for at least two years. This makes it your primary residence, eligible for the capital gains exclusion of $250,000 for a single taxpayer and $500,000 for a married couple filing jointly.

The Least You Need to Know

➤ Vacation homes are a lifestyle choice, but they may become a better investment as demand grows.

➤ Tax breaks can cut the cost of ownership, but tax breaks are tied to whether you use the home yourself, treat it as rental property, or do some of each.

➤ Time-share units are tough to resell, making resale units a bargain for buyers in many places.

➤ A second home can be a trial retirement home, if you choose the location wisely.

➤ There is no capital gains tax break when you sell a vacation home used for pleasure—unless you've made it your permanent residence for at least two years.

Part 3
Kids Cost, Kids Save

Those little bundles of joy can cost megabucks to raise, but they can also produce some nifty tax shelters along the way.

In this part of the book, you'll learn about tax credits, tax-sheltered ways to save for college, special education tax breaks, and last—but not least—what grandparents can do to help while minimizing their own taxes.

Chapter 6

UGMA, UTMA, Kids and Taxes

> ## In This Chapter
>
> ➤ Finding that children yield a tax bonus in exemptions and credits
>
> ➤ Discovering that children's earned and unearned income above specified amounts is taxable
>
> ➤ Including children's income on your tax return, or filing separate tax returns for each child
>
> ➤ Saving for your children in your name or theirs

It costs a lot of money to have and raise children these days—upwards of $200,000, and that's before they reach college. But tax breaks along the way can ease some of the financial pain.

This chapter describes the impact kids have on your tax picture and then explains the ins and outs of saving money in children's names versus your own. Which is better isn't as clear cut as you might think. Read on.

Kids and Taxes

As every expectant parent knows, a baby born on December 31 is a tax-bonus baby. That's because you immediately earn a personal exemption on your federal income tax return. The exemption is for the year the child is born—and every year thereafter that the child is a dependent—whether the child is around for just 1 day or all 365 days.

Exemptions go up along with the cost of living. For the 1999 tax year, the exemption for each dependent was worth $2,750; for 2000, it went up to $2,800.

But the personal exemption is just the beginning. There are other tax bonuses as well.

Children Get Credit

A $500 tax credit is available for each child under age 17 for married couples filing jointly whose adjusted gross income is $110,000 or less, and for singles with AGI of $75,000 or less. Above those income levels, the total credit is reduced by $50 for every $1,000 in additional income, phasing out entirely for a married couple with one child at income of just over $119,000.

The exemption plus the $500 tax credit can make a big difference in your taxable income. Here's an example from tax publishers CCH Incorporated.

Let's say you're a married couple with no children and $60,000 of adjusted gross income. Taking the standard deduction and two personal exemptions brings your taxable income to $47,050, putting you in the 28 percent tax bracket, as shown in the table in Chapter 1, "The Toll Taxes Take." This produces a federal income tax bill for the year 2000 of $7,436. If you add one child to the mix, taking the additional exemption of $2,800 and the credit of $500, the tax drops to $6,190. That's a savings of $1,284.

If you have a second child, it gets even better. Another exemption brings taxable income down to $41,450, dropping you from the 28 percent bracket to the 15 percent bracket according to the year 2000 tax brackets. That additional $500 credit brings your federal income tax bite down to $5,218.

Tax Tips

Want to claim an exemption for your newborn? Be sure to apply for a Social Security number for the baby right away. You must have it for the federal income tax return you file for the year when the child is born.

Tax Tips

If a bundle of joy is on the way, be sure to file a revised W-4 withholding form with your employer. The new $500-per-child credit is built into the forms, so your withholding will drop and your take-home pay will increase.

Caring Gets Credit, Too

Then there's the childcare credit, a boon to working parents of children under age 13—and older children as well, if they are unable to care for themselves because of a physical or mental disability. The credit can be claimed for the cost of childcare while you work; that care can include day care, after-school programs, and even summer day camp.

There is no upper limit on income for the childcare credit, although the amount you may claim decreases as income rises to $28,000. For parents with income up to $10,000, the credit is a maximum of $720 for one child or $1,440 for more than one. It is calculated as 30 percent of qualifying expenses up to $2,400 for one child and $4,800 for two or more children. The credit gradually decreases to 20 percent of allowable expenses at AGI of $28,000 or more.

Your Child's Income

Things get really interesting on the tax front when your children start to have money of their own.

Whether they have unearned income from investments you've made in their names (more about this later) or earned income as the fruit of their own labors, Uncle Sam wants his due.

In brief, these are the rules:

➤ No tax is due on a child's earned income in amounts up to the standard deduction for single taxpayers; in 2000, this is $4,400. Beyond that level, money children earn for themselves is always taxed at their own income tax rate.

Want to give your youngsters a big boost toward future financial security? Once they have earned income in a given year, let them spend their earnings (forced savings don't work) but give them a matching amount (up to $2,000) to contribute to an individual retirement account. A Roth IRA (contributions are not tax-deductible, but withdrawals after the age of 59½ are never taxed; see Chapter 12, "On Your Own [IRA] Account") can yield big benefits down the road. Contribute $2,000 a year for 10 years, and then leave the account alone to continue compounding at a very conservative 8 percent for 40 years. Your youngster will have a retirement nest egg of $255,520. Not bad for starters.

➤ Investment income is a different story. The first $700 is not taxable. For children under age 14, amounts between $701 and $1,400 are taxed at the child's rate; amounts over $1,400 are taxed at the parent's (typically higher) income tax rate. For children 14 and over, everything over $700 is taxed at the child's own (typically lower) income tax rate.

➤ When a child has both earned income and investment income, the calculations get more complicated. You must add $250 to the child's earned income, and then take the larger of the resulting amount or $700. Then

Tax Tips

When parents are divorced, the custodial parent may claim the childcare credit even if he or she does not claim the child as a dependent.

compare that number with the standard deduction for single taxpayers ($4,400 in 2000) and use the smaller figure to determine the tax that is due. While this sounds complicated—because it is—it actually produces an improvement over prior law, where the first dollar of a child's unearned income was often subject to tax.

Tax Treats

Although the tax rules applying to children are complicated, you may come out ahead. Mark Luscombe, a federal tax analyst with CCH Incorporated, points out that an investment producing $1,400 of income will cost $392 in taxes for an adult in the 28 percent tax bracket. The same investment income in a child's name will cost only $105 in taxes—because the child can subtract the nontaxable $700 and then pay 15 percent of the remaining $700. That's a tax saving of $287.

The Kiddie Tax

Before 1986, a favorite tax-saving strategy for parents involved putting investments in the names of children so that income would be taxed at their lower tax rates. This shifting of income from parent to child saved tax dollars for the family as a whole.

As part of the Tax Reform Act of 1986, however, Congress changed the rules. The "kiddie tax," as it's called, divides children between those under the age of 14 and those 14 and over. Younger children are taxed at their parents' rate, as indicated above, so that there is no longer any advantage in putting sizable investments in their names.

But wise planning can minimize the impact of the kiddie tax. For example, you might follow one of these approaches:

➤ Have children own assets that don't generate much (if any) current income, such as growth stocks and stock mutual funds aimed at capital appreciation. Index funds are another good bet because they tend not to generate large capital gains distributions.

➤ Delay taking capital gains until the child turns 14. At that time, when the youngster's unearned income is taxed at his own rate, the long-term capital gains tax bite will be just 10 percent for a child in the 15 percent tax bracket, or 8 percent if the asset has been held at least five years.

Who Files What

If tax-saving strategies don't eliminate tax on their unearned income, you'll have to decide whether you should file separate tax returns for your children or include their income on your own return. If you file returns for them, you must use Form 8615 and attach it to the child's 1040. If you include the children's investment income on your return, you must use Form 8814 and attach it to your own 1040.

If your children have any earned income, or if their gross income (earned and unearned) is $7,000 or more, you won't have a choice. You'll have to file separate federal income tax returns for them.

When you do have a choice (when their income is solely from interest and dividends), which way should you go?

Tax Tips

By understanding the tax laws, you can make them work in your favor. Consider this example from CCH Incorporated: Paying private-school tuition for a 15-year-old by selling 100 shares of stock purchased for $20 a share that is now worth $50 a share will generate a long-term capital gains tax of $600 (20 percent of the $3,000 profit). By first giving the stock to the child and having him make the sale, the capital gains rate is cut in half from your 20 percent rate to a 15 percent-taxpayer's 10 percent rate. The result is a tax saving of $300.

Including the child's income on your tax return is certainly easier. But filing separate returns may be more beneficial. Adding your child's income to your own on your tax return could mean that you lose deductions tied to adjusted gross income. As described in Chapter 1, "The Toll Taxes Take," these may include medical expenses, casualty losses, and miscellaneous itemized deductions.

Adding the child's income to your own also could subject you to the personal exemption phaseout. You could miss out on deductible IRA contributions or a Roth IRA conversion (see Chapter 12) if your child's income pushes you over the income ceilings for eligibility.

You may have to do the calculations both ways—or use a professional adviser—to see which way is best.

Your Name or the Kid's

Serious saving for children involves putting away sizable sums. Here's where the annual gift tax exclusion comes into play. You are allowed to give up to $10,000 a year to each of as many people you like, free from federal gift tax. If you are married, you and your spouse together can give up to $20,000 to any one person each year. For parents who can spare the cash, this is a very good way to shelter assets from eventual federal estate tax. For more on gift and estate tax, see Chapter 24, "You Can't Take It with You."

Let's say that you want to make gifts to your children to fund their college education. You could simply give them the money. But few parents want to give hefty sums to young children free and clear. Fortunately, there are other choices.

You might save in your own name, in an account you designate for the child's benefit. This gives you the most flexibility in controlling the money because you can use it for something else if your circumstances change, but it does leave you paying tax on the assets at your own income tax rate. Two other choices are custodial accounts and trusts.

Tax Talk

The **Uniform Gifts to Minors Act** (**UGMA**) permits the transfer during your lifetime of bank deposits, securities (including mutual funds), and insurance policies. The newer and more flexible **Uniform Transfers to Minors Act** (**UTMA**) allows you to put almost any asset in a child's name, including real estate and royalties, both during life and in your will. UTMA statutes have replaced UGMA in most, but not all, states.

A Custody Case

Most money that's put away in children's names is money intended for college. Most of that money goes into custodial accounts under arrangements known as the *Uniform Gifts to Minors Act* (UGMA) or the *Uniform Transfers to Minors Act* (UTMA). Which one you can use depends on the laws of your state.

It's easy to open a custodial account. Just fill out the appropriate forms at a bank, stockbrokerage firm, or mutual fund. Just don't expect the clerks who hand you the forms to explain the practical consequences and financial ramifications of the arrangement. Think it through before you open a custodial account, keeping the following in mind.

Custodial accounts can be a great vehicle for college savings. They are easy to open. Other people—such as grandparents or a doting aunt—can add to the account. They work well for the steady saving of small sums.

But blindly saving for college through a custodial account may not be a wise idea. You might be better off simply saving in your own name. There are at least three reasons why this is so.

First, since the introduction of the kiddie tax in 1986, putting income-producing assets in children's names does not make as much sense as it once did in tax terms. For children under age 14, as we've seen, income over $1,400 is taxed at the parent's rate. You might do better in one of the college savings plans described in Chapter 8, "Education Tax Breaks."

But the tax consequences of saving in your name or your child's are only one part of the equation.

The second potential disadvantage is that the assets in the custodial account are an irrevocable gift to the child. You control the money—but only until the child reaches legal age under the laws of your state. In most states, the age of majority is either 18 or 21. At that time, if Suzie wants to run off with a rock band or Junior decides to blow the money on a red Porsche instead of going to college, there will be nothing you can do to stop them. (In one difference between UGMAs and UTMAs, however, some states permit parental control of UTMAs until age 25.)

Tax Tips

If you are able and willing to give away the full amount excluded from gift taxes each year, hold back just a little. Maybe transfer $9,500 into each child's name instead of $10,000. That gives you some leeway for cash birthday and holiday gifts and is less likely to trigger alarms at the IRS. It even lets you pay the tax on the child's income, if you choose to do so.

The third problem crops up when your youngster is ready for college and you apply for financial aid. This is the real bummer because colleges figure that 35 percent of assets in the child's name are available for college, against only 5.6 percent of assets in the parent's name. So, money you've scrupulously squirreled away for college actually hurts your child's chances of receiving financial aid. (For more on financial aid, see Chapter 8.)

Trusting In Your Kids

UGMAs and UTMAs aren't the only devices that can minimize tax on college savings. If you plan to put aside significant sums—enough to make the cost of setting up a trust worthwhile—you might consider using a "minor's trust" because it can keep money out of children's hands at least until they reach age 21. When structured properly—be sure to get professional advice—a trust can be set up to make distributions to the beneficiaries at whatever age or ages you think best. Many parents stagger distributions, often using ages 25, 30, and 35.

One disadvantage to using trusts, however, is that their income is taxed at a higher rate than that of individuals. In 2000, as an example, income above a $100 exemption plus $1,750 is taxed at 28 percent. An individual taxpayer doesn't hit the 28 percent bracket until taxable income reaches $26,250.

Tax Traps

If you contribute the money to your child's UGMA or UTMA account, if you are the custodian, and if you die before the child is of legal age, the assets in the account will be included in your taxable estate. One way around this is to name someone else as custodian. This is particularly wise advice for grandparents setting up custodial accounts for grandchildren; in this case, it's a smart move to name one of the child's parents as custodian.

Tax Tips

You can't assume that your children will never find out about the money you stashed away in custodial accounts for them. *Forbes* recently reported that one young woman found out when the IRS sent her a notice asking about unreported income. She sued her parents for legal fees plus triple the amount in the account, claiming both theft and breach of fiduciary duty.

If the assets in the trust are earning 8 percent, you could have a bit more than $23,000 in a minor's trust before the income would reach $1,750 and be taxed at more than 15 percent. But if you do want to establish a trust and keep it going for many years, you should fund it with assets that don't throw off much current income.

When the Game Ends

When your child reaches legal age and you want to transfer the assets in the custodial account, you'll have to fill out the forms provided by the bank, mutual fund, or stock transfer agent.

But what if your child isn't yet responsible enough to manage sizable sums? What if you've miscalculated and need the money yourself?

Anything placed in a child's name in a custodial account is irrevocably given. It belongs to the child. You can't change your mind and take it back, even in the face of real financial need. The only thing you can do to reduce the account before the child reaches legal age is use some of the money for the child's benefit in ways that go beyond your normal support obligation as a parent. State laws and court rulings differ, but the general consensus is that such items might include a computer, private tutoring, or summer camp.

Of course, you also can use the money to pay for college. Plan your investment strategy—whether the money is in your name or your child's—so that cash will be available when tuition bills come due. That means growth investments in the early years, while your child is still some years from college, shifting gradually to fixed-income investments as freshman year gets closer. Ideally, you will be able to continue investing some of the money for growth even after the start of college because the last tuition payment is still three years away.

But be prepared for the moment of truth. When your youngsters reach legal age, the money is theirs. Period. End of report. If you are on good terms with your child, though, you don't actually have to turn over the account on the 18th or 21st birthday. You can continue to manage the money on your child's behalf.

Things get sticky when parents and children are not on particularly good terms. In really nasty situations, children have been known to sue their parents to gain control of the funds. In the 1960s and 1970s, there was a lot of this sort of thing as young adults joined cults and fell under the influence of charismatic leaders who wanted their worldly goods. But it can and does still happen when there's a rift in the family.

Of course, that won't happen to you. But you do need to know that a custodial account is an irrevocable gift. The child who is the light of your life at 6 may prove to be irresponsible at 20 and need more time to grow up. Don't lightly turn over control of assets to your child by way of a custodial account. Give it serious thought—especially because the tax benefits are minimal and the impact on financial aid may be substantial.

What Your Kids Need to Know

Even as you manage their college funds on their behalf, give your children some basic lessons in money management before they go off to college. Otherwise you may find them majoring in "Pizza 101" or expecting an automatic teller machine to dispense greenbacks even when the bank account is running on empty.

When they are in elementary school, start by giving a regular allowance. Peg the amount somewhere between having so much that they can do everything they want to do and having so little that they're frustrated by not being able to do much of anything. Decide the amount in consultation with the child, based on things he or she must pay (lunch money and Scout dues, for example) and the discretionary "bubble-gum money" that lets them have fun with their friends.

Look at the allowance as a learning tool, and don't attach strings in the way of good grades or doing household chores. Having a set amount of money, given at regular intervals, teaches children to set priorities and make decisions. They should earn grades to the best of their ability, without monetary incentive. And they should do daily chores because they are members of the family—although, if you choose to do so, you can offer pay for occasional special jobs such as cleaning out the basement or washing the car.

By the high school years, the allowance should be large enough to cover most activities. You might also want to introduce a separate clothing allowance. Now is definitely the time to teach how checking accounts work, what ATM machines do, and the responsible use of credit.

By the time youngsters go off to college, they should know how to write checks and balance the checkbook. They should be able to balance a craving for midnight pizza with the need to buy the semester's textbooks. They should understand the limitations of cash machines. And they should know that flashing plastic means that bills must be paid at the end of the month.

These last points are vitally important. Astonishing as it may seem, some college students (and a few adults as well) believe that a checking account has money in it because there are blank checks in the checkbook. Some don't understand that cash can't come from automatic teller machines unless there is money in the bank account. And some are head-over-heels in debt by the time they leave college because they are bombarded with credit card offers, accept all the cards, and use them.

The Least You Need to Know

➤ It costs a lot to raise children, but tax exemptions and credits can ease the burden.

➤ Children's earned income above the standard deduction is taxed at their own income tax rate.

➤ Investment income is taxed at the parent's rate until a child reaches age 14, when it is taxed at the child's own rate.

➤ Although you may be able to include your child's income on your own tax return, it is often better to file separate returns for the children.

➤ Custodial accounts have significant drawbacks: The kiddie tax reduces tax benefits, the money is an irrevocable gift to the child, and financial aid may be reduced.

Chapter 7

Uncle Sam's IOUs

> ## In This Chapter
>
> ➤ Savings bonds can be bought for as little as $25
>
> ➤ Savings bond interest is subject to federal income tax, but not state and local tax
>
> ➤ Tax on the interest can be deferred until the bonds are redeemed or reach final maturity
>
> ➤ Interest may be tax-exempt when proceeds are used for college tuition and parents meet income limitations
>
> ➤ I-bonds and HH-bonds are alternatives to familiar EE-bonds

If you're seeking an absolutely safe investment, one that can be acquired with as little as $25, Uncle Sam's savings bonds are for you. Either—or both—of the familiar EE-bonds or the new inflation-indexed I-bonds are easy to buy and may find a place in your investment mix.

While savings bonds are inexpensive and easy to buy, however, they can be complicated when it comes to determining interest rates and maturity dates. This chapter introduces you to the ins and outs of savings bonds, with special attention to their value for your children and grandchildren.

A Tax-Deferred Delight

EE-bonds are sold at half the face value printed on the bond. That is, you pay $25 for a bond that will be worth $50 at original maturity, and $50 for a bond that will be worth $100.

Bonds are issued in $50, $75, $100, $200, $500, $1,000, $5,000, and $10,000 denominations. An individual may spend no more than $15,000 on EE-bonds in any one year; $15,000, of course, will buy $30,000 worth of bonds at their face value.

Tax Tips

Decades ago, patriotic school-children saved their pennies and bought Savings Stamps. Complete books of stamps could be traded in for savings bonds. Incomplete books of stamps still surface from time to time and can be re-deemed at their face value or applied toward the purchase of a new savings bond. If you have such stamps, write to the Bond Consultant Branch, Bureau of the Public Debt, Parkersburg, WV 26106-1328.

If you have $10,000 or $15,000 to invest all at once, however, you're probably much better off investing in the stock market or in the U.S. Treasury bills, notes, and bonds described in Chapter 19, "Uncle Sam Treasures You." Savings bonds are a better alternative to certificates of deposit, especially if you want to save small amounts on a regular basis. Some folks save up pocket change and buy an EE-bond every time the total reaches $25.

How to Buy

Savings bonds are easy to buy. They have been available for many years at most local banks, through branches of the Federal Reserve Bank, and through payroll deduction programs at many employers. Today they are also available online, at www.savingsbonds.gov, and through automatic debit to your bank account via the Treasury's new EasySaver program. For information about EasySaver (minimum purchase is two bonds a year), call 1-877-811-7283, or go online at www.easysaver.gov. No sales charge or commission is applied, no matter where you buy.

When you buy a bond, you can designate the owner in one of three ways:

➤ **Individual ownership**—If John H. Smith is the registered owner, he is the only one who may redeem the bond. On the death of the owner, the bond becomes part of the owner's estate.

➤ **Co-ownership**—If "John H. Smith or Marsha L. Smith" are named as co-owners, either one may cash the bond without the knowledge or approval of the other. On the death of one, the other becomes the sole owner of the bond.

➤ **Beneficiary**—If the face of the bond reads "John H. Smith POD Marsha L. Smith," then only John Smith may redeem the bond during his lifetime. POD means "pay on death," so Mary Smith automatically becomes the sole owner at his death.

Once registered, savings bonds are not transferable; you cannot simply sign them over to someone else. They can be reissued to indicate a change of ownership only under some circumstances. One example would be when a co-owner dies; the surviving owner can then name a new co-owner or beneficiary. Also, an individual owner can add a co-owner or beneficiary. Caution: Some reissues create a taxable event.

Tax Treats

A minor may own savings bonds in his or her own name. This, plus the fact that bonds can be purchased in such small amounts, makes them popular gifts for births, birthdays, confirmations, bar mitzvahs, and similar occasions. If you're buying a bond as a gift, try to obtain the recipient's Social Security number. Otherwise, your own number will appear on the bond. Although you won't be liable for the taxes when the bond is redeemed, if you are not the owner, this may cause some confusion down the road.

How Much Will You Earn?

Savings bonds are fixed-income investments. But *fixed-income* doesn't mean that there is a guaranteed rate. Bonds issued prior to May 1995 earn either a guaranteed rate or a blend of market rates, depending on when they were purchased. Since May 1995, bonds have earned a variable market-based rate. For bonds issued from May 1995 to April 1996, the rate is pegged at 85 percent of the average of six-month T-bills during the first five years, and then at 85 percent of the average yield on five-year Treasuries.

In 1997, the Treasury Department took two steps in an effort to attract more buyers. It began adding interest monthly instead of semiannually, although bond interest is still compounded semiannually. It also beefed up yields. Today the rate is pegged at 90 percent (instead of 85 percent) of the average yield on five-year Treasuries (instead of six-month T-bills). A new rate is set every six months and is

Tax Traps

It's a mistake to think that all EE-bonds earn the same rate of interest, says Daniel Pederson, president of the Savings Bond Informer. Most earn between 4 percent and 6.1 percent—but how much your bonds are actually earning depends on when you bought them. Older bonds may actually pay more than newer bonds.

announced each May and November. As an example, for EE-bonds issued on or after May 1, 1997, the rate for May through October 1999 was 4.31 percent. The rate on the same bonds for November 1999 through April 2000 became 5.19 percent.

Floating market-based rates were meant to make savings bonds more competitive. They certainly have made them more confusing. You can't predict how much you'll actually earn on bonds purchased prior to May 1995 because the government averages every semiannual interest rate and then compares that to the guaranteed rate to arrive at a redemption value.

For newer bonds, those issued in May 1997 and thereafter, there is one certainty: These bonds earn the full rate of interest right from the start, as long as you hold the bonds for at least five years. If you cash in a savings bond before five years, you will lose three months' interest. Note, too, that bonds cannot be redeemed at all during the first six months.

How Much Your Bonds Are Currently Worth

If you want to know how much your bonds are currently worth, try the following:

➤ Go online at www.savingsbonds.gov and download the program called the Savings Bond Wizard.

➤ Request "Tables of Redemption Values" from the Bureau of the Public Debt, 200 Third Street, Parkersburg, WV 26106-1328.

➤ Check out the Bond Values information on the Web site of the Federal Reserve Bank of New York, at www.ny.frb.org.

➤ Go online at www.bondhelp.com, or call 1-800-927-1901. For a fee (starting at $15 for up to 10 bonds), a company called the Savings Bond Informer will prepare a customized statement on your bonds. The statement shows vital information you can't get anywhere else, including past performance and anticipated future performance, which will help you time redemptions and exchanges so that you won't lose interest.

Does Mature Mean Grown-Up?

There is a difference between the "original maturity date" of a bond and the date it reaches its final maturity. The original maturity date is the date a bond reaches its face value. The final maturity date is the date after which Uncle Sam no longer pays interest.

When will your bond reach its original maturity date? Believe it or not, unless it already has, no one can answer that question. When bonds paid a fixed rate of interest, maturity dates were predictable. A bond earning 6 percent would reach face value in 12 years. Want a simple way to calculate returns when you know the interest rate?

The "rule of 72" lets you estimate the number of years it will take your money to double; all you need do is divide 72 by the annual interest rate.

Rule of 72

Annual Interest Rate	Approximate Number of Years to Double Your Investment
3%	24
4%	18
5%	14
6%	12
7%	10
8%	9
9%	8
10%	7.2

For bonds paying only a market-based rate of interest—that's all EE-bonds issued since May 1995—the original maturity date can't be predicted in advance.

The level of interest rates during the holding period determines when your bonds reach their face value. However, if market-based rates are not sufficient for an EE-bond to reach face value by 17 years from its issue date, the Treasury will make a one-time interest rate adjustment to increase the redemption value to face value at that time. So, you'll never have to hold an EE-bond more than 17 years to collect the amount shown on its face at redemption. Along the way, however, you may need help in figuring out exactly how much your bonds are worth.

E-I-E-O-U

Although EE-bonds are the best known of Uncle Sam's family of savings bonds, there are two other bond choices. Inflation bonds, known as I-bonds, have been issued since September 1998. HH-bonds, providing semi-annual interest income, may be obtained in exchange for E- and EE-bonds.

Both deserve a closer look.

I-Bonds to Beat Inflation

Series I-bonds work exactly the same way as EE-bonds in terms of how bonds may be registered, when interest is added, when and how interest is taxed, and so on. Instead of being sold at half their face value, however, I-bonds are sold at their face value. A $50 I-bond costs $50. Also unlike EE-bonds, you may spend up to $30,000 on I-bonds in a single year.

But the big difference between EE-bonds and I-bonds is in how the income is determined.

The earnings rate on I-bonds is a combination of two separate rates: a fixed rate and a variable inflation rate. The fixed rate in effect when the bond is purchased remains in effect for the life of the bond. The inflation rate is adjusted every six months in accordance with the changes in the Consumer Price Index (CPI).

For example, I-bonds bought from May through October 1999 earned a combined rate of 5.05 percent for the first six months, a combination of a fixed rate of 3.3 percent and a variable rate of 1.72 percent. I-bonds bought from November 1999 through April 2000 earned a combined rate of 6.98 percent for the first six months, made up of a fixed rate of 3.4 percent and a variable rate of 3.52 percent.

I-bonds also come with a guarantee: Even in periods of deflation, you will never lose money. Uncle Sam has promised to keep your principal intact.

If you're a risk-averse investor who is worried about inflation picking up steam, I-bonds may deserve a place in your portfolio—although you're more likely to beat inflation over the long haul with equities. The following table summarizes the difference between EE-bonds and I-bonds.

EE-Bonds	I-Bonds
Issued at 50 percent of face value	Issued at face value
Interest is 90 percent of average yield of five-year Treasuries	Interest combines a fixed rate of return and a variable rate based on the CPI and changed semiannually
Guaranteed to reach face value in 17 years	Future value is unpredictable
Can be exchanged for HH-bonds	Cannot be exchanged for any other savings bonds

HH Is for Hesitate

If you're reaching retirement age with a bunch of old E- and EE-bonds that are reaching the end of their interest-paying years, you can redeem the bonds. If you do, of course, you'll owe a hefty tax bill on all the accumulated interest over the years.

Many retirees choose to convert their E- and EE-bonds to HH-bonds instead. Converting to HH-bonds lets you defer tax on the accumulated E- and EE-bond interest for as much as another 20 years. However, tax must be paid each year on the interest earned on the HH-bonds.

To convert to HH-bonds, you must have at least $500 in EE-bonds. If you have more than $500 but less than a multiple of $500, you can make up the difference in cash or take the difference in cash. To make an exchange, your EE-bonds must be at least six months old. At the other end of the savings spectrum, E-bonds that reached final maturity more than one year earlier are not eligible for conversion.

HH-bonds pay semiannual interest, by direct deposit to your bank account. What's the down side of making a conversion? HH-bonds have an interest-paying life of 20 years, with the initial interest rate locked in for 10 years. The change after 10 years can be abrupt—the 7.5 percent rate of the mid-1980s is now 4 percent. That's a pretty low rate to lock in for 10 years.

Tax Treats

If savings bonds have been lost, stolen, mutilated, or destroyed, they usually can be re-placed. So, if you can't locate the bonds you were given for your high school graduation, or if bonds were damaged in a fire, you should fill out a claim form. Most local banks have the forms—ask for PDF 1048—or go online to www.savingsbonds.gov. Then send the form to the Bureau of the Public Debt, Savings Bonds Operations Office, Parkersburg, WV 26106-1328. It will help if you know the issue dates, serial numbers, and the exact name in which the bonds were registered.

Tax Ramifications

Savings bonds are issued by the U.S. Treasury. Like other Treasury obligations, as de-scribed in Chapter 19, the interest is subject to federal income tax, but not to state and local income tax. This can make them a wise buy for residents of high-tax states.

EE-bonds are a rare breed, however, because you have a choice of when to pay the federal income tax on the interest. Most folks defer tax on the interest until the bonds are redeemed; of course, you must report the interest at final maturity if you haven't done so earlier or if you don't exchange the bonds for HH-bonds. If you don't make a specific election to do otherwise, you will defer paying tax. But you are al-lowed to pay the tax each year—in some cases, it may make sense to do so.

Whether you elect to pay the tax each year or defer the tax until the bonds mature or are redeemed, you must use the same method for all E-, EE-, and I-bonds you own. A change from deferral to annual reporting can be accomplished simply by reporting all interest accrued to the date of the switch. If you want to change from annual report-ing to deferred reporting, you must request permission from the IRS. Permission is au-tomatically granted, but the statement must be filed with your tax return for the year of the change.

Tax Traps

If you elect to declare the interest each year for tax purposes, be sure to keep a copy of the federal tax return you file stating this intent. You will need to document this election when the bonds are redeemed, or tax will be owed on the entire accumulated interest over the life of the bonds. In other words, if you're not careful, you'll wind up paying taxes twice on the same interest income. Or, if you own the bonds when you die, your beneficiaries may pay tax you've already paid.

If you are buying EE-bonds or I-bonds in the hopes of using tax-free proceeds to pay tuition (see "Tax-Free for Some Folks" later in this chapter), you'll want to defer the tax because you may not have to pay it at all. If you want the proceeds to be used for tuition but know that your income is too high to qualify for the tax break, you may elect to declare the interest as you go along so that it will be taxed at your child's lower tax rate.

If this is the course you choose, buy the bonds in your child's name. Then, after the year in which you make the purchase, file a federal income tax return in the child's name reporting the accumulated accrued interest to that point on all the bonds owned by the child. Indicate on the return that it is being filed with the intent of reporting savings bond interest annually.

By electing this method, you take advantage of the fact that no income tax need be paid by a child with interest and dividends of less than $700 in a single year. (See Chapter 6, "UGMA, UTMA, Kids and Taxes," for more on the taxes owed by children.) You won't have to file another tax return until the child's unearned income exceeds $700 or until she earns taxable income. Then, when the bonds are redeemed, only interest earned in the last year will be subject to tax.

Tax-Free for Some Folks

If you meet the income limitations and follow all the rules, the interest on EE-bonds and I-bonds issued after 1989 may be completely tax-free when the proceeds are used for college tuition and fees. Incidentally, those proceeds can pay tuition for your child or for you or your spouse.

These are the rules:

➤ The bonds must be registered in the name of an adult who is at least 24 years old on the first day of the month in which the bonds are issued. The bonds cannot be registered in the name of a child, although the child may be named as beneficiary.

➤ The bonds must be redeemed in the same calendar year that "qualified educational expenses" (currently defined as tuition and fees) are paid. Expenses for room and board do not qualify.

➤ The bonds may be redeemed earlier if the proceeds are contributed to a state-sponsored tuition program or to an Education IRA.

➤ File Form 8815 with your federal income tax return for the year in which bonds are redeemed and used to pay educational expenses.

➤ You must meet the income limitations in the year in which the bonds are redeemed. The amount goes up each year. For the year 2000, married couples filing jointly can claim a full exclusion of savings bond interest at a modified adjusted gross income of $81,100; the exclusion phases out entirely when income reaches $111,100. For single taxpayers, the income amounts are $54,100 to $69,100.

Tax Traps

If you inherit savings bonds, there is no step-up in basis as there is on other inherited securities. If the taxable estate exceeds the amount that is exempt from federal estate taxes—$675,000 in the year 2000, rising gradually to $1 million in 2006 and thereafter—the full value of the savings bonds, including accrued interest, could be subject to estate tax.

It's important to note that the income limits apply when the bonds are redeemed, not when they are purchased. If your income could be a lot higher when your youngsters are ready for college, you may want to buy savings bonds in your children's name rather than your own. Doing so, as indicated previously, lets you elect to report the interest each year and eliminate much of the tax.

If you plan to take advantage of the tax exemption on savings bonds used for tuition, be sure to keep good records of these items:

➤ The serial numbers, face amounts, and issue dates of the bonds.

➤ The redemption dates and total proceeds received, broken down by principal and interest.

➤ The amount of tuition and fees, the dates payments were made, and the name of the college or university your child attends. Canceled checks are a good backup for your records.

Holding On

According to Dan Pederson, author of *Savings Bonds: When to Hold, When to Fold, and Everything in Between,* more than $7 billion worth of savings bonds that have stopped paying interest are still out there somewhere. Many are in safe deposit vaults or dresser drawers. Some have been inadvertently trashed by heirs who never knew they existed.

There are two messages here:

➤ First, tell your beneficiaries that you own savings bonds—Uncle Sam doesn't send statements. Keep a record of your bond holdings with your important permanent papers.

➤ Second, keep track of when savings bonds no longer pay interest. Uncle Sam won't remind you, but the following table has the information.

Savings bonds don't pay interest indefinitely. Check the issue date on any older bonds you own—it's usually found in the upper-right corner of each bond—against the following table:

Issue Date	Final Maturity Date
Series E-bonds issued before December 1965	40 years
Series E- and EE-bonds issued after November 1965	30 years
Series H-bonds issued between 1959 and 1979	30 years
Series HH-bonds issued since 1980	20 years
Series I-bonds	30 years

Note that E-bonds issued before 1960 are no longer paying interest. Neither are E- and EE-bonds issued between December 1965 and sometime after mid-1970 (depending on exactly when you're reading this book). Because E- and EE-bonds stop paying interest after 30 years, take a look at any bonds you're holding that were issued in 1970 and beyond. Some H- and HH-bonds have also reached their final maturity date. Any such bonds that you hold should be redeemed.

But be careful when you sell your EE-bonds (or exchange them for HH-bonds), lest you run afoul of tricky rules and lose as much as six months of interest. One day can make a difference because interest is credited to many bonds just twice a year. For example, if your bond registers its semiannual interest payment on November 1 and you cash it in on October 31, the Halloween goblins will get you—or at least they'll get the six months of interest you could have had by waiting a day.

When you do redeem your bonds, do so as early as possible in the month. If your bond increases in value in November, cashing it in on the first of the month will earn you the full interest for the month, the same exact amount you will receive if you redeem the same bond on November 30.

Tax Traps

When a bond reaches final maturity, that's it for the interest. Unless you cash it in, you've got a dead piece of paper on your hands. Worse yet, the accrued interest is taxable in the year a bond reaches final maturity. If you didn't pay the interest then, you can file an amended tax return for up to three years. Beyond that? Talk to your tax adviser.

If you plan to redeem only some of the bonds you own, be sure to find out first how much each is currently paying in interest. The strategy Dan Pederson calls "selective redemption" can make a big difference in how much money you ultimately have.

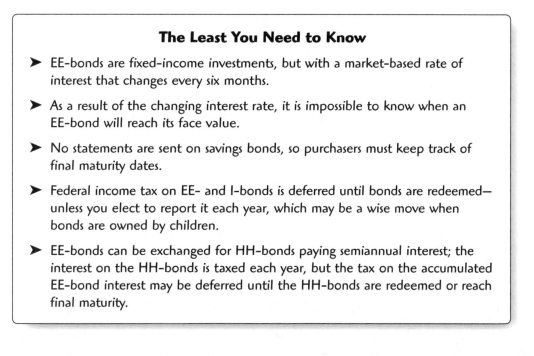

The Least You Need to Know

➤ EE-bonds are fixed-income investments, but with a market-based rate of interest that changes every six months.

➤ As a result of the changing interest rate, it is impossible to know when an EE-bond will reach its face value.

➤ No statements are sent on savings bonds, so purchasers must keep track of final maturity dates.

➤ Federal income tax on EE- and I-bonds is deferred until bonds are redeemed—unless you elect to report it each year, which may be a wise move when bonds are owned by children.

➤ EE-bonds can be exchanged for HH-bonds paying semiannual interest; the interest on the HH-bonds is taxed each year, but the tax on the accumulated EE-bond interest may be deferred until the HH-bonds are redeemed or reach final maturity.

Chapter 8

Education Tax Breaks

In This Chapter

➤ Finding tax breaks to help in meeting the high cost of college

➤ Using Education IRAs to put away $500 per year per child

➤ Using the HOPE and Lifetime Learning credits for dollar–for–dollar reduction in taxes

➤ Using state college savings plans as a tax–sheltered way to save for college

➤ Using loans and grants to fill the gap

In January 2000, as President Clinton entered his last year in office, he proposed to leave a legacy in the form of a $30 billion tax cut to help middle-income families pay the cost of college. The highlight of the proposal was a tax deduction or tax credit that would ultimately save families about $2,800 in taxes.

If the proposal makes it into law (which is unclear at this writing) it will join a host of other tax breaks designed to help defray the high cost of college. Like home owner-ship, higher education is considered a praiseworthy goal; both are supported with tax breaks.

This chapter explores a number of current college-related tax deductions and credits, and helps you decide which is best for you. Because tax breaks don't always do the trick, this chapter also describes the basics of financial aid and steers you to sources of more information.

The Cost of College

For years, college costs have been increasing faster than the rate of inflation. Although the increase is less than 5 percent for the 1999–2000 academic year, that still exceeds an inflation rate hovering at about 3 percent.

According to an annual survey by the College Board, the average cost of one year at a private college or university in the 1999–2000 academic year—including tuition, fees, room, and board—was $20,688. The average cost of one year at a public institution was $8,086. "Average," of course, means that some institutions cost less and that others cost considerably more.

High as they are, the numbers don't include transportation, books, clothes, social activities, and the inevitable late-night pizza.

Taken altogether, the cost of one year at a private college by the time today's 4-year-old completes high school could be $50,000. The cost of a four-year education—don't even think about graduate school—could exceed $200,000. To accumulate $200,000 in 15 years, you would have to earn a steady 10 percent on monthly savings of $500. Earn less, start late, or skip some months, and you'll have to save considerably more.

Even if you've diligently saved since Junior was born, you probably need all the help you can get. Fortunately, help is available.

Education IRAs

Education IRAs came into being as part of the tax law passed in 1997, effective in 1998. The term IRA (which stands for Individual Retirement Account) is actually somewhat misleading because these accounts have nothing to do with retirement. Instead, they allow you to put away up to $500 a year per child toward higher education—if you meet the income limitations of $110,000 for a single taxpayer, or $160,000 for a married couple filing jointly.

Eligibility starts to phase out at $95,000 in adjusted gross income for a single taxpayer and $150,000 for a married couple. But Mark Luscombe, a federal tax analyst with CCH Incorporated, points out that children and grandparents may meet the income limitations and be able to fund an Education IRA even if parents cannot.

Contributions are not deductible, but the money won't be taxed at withdrawal if it is used for "qualified education expenses." In the case of the Education IRA, qualified expenses are tuition and fees. Room and board qualify only if the student is attending school at least half-time.

But $500 a year won't produce enough to pay for college, even after 18 years of diligently saving. Even if you could earn 10 percent a year—a rate beyond the reach of most investors in most years—you would have only a bit more than $25,000. That would pay for one year at a private college today. In 18 years, it won't be much more than a drop in the bucket of a four-year college education. Fortunately, other, better alternatives are available.

HOPE Springs Eternal

Two federal tax credits were also introduced with the 1998 tax year. As credits, rather than deductions, they represent a dollar-for-dollar tax saving. Get a $1,000 credit, and you save $1,000 in taxes. By contrast, a $1,000 deduction saves just $280 for a taxpayer in the 28 percent bracket.

Both credits may be taken in full by single taxpayers with an adjusted gross income of up to $40,000, phasing out at $50,000. For married taxpayers filing jointly, the full credit applies at an AGI of up to $80,000, phasing out at $100,000.

The HOPE credit applies to tuition and fees in the first two years of college. It does not apply to books, room and board, transportation, or any other college-related expenses. The credit also can't be taken beyond the sophomore year.

The HOPE credit is calculated as 100 percent of the first $1,000 in eligible expenses, and 50 percent of the next $1,000, for a maximum credit of $1,500. It may be taken for each student in the family.

The Lifetime Learning credit is 20 percent of qualified tuition expenses, up to a maximum of $1,000 per family, for any year in which the HOPE credit is not claimed. The maximum per-family credit becomes $2,000 in 2003 and thereafter. While the HOPE credit applies only to the first two years of undergraduate education, the Lifetime Learning credit may be taken for undergraduate and graduate tuition as well as for job training.

States Get in Line

Taking advantage of recent federal legislation authorizing tax breaks for college savings, the states are making big strides in offering help with college.

Ten years ago, just three states offered college savings plans. Today, 21 states offer prepaid tuition programs under which today's payment guarantees tomorrow's tuition. Thirty-three states offer savings

Tax Traps

Money can be contributed to an Education IRA only until the beneficiary reaches age 18. Once most youngsters are in college, therefore, no more contributions can be made. In addition, money in an Education IRA must be used by the time the child reaches age 30. If one of your children doesn't use it, it can be transferred to another younger child. Otherwise, the account will be subject to federal income tax plus a 10 percent tax penalty.

Tax Tips

If your income is too high to qualify for the education credits but your youngster has income in his or her name, consider having the student claim the credit—even if you are paying the tuition. You won't be able to claim the child as a dependent on your income tax return, but the net return may be beneficial to the family.

plans producing market-based returns. Some states offer both types of "Section 529" plans, named for the authorizing statute, but the more flexible savings plans are pulling ahead of the more limited prepaid tuition plans.

Perhaps the best thing about both prepaid tuition and college savings plans is that there are no income limits. Anyone, at any income level, can take advantage of these programs to save for college.

Locking in Low(er) Prices

Under prepaid tuition plans, parents can pay a lump sum or make monthly payments to lock in the price of future tuition at a state college based on today's prices. The state invests the pooled contributions in the plan to meet projected increases in college costs. You are guaranteed that tuition costs will be met, regardless of the pace of inflation.

Tax Traps

No double-dipping allowed! You can't contribute to an Education IRA and a state tuition plan for the same student in the same year. In addition, taking a tax-free distribution from an Education IRA makes a student ineligible for the HOPE or Lifetime Learning credits for the same year.

Your payments are based on the current age of the child (the younger the child, the less you contribute), the projected date of college entrance, and the number of years you want to fund. Where many state prepayment plans initially were designed to cover only tuition, federal law now allows them to accept prepayments for room and board as well. Some plans do, some don't; check the details of your own state's plan.

The plans have recently become more flexible in another way. At one time, the money could be used only at an institution within the state—and, in some cases, only at a public institution. Now, however, many permit it to be used anywhere in the country and at any qualified institution. If the college your child attends costs more than you've prepaid, you'll just have to make up the difference.

What if your child chooses not to attend college at all? Before you sign up, check the plan's policy on refunds but be aware that tax penalties may also be levied. The section later in this chapter, "Choosing the Right Plan," outlines other questions to ask before you commit to a specific college savings plan.

Contributions to prepaid tuition plans are not tax-deductible, but no federal income tax is due on earnings until the money is withdrawn. At that time, it will be taxable at the student's lower rate. This is a big improvement over the earlier situation, which stalled the plans for some years in which federal income tax was assessed at the parent's (typically higher) tax rate.

As an added plus, many states exempt earnings from state income tax. Some also allow families to deduct at least part of their contributions from state income taxes.

Tax Treats

There's one possible double use of college tax breaks. If your family meets the income requirements, you can claim the HOPE and Lifetime Learning credits, even if your youngster is using money in a tax-sheltered college savings plan to pay for college.

Growing Your Money

The newest kid on the block—and growing fast—is the college savings plan. The plans go by different names in different states—examples are Arizona's Family College Savings Program, Colorado CollegeInvest, Massachusetts's U. Fund, and New Jersey's Better Educational Savings Trust (BEST).

Federal income taxes are deferred on earnings, as they are in prepaid tuition programs, and no state income tax is levied on earnings. When federal income taxes do come due, at the time money is withdrawn, you'll need to find the money outside the plan to pay the taxes. Because taxes aren't a "qualified educational expense," using plan proceeds to pay the taxes would result in a 10 percent penalty. (In 1999, Congress passed a law eliminating federal income tax on proceeds used for education. The measure was vetoed, but it could come up again.)

Moreover, unlike the prepaid plans that guarantee to pay tuition, these plans produce a market return that could be higher. On the other hand, there is no guarantee that earnings will cover tuition; investments could go south. But these plans are also more flexible than prepaid tuition plans.

Contribution limits vary by state, but you generally may put away from $100,000 to $150,000 for any one student, in either a lump sum or in periodic contributions. At the other end of the contribution range, some states have minimum investments of $250 and offer automatic investment programs starting at $25.

There is no federal tax deduction for the contribution, but there are state tax deductions in some states. In New York, as an example, state residents may deduct up to $5,000 a year for contributions to the New York plan. For a married couple, that's a $10,000 deduction—or a savings of almost $700 in the highest state tax bracket, close to $1,000 in high-tax New York City.

The state savings plans are new, and some glitches still have to be worked out. In addition, there are two possible disadvantages: First, you'll face penalties if the money is not used for education. Second, you don't usually choose the investments. As a rule, the money is placed in a special account. Some are managed by the same folks who manage the state's pension accounts; others are managed by an investment advisory firm, such as TIAA-CREF, Fidelity, or Merrill Lynch. Some invest very conservatively, so you'll want to check out the investment philosophy before you make a commitment.

Although equities generally are considered the best place to be for a toddler's college fund, with years to ride market fluctuations, some of the state plans tend to be more conservative. Although the mix may shift from equities to fixed-income investments as a child nears college age, the initial mix may lean more toward fixed-income investments than you would do on your own.

Consider this example: In New York, contributions for a 3-year-old are split by fund manager TIAA-CREF at 55 percent for growth and 45 percent for fixed-income investments. In Massachusetts, New Hampshire, and Delaware, money for a 3-year-old is invested by fund manager Fidelity Investments at 77.4 percent in domestic equity funds, 10 percent in international equity funds, and 9.4 percent in high-yield fixed-income funds. That's not bad.

Tax Treats

Most states don't give college savings plan contributors any investment choices. But the picture may be changing. In January 2000, American Century announced a new Kansas program in which contributors can choose one of three investment tracks: conservative, moderate, and aggressive. Within each track, asset allocation portfolios of mutual funds automatically adjust to a more conservative mix as the beneficiary approaches college age. Look for more states to follow.

Money generally must be invested in these plans at least three years before the beneficiary is to start college. If you start that late, however, you'll find far more conservative investments. All four states mentioned in the last paragraph invest 10 percent of the contributions for a youngster 15 or older in growth funds, with the balance divided (and tilted slightly one way or the other) between fixed-income funds and money market funds.

You don't have to wait until your state offers a college savings plan, and you're not limited to a plan offered by your state. Several plans, including New York's, are open to residents of any state. For information, including a complete list of state programs and their telephone numbers, call the College Savings Plan Network at 1-877-277-6496, or visit them online at www.collegesavings.org.

Choosing the Right Plan

Prepaid tuition plans may suit you if you want a firm guarantee that tuition will be paid. Savings plans may meet with your approval if you are willing to take a chance in exchange for potentially higher returns. Some plans use a conservative investment mix, but there is still no guarantee that college costs will be met.

Before you decide which way to go and which specific plan is right for you, consider the following:

Tax Tips

Looking for another advantage to contributing to a college savings plan? Unlike custodial accounts under the Uniform Gifts to Minors Act or Uniform Transfers to Minors Act, this money doesn't get turned over to the kid at any particular age. You stay in control, so you can be sure that the money gets spent on education instead of a backpacking journey through Latin America. If child number 1 doesn't choose to go to college, you can designate child number 2 as the beneficiary. You can even use the money to take courses yourself.

➤ What is your tax bracket? Will you benefit from federal income tax deferral or from state income tax exclusion?

➤ Is your child likely to be awarded financial aid? If so, you may want to wait until the rules are clarified. Right now, no one is sure whether money in a college savings plan will be assessed at the parent's lower rate or the child's higher rate. In fact, it could be treated differently for the purposes of government-funded financial aid and that provided by colleges.

➤ Does the program cover all the costs associated with college? Or does it cover just tuition and fees?

➤ What does the plan cost? Some states have application fees, and some charge a percentage of the account's earnings each year. In addition, you can expect to pay the annual expenses of the mutual funds where the money is invested.

➤ Are you comfortable with the asset mix in the plan? Might you be better off investing on your own? Do you want to choose your own investments rather than rely on your state or its financial adviser to do so for you?

➤ What are the penalties if the money isn't used for education? Federal law states that the money will be taxed—at your rate, not your child's—and that a 10 percent federal tax penalty will be levied on the earnings. States may impose additional penalties.

The following list compares educational funding options:

➤ **State savings plans**—There are no income limits on participation. Earnings grow tax-deferred, may be exempt from state tax, and are federally taxed at the child's rate. Tax penalties are assessed if the money is not used for college.

➤ **Prepaid tuition**—There are no income limits on participation. The tax advantages are the same as state college savings plans. Funds may cover only tuition, and benefits may be reduced at an out-of-state school.

➤ **Education IRA**—Single taxpayers are limited to $95,000–$110,000 AGI; joint filers are limited to $150,000–160,000 AGI. The proceeds are tax-free if used for college tuition, but are subject to penalty if you fund a state tuition plan in the same year.

➤ **Custodial accounts**—There are no income limits. The first $700 of earnings is not taxed, the next $700 is taxed at the child's rate if he or she is under age 14, and the balance is taxed at the parent's rate. At age 14 and over, all funds are taxed at the child's rate. Placing assets in a custodial account is an irrevocable gift to the child; the child controls the account at age 18 or 21.

Filling the Gap

Okay, you've saved on your own and through your state's savings plan, you've taken advantage of all the other tax breaks you can—but you're still coming up short. If willing grandparents aren't available to take up the slack (see Chapter 9, "For Grandparents Only"), grit your teeth and apply for financial aid. I say "grit your teeth" because both the rules and the application forms are complicated. Some observers say they're worse than the tax code and income tax forms. But qualifying for aid makes it all worthwhile.

Think you earn too much money to qualify for financial aid? Don't give up hope. According to the U.S. Department of Education, about 14 percent of students from families of $100,000-plus in income receive financial aid. Some recipients have family incomes of more than $200,000.

Factors that can enhance eligibility for high-income families include several family members in college at one time, high medical bills, and parents nearing retirement. You can also take steps to reduce your income in your youngster's crucial junior year of high school, as noted in the list that follows. But heed the words of Anna Leider, author of *Don't Miss Out: The Ambitious Student's Guide to Financial Aid*, and recognize the "fine line between getting your fair share and abusing financial aid rules at the expense of needier students."

In other words, don't overdo the finagling to qualify for financial aid; just take advantage of legitimate loopholes.

➤ Spend money on the child that you've saved in your child's name—perhaps Susie wants a more powerful computer, or Johnny would enjoy music lessons.

➤ Defer taking capital gains until after financial aid calculations are made. Instead of holding on, take a loss on any losers in your investment portfolio.

➤ Make capital expenditures for your small business, or start a part-time home business. If it's a legitimate business intended to make a profit, start-up and operating costs may be deductible.

➤ Put as much money as possible into a tax-qualified retirement plan. If you're above the maximum funding limits, consider an annuity. Assets in these vehicles don't count in the financial aid formula at most schools.

➤ Instead of using a credit card, use savings or borrow against your securities portfolio to pay for a major purchase, thereby reducing your reportable assets. In fact, you should use reportable assets to pay down outstanding credit card debt.

➤ Convert credit card debt to home equity debt to lower the amount of available equity in your home. Although home equity doesn't count as an asset for government financial aid, it does count in the financial aid assessment by private colleges. Reducing home equity may increase the chance of receiving financial aid.

Tax Tips

Did a financial aid office "just say 'No'"? Don't give up hope. You can politely let the office know if some crucial fact didn't show up on the financial aid application or if circumstances have changed since you filed the application. Maybe that hefty income you reported last year included a once-in-a-lifetime bonus. Perhaps a parent lost a job or contracted a serious illness. Maybe there's a recent obligation to care for an aging grandparent. Bring such things to the attention of the financial aid office and ask for reconsideration.

Tax Tips

If you have EE-bonds that you bought to use for college bills, hold off on cashing them in until after the student is midway through college. Before then, the proceeds will be counted in your income and could reduce financial aid.

Applying for financial aid starts with filing the Free Application for Federal Student Aid (FAFSA) and also, if a private institution is in the student's plans, the College Board's Profile form. You can find the FAFSA online at www.fafsa.ed.gov and the Profile at www.collegeboard.org.

Accuracy counts in filling out the forms. Financial aid officers don't appreciate under-reporting in an effort to get aid that should properly go to someone else. They want to know about your vacation home as well as your securities. But they also want to know about things that may enhance the student's eligibility, such as other family members in college or a parent nearing retirement.

Types of Aid

Many colleges have moved away from completely need-based financial aid in recent years. In addition to need-based aid, these schools award merit scholarships in an effort to boost the level of the student body.

Most financial aid, however, is still in the form of loans rather than outright grants. Federal programs include three types of loans:

➤ The Perkins loan, with a 5 percent interest rate, is designed for lower-income families. Up to $4,000 per undergraduate year may be borrowed, to a total of $20,000. The money for Perkins loans comes from the government but is dispensed by the colleges.

➤ The Stafford loan, in both subsidized and unsubsidized versions, is available directly (at participating schools) and from commercial lenders. The interest rate tops out at 8.25 percent but often runs lower. Freshmen may borrow up to $2,625, sophomores may borrow up to $3,500, and juniors, seniors, and fifth-year undergraduates may borrow up to $5,500 per year. The maximum undergraduate loan amount is $23,000. The Stafford may be the most widely used student loan.

➤ The PLUS loan may be taken by students or parents. It is unsubsidized, but the interest rate tops out at 9 percent.

For information about federal programs and help in filling out the financial aid applications, call the Federal Student Aid Information Center, toll-free, at 1-800-433-3243.

Loan Consolidation

Most federal student loans must be repaid within 10 years. When a graduate is burdened with hefty interest payments on several student loans during the low-income years of a first job, consolidation may be an answer. A consolidation loan combines several smaller loans into one bigger loan from a single lender. The proceeds of the larger loan are used to pay off the other loans.

Consolidation can reduce monthly payments by stretching out the term of the loan, depending on the dollar amount, to as much as 30 years. There's a trade-off though: Even though the interest on consolidation loans can't exceed 8.25 percent, you'll pay much more in total interest over the longer period.

Before considering a consolidation loan, look at some of Uncle Sam's alternative arrangements for paying off student loans. These include monthly payments based on your annual income, an extended repayment plan, and a graduated repayment plan. As an example, an income-sensitive plan might reduce a monthly payment of $122 on a $10,000 Stafford loan to $69 a month for the first five years, but payments for the remaining five years would jump to $204. Ask your lender for details.

Beyond Financial Aid

If you're down to the wire with college about to start, and you haven't saved enough or been able to secure enough financial aid, you still have some options. Consider the following:

➤ Tap your 401(k) plan. You can borrow up to 50 percent of your money, to a maximum of $50,000, but you'll have to repay the loan within five years—sooner if you leave your job for any reason. A hardship withdrawal is also a possibility, but you'll lose your retirement nest egg and owe an immediate tax on the money.

➤ Use your IRA. There's no tax penalty if you take money from either a traditional IRA or a Roth IRA, even if you're under age 59½, if the money is used for higher education. You will owe ordinary income tax on money taken from a traditional IRA, but withdrawals from a Roth are tax-free up to the amount of your original contribution. (All withdrawals from a Roth are tax-free if you are over age 59½ and have maintained the account for at least five years.)

➤ Take out a life insurance loan. As described in Chapter 23, "Your Money for Your Life," life insurance loans do not have to be repaid at all. If the loan is not repaid, however, the borrowed amount plus interest will be subtracted from the death benefit.

➤ Take out a home equity loan or line of credit. The interest on loans secured by your home, as described in Chapter 3, "The Roof Over Your Head," is generally tax-deductible.

In making your choice, compare the interest rate and other loan features. For example, the most you can lose by taking a life insurance loan and not paying it back is a portion of the death benefit. The most you can lose if you borrow against home equity and fail to repay is your house.

The Least You Need to Know

➤ Check out the wide variety of tax-advantaged ways to save for college.

➤ The Education IRA, with its parental income limits and annual contribution limit of $500, may be the least useful.

➤ State prepaid tuition plans, which guarantee that the cost of tuition will be met, can be a reassuring option.

➤ State college savings plans, combining federal tax deferral and state tax breaks with market-based returns, are attractive to many parents and grandparents.

➤ Any remaining gap between savings and college costs can be filled with financial aid and by tapping tax-advantaged assets such as retirement plans and home equity.

Chapter 9

For Grandparents Only

In This Chapter

➤ Grandparents can be in an ideal position to help grandchildren

➤ Tailoring gifts to yield tax advantages

➤ Using a custodial account or establishing a trust

➤ Contributing to a state college savings plan

There's a bond between grandparents and grandchildren that has nothing to do with money. Even so, when grandparents have more than they need, one of the nicest things they can do is help their grandchildren.

If you're in that happy position, think about going beyond gifts of clothing and toys: Help your children meet the high cost of higher education for their children.

If you structure your gifts wisely, you can reap some tax advantages as well. This chapter leads the way to tax-wise giving for grandparents.

Sharing the Wealth

Leave money to your grandchildren in your will, and they will remember you fondly. Give them money now, to help them achieve their dreams, and you can share their pleasure.

There are many ways to make life easier for the youngest sprigs on your family tree, from pitching in on college costs to providing the down payment on a house. How much any grandparent wants to do, of course, is a matter of individual choice. But if you are both able and willing to help, you'll want to follow the rules laid down by Uncle Sam.

That means understanding the unified gift and estate tax, which dictates how much you can give without increasing your tax bills.

Amounts Excluded from Gift and Estate Tax

Year	Amount
1999	$650,000
2000	$675,000
2001	$675,000
2002	$700,000
2003	$700,000
2004	$850,000
2005	$950,000
2006 and thereafter	$1,000,000

What's "Unified" About This Tax?

The unified gift and estate tax, described more fully in Chapter 24, "You Can't Take It with You," taxes transfers of wealth whether they are made during life or at death. Sizable sums are excluded, as shown in the previous table, but when an estate exceeds the excluded amount the federal tax rate starts at 37 percent and rises to 55 percent. For the truly wealthy who leave estates in excess of $10 million, a surtax brings the total tax to 60 percent.

But there are ways around the tax. For example, you can give up to $10,000 in any one year to as many people as you like without affecting your gift and estate tax exclusion. If you and your spouse make joint gifts, each gift can be for as much as $20,000. The recipients don't have to be relatives, but many grandparents use the gift tax exclusion to help their grandchildren. The gifts produce two tax benefits for the grandparents, reducing current income taxes (because future income on the gift is transferred to the child) and reducing their own taxable estates.

Grandparents who expect to leave enough to be subject to the federal estate tax may want to reduce their taxable estates by making annual gifts to children and grandchildren. The gifts can be made outright but if the grandchildren are minors, it may be preferable to make the gifts via a custodial account or a trust.

The biggest drawback to a custodial account, as described in Chapter 6, "UGMA, UTMA, Kids and Taxes," is that the money belongs to the child when he or she reaches legal age. If you think that will be too soon for your grandchild to come into money, consider using one of the trusts described later in this chapter, in the section titled "Trusting in Tax Breaks."

If you use a custodial account under either the Uniform Gifts to Minors Act or the Uniform Transfers to Minors Act of your state, think about naming one of the youngster's parents as custodian. If you give the money and are also the custodian, any money in the account will be included in your taxable estate if you die while the child is still a minor.

Just Write a Check

Another way of helping your grandchildren without running into gift tax complications is to pay for their medical or educational costs. Don't give the money to your children or grandchildren so that they can pay the bills. Any amount paid for medical and educational expenses—even sums well above the $10,000 a year otherwise eligible for the gift tax exclusion—are excluded from tax, but only if you pay the institution directly.

This tax break can come into play in many ways. The expense doesn't have to be for college. You could help out your kids—and at the same time provide quality education for your grandchildren—by writing a check for nursery school or art lessons. On the medical front, you could help to defray the cost of teeth-straightening braces.

More Is Better

While the federal tax rate is exactly the same on gifts and estates, ranging from 37 percent to 55 percent, it actually works out more favorably in dollars to make taxable gifts during life than to leave the same amount at your death.

Tax Tips

Although you can give up to $10,000 per year per person without gift tax, it's wise to keep gift amounts slightly below the maximum amount. Then, if your tax return is audited, you won't have to explain why you didn't file a gift tax return for a $50 birthday check added to a $10,000 estate-reducing transfer. You'll also have some leeway to pay the income taxes for the child, on interest and dividends generated by the gift, if you choose to do so.

Tax Traps

Be careful when you write that check to the college. Only amounts paid for tuition qualify for the tax-free gift. If you want to pick up the additional cost of room and board, you'll have to do it under the standard $10,000-a-year gift tax exclusion.

Tax Tips

Amounts paid directly to an institution for medical or educational expenses do not count toward the annual gift tax exclusion. But that doesn't mean that they also may be claimed as income tax deductions. Your own medical expenses may be deductible; amounts you pay toward someone else's expenses are not deductible by you unless that person can be claimed as a dependent on your income tax return.

Tax Traps

Giving away a cash value life insurance policy on your life is one way to make a lifetime gift. But if you plan to give away a life insurance policy, don't wait. The Internal Revenue Service frowns on "deathbed gifts" of life insurance. Such gifts given less than three years before you die will be added back into your gross estate in calculating estate taxes that may be due.

That's because the estate tax is paid on the gross amount, including the tax itself, while gift tax is paid on the net amount of the gift. In lawyer-speak, the estate tax is tax-inclusive, while the gift tax is tax-exclusive.

As a simple example, let's assume that you are already over the amount excluded from gift and estate taxes when you leave your children $1 million in your will. At a 50 percent estate tax rate, they wind up with $500,000.

If you give them the same $1 million while you're alive, you pay a gift tax of $333,000 and the children receive about $667,000.

As another incentive to lifetime giving, you have to file a gift tax return, but you don't actually pay the tax until the total amount you've given exceeds the combined gift and estate tax exclusion. With a $1 million lifetime gift—unless it is a combined gift from husband and wife and is therefore within the excluded amount—the tax would be due when the gift tax return is filed the following spring. With gifts under the excluded amount—remember, that's $675,000 per person in 2000, rising to $1 million in 2006—the tax may not be due until after your death. Then it will come directly from the estate.

Trusting in Tax Breaks

Instead of putting $10,000 into an UGMA or UTMA account (as described in Chapter 6) for each grandchild, in which case the money will belong to the child at age 18 or 21, you may want to establish a trust.

A trust is simply a three-party legal agreement whereby you (the donor) name a trustee to manage assets for a designated beneficiary. There are as many types of trusts as there are lawyers to create them, and you can tailor-make a trust to suit your personal objectives.

But different types of trusts have different financial and tax consequences. Read the following sections, consult the additional materials listed in Appendix A,

"Resources" (*The New Book of Trusts* is especially good), and then, if you want to establish a trust, consult an experienced attorney who specializes in trusts and estates.

Pick and Shovel

With a trust, you can set the terms. For example, if you care strongly about higher education, you might specify that the money is to be used for college costs and that any money left over will be distributed to the child at age 25 or 30. The trust document might also say that if the child chooses not to attend college, she will receive half the money at age 35 and half at age 40.

Tax Tips

A single trust can be created to benefit all your grandchildren, with the trustee directed to make distributions to pay college costs for the named beneficiaries and then distribute the remaining principal at specified times. With custodial accounts, by contrast, you will need a separate account for each grandchild.

To accomplish this end, and not have a minor's trust end at age 21 as it otherwise must, the trust document must require that the beneficiaries have a brief window following each contribution to the trust in which they can elect to withdraw that contribution. The trustee will notify the children, through their parents while they are very young, that a contribution has been made. They then have a period of time, typically 30 to 45 days, in which to request the money. This provision is called a "Crummey power," after a landmark court case involving a person named Crummey.

Of course, you expect them to ignore the notice and leave the money in the trust. If an older beneficiary did turn contrary and elect to withdraw an annual contribution, you simply wouldn't put any more into the trust. Earlier contributions would remain intact and be distributed according to the provisions of the trust document.

Skipping Generations

Perhaps you've done exceedingly well in the market, sold a successful business, or exercised some profitable stock options. If you don't need the money, and if your children won't need the money, you may want to establish a trust to benefit your grandchildren.

The clear advantage lies in skipping one set of estate taxes. If you leave the money to your children and they leave it to their children, amounts in excess of the federal exclusion will be taxed at your death and again at each child's death. This outcome can be avoided by creating a trust with income going to your children during their lifetimes and the principal going to their children, your grandchildren, when their parents die.

Tax Tips

The generation-skipping tax applies, as you would expect, to gifts that skip a generation. That includes your grandchildren—but not if your child, their parent, dies first. In that instance, the children move up a generation and there is no GST. (Although rejecting an inheritance—"disclaiming" it, in legal jargon—normally has the same effect as death, by letting an inheritance go to the next generation, it doesn't work as a mechanism to avoid the GST.)

Tax Talk

A **dynasty trust** can shelter family wealth for generations. This is in sharp contrast to most state laws governing trusts, which generally allow trusts to extend only until the last to die of the named individuals living when the trust was created, plus 21 years.

Be careful. Special rules—and onerous taxes—apply to gifts that skip a generation. You are allowed to give up to $1,030,000 in 2000 (twice that amount, if your spouse consents to the gift), without incurring the generation-skipping tax (GST). The amount is indexed to inflation but is not per-recipient. Instead, it is the total amount that any one donor may give free of the GST to any number of people. The ceiling is figured going in, not coming out. The $1 million you give today could be worth many times that by the time it goes to your grandchildren, and it will not be subject to the additional GST tax on the intervening growth.

If you give more, though, the excess will be subject to a flat GST of 55 percent. If a generation-skipping trust isn't very carefully drawn, that tax may be levied on top of estate taxes. The combined amount could virtually wipe out a large estate.

To use a trust to extend beyond the two generations of your children and your grandchildren, you must generally establish a *dynasty trust*. Only a few states—including Delaware, South Dakota, New Jersey, Wisconsin, and Alaska—currently permit these trusts that can span several generations. The laws vary slightly from state to state, but you must use an institution in the state you choose. You won't necessarily have to travel. Major banks and money management firms in large cities such as New York have established affiliates in states permitting dynasty trusts.

College Bound

Many of the same college-funding techniques described in Chapter 7, "Uncle Sam's IOUs," and Chapter 8, "Education Tax Breaks," may be used by grandparents as well as by parents. But take note of the following provisions.

EE-bonds are tax-free when used for college by parents who meet the income qualifications. But the bonds must be owned by—issued in the name of—the student's parent. If you want to use EE-bonds to help pay for the cost of college for a grandchild, be sure to buy the bonds in the parent's name or give the parent the money to buy the bond. Don't buy the bond in your name or in your grandchild's name, or it won't qualify for the tuition tax break.

Grandparents can contribute up to $500 a year to an Education IRA for each grandchild. This is on top of the maximum of $2,000 a year that you may contribute to your own IRA.

Education IRAs can be opened by single taxpayers with adjusted gross incomes of $95,000 to $110,000, and by married taxpayers filing jointly with AGI of $150,000 to $160,000. If your income is too high but your child's income is under the ceiling, give your child the money to open the Education IRAs for your grandchildren.

Education IRAs must be used by the time the beneficiary reaches age 30. If your oldest grandchild elects not to go to college, however, you can change the beneficiary on the Education IRA to his sister or brother. If the money is not used for tuition by the time the youngest child in the family reaches age 30, however, it will be subject to a 10 percent tax penalty.

529 and Counting

More states each year are offering tax-deferred opportunities to save for college via the *Section 529 plans,* described at length in Chapter 8. The plans take two forms. Some are prepaid tuition plans, and some are college savings plans. Both offer tax deferral on growth in the accounts, with taxes on withdrawal paid at the student's (typically lower) tax rate. In some cases, there are state income tax deductions as well.

Tax Traps

Watch out for rules against double-dipping. No contribution may be made to a state-sponsored college savings plan—by anyone—in the same year a contribution is made to an Education IRA for the same child.

Tax Talk

Section 529 plans, named for the applicable section of the tax code, include both prepaid tuition plans and the increasingly popular college savings plans. Some states have one, some have the other, and some offer both.

Prepaid tuition plans let parents and/or grandparents make advance payments, based on current college costs, to guarantee tuition payments when the youngster is ready for college. Some of these plans also cover room and board.

State college savings plans also accept contributions toward the future cost of college. Instead of guaranteeing enough to cover tuition, however, these plans invest the money—typically in a portfolio of stock funds, fixed-income funds, and money market mutual funds—so there may be more or less money at the end.

Some state savings plans are tilted toward the fixed-income end of the investment spectrum, while others use more equities for younger children. Because the end result is not guaranteed, as it is with prepaid tuition plans, you should check the investment strategy before you make a contribution. The plans are so new that you won't find much of a performance record, but you can at least judge the investment mix.

The rules vary by state, but college savings plans can generally be funded with contributions as small as $25 (if made as automatic debits from a bank account) and as large as $50,000. Once an account is established, other people can add to it. So whether you open the plan or your children do, relatives and friends can add their own contributions to mark birthdays, holidays, and special events.

College savings plans also have special gift and estate planning wrinkles of special interest to grandparents:

➤ A contribution of up to $50,000 may be made in a single year without triggering gift taxes or using any of your generation-skipping tax exemption. The only stipulation is that you cannot then give additional tax-free gifts to the same beneficiary for the next four years.

➤ Contributions are immediately excluded from your taxable estate even though you retain the right to change the beneficiary and can even, subject to tax penalties, withdraw the money. According to the accounting firm Ernst & Young, this is a unique situation in the realm of estate tax. However, if you make a gift of $50,000 and die within five years, a pro-rata proportion of the contribution will be counted toward your taxable estate.

➤ Unused money in a college savings account may be transferred without penalty to another child in the same family. But, under current rules, you can't transfer the money to a grandchild in a different nuclear family. So, if your son's child elects not to attend college, your daughter's child can't use the money—at least, not without your withdrawing the money, paying a tax penalty, and then opening an account for the second child. Before you open a college savings plan, check current rules with a knowledgeable tax adviser.

➤ Find out what happens if you, as the owner of the account, die before the child attends college. Because many states have no provision in their plans for successor owners, you may want to give your child the money to open the plan for the benefit of his or her child. Again, consult a knowledgeable tax adviser.

Investing on Your Own

Instead of meeting the restrictions of a formal college savings program, you might simply invest for your grandchildren by buying shares of stock or stock funds for them. Some grandparents make a habit of doing this at a grandchild's birthday every year.

There isn't any particular tax break, unless you place the shares in a custodial account for the children, but it can build a college fund for your grandchildren. It can also help them develop regular savings habits and, when the children are old enough, learn about investing.

Buying Shelter

Here's one more idea for helping grandkids through college: Buy a condominium unit or a house near campus. It can house your grandchild during the college years while taking in rents from other students. At the same time, it can yield valuable tax deductions for you in the way of depreciation, mortgage interest, and property taxes. With a house or multiapartment building, hiring your grandchild as the property manager can provide him with spending money while allowing you to deduct the salary against the rental income.

Don't count on reaping big profits when you sell, especially if it's a short-term investment. But you can enhance the odds of coming out ahead by buying in an area where dormitory space is in short supply, enrollments are growing, and the local housing market is stable.

Grandchildren sometimes need help beyond the college years. If you are asked for a loan—perhaps as a down payment on a house—understand the tax consequences before you say "Yes."

The general rule is that you must charge what's called the "applicable federal rate" of interest. The AFR is published in the Federal Register and changes each month. In December 1999, it was 5.74 percent on loans of less than three years, 6.2 percent on loans of three to nine years, and 6.47 percent on longer loans.

You can't ignore the AFR by telling your grandchild to forget about the interest. If you make an interest-free loan, you will owe income tax on the interest you would have received if you had actually charged the AFR. You may also face gift tax on the interest you should have charged.

But there are two exceptions to the rule:

➤ First, if the loan is for less than $10,000, you don't have to charge interest or report the interest income.

➤ Second, you don't have to charge interest on loans of up to $100,000 as long as the borrower doesn't use the money to invest. Instead, you report as income on your own federal income tax return the amount of the borrower's taxable unearned income for the year. If the borrower has less than $1,000 of unearned income for the year, you don't have to report anything at all.

The Least You Need to Know

➤ There is no gift tax on gifts of up to $10,000 a year, on gifts up to $20,000 for a married couple making a joint gift, or on any amounts paid directly to a medical or educational institution.

➤ Although the tax on gifts and bequests is identical, the way it is applied means that it costs less to make taxable gifts during life.

➤ Custodial accounts work well for small sums given to grandchildren, while trusts may be a better mechanism for larger sums or multiple beneficiaries.

➤ The generation-skipping tax can take a big bite out of gifts of more than $1 million.

➤ Grandparents can help grandchildren and garner tax breaks by contributing to Education IRAs, prepaid tuition plans, or college savings plans.

Part 4

Buying Futures

Tax-deferred retirement plans are among the best tax shelters available. But they sure can be confusing.

This part of The Complete Idiot's Guide to Tax-Free Investing *cuts through the thicket of 401(k) plans, employer-paid pensions, Individual Retirement Accounts, and special retirement options for the self-employed.*

This part also addresses the infernally complicated rules affecting withdrawals of retirement plan money, and describes annuities as a way to supplement retirement income.

Chapter 10

Building Your Nest Egg at Work

In This Chapter

➤ Discovering why 401(k) plans are today's most popular retirement saving vehicle

➤ Contributing the maximum and investing it wisely to produce retirement income

➤ Using matching contributions from your employer to boost returns

➤ Knowing that the money is designed for retirement but available in case of emergency

Your grandfather probably retired with a pension, a monthly check offered as a reward for years of service. Employer contributions funded the pension, and the employer made the investment decisions.

Forget about it. Today, you are far more likely to find a 401(k) plan where you work than a promised pension. These increasingly popular employer-sponsored retirement plans are based not on a promised benefit, but on your contributions—although there may be an employer match as well.

The 401(k) plan is the cornerstone of most workers' retirement savings today. With a 401(k) plan, how much money you eventually receive depends on how much you contribute over the years and how wisely you invest your contributions. This chapter explains how to make your 401(k) work harder for you.

Playing by the Rules

The 401(k) plan didn't even exist a scant 20 years ago. It took a brainstorm on the part of a man named Ted Benna, then a young benefits consultant and currently the president of the 401(k) Association, to recognize that Section 401(k) of the Internal Revenue Code afforded the opportunity for tax-sheltered savings for retirement.

Since then, the 401(k) plan has spread like wildfire. According to research by the Spectrem Group, a research and consulting firm in Windsor, Connecticut, there were 94,000 plan sponsors, 11 million participants, and $155 billion in assets in 1986. By 1998, there were 283,000 plan sponsors, 28 million participants, and $1,140 billion in assets. You, your employer, and your money may be counted in this total.

The 401(k) plan has both disadvantages and advantages when compared to the traditional defined benefit pension plan. Its primary disadvantage is obvious: You pay for it, and your employer doesn't have to contribute at all. But its advantages are significant: Your pretax dollars can grow tax-deferred. Just as important, a 401(k) is portable. If you change jobs, as so many workers do, you can't take a traditional pension along, but you *can* take the money in your 401(k).

Tax Tips

In most cases, you must choose to participate in a 401(k) plan offered by your employer. If you don't elect to participate (even though it's a big mistake), you're out of the loop. But you may lose the ability to opt out under a recent Internal Revenue Service ruling that authorizes employers to automatically deduct 401(k) contributions from your paycheck. Some large companies have begun automatic deductions; others are expected to follow.

At this writing, you are allowed to contribute a maximum of $10,500 a year to a 401(k) plan. That's Uncle Sam's ceiling, and it goes up from time to time along with rises in the cost of living. Your employer's plan also sets its own rules. It may require you to be on the payroll for a year before joining the plan. In addition, it may allow you to contribute a specific percentage of your salary (often about 6 percent) and may set a lower maximum contribution.

Many workers have trouble putting aside the maximum contribution, but you should try to contribute as much as possible. Not only will you have far more money when retirement rolls around, but there are two distinct tax benefits to maxing out your contribution.

First, you recognize an immediate tax benefit. Your contributions are pretax—that is, they reduce your salary for income tax purposes, although they are still subject to Social Security and Medicare tax. If you contribute $1,000 to a 401(k), the entire $1,000 is invested toward your future while your taxable income is reduced by the same amount.

Take that same $1,000 in the form of salary, and you'll pay income tax on it before you can invest what's left. If you're in the 28 percent federal income tax bracket, you'll pay $280 in taxes on $1,000 and have $720 left to invest. If your state levies an income tax, as most do, you'll have even less.

Second, you see an ongoing tax benefit. Earnings and appreciation on the invested contributions are not taxed until they are withdrawn from the plan. Ideally, that will be at retirement, when your tax bracket may be lower.

Playing with Matches

The desirability of participation in a 401(k) plan ratchets up a notch when you realize that more than 80 percent of 401(k) plan sponsors match a portion of their employees' contributions. The most common match, according to the Spectrem Group, is 50 cents on the dollar, up to 6 percent of pay.

About 15 percent of the plans in a 1998 William M. Mercer, benefits consultants, survey used a tiered match, such as matching 100 percent of the first 3 percent of pay and 50 percent of additional contributions. Some employers even match *after-tax* contributions.

What does all this mean to you? Think of your employer match as free money, or as a risk-free return on investment. Both are true. If your employer puts up 50 cents for every dollar you contribute, you are receiving the 50 cents free. You are also receiving an immediate guaranteed risk-free rate of return. Where else can you earn a guaranteed 50 percent?

So, even if you can't cough up enough dough to make the maximum allowable contribution to your 401(k) plan, you should definitely contribute to the level of the employer match. Not doing so is simply throwing money away.

Playing It Close to the Vest

Your contributions are yours. The money belongs to you, even if it has been put into the 401(k) plan. Employer contributions, however, are another matter. Your employer can—and often

Tax Talk

After-tax contributions are made from salary that has already been taxed. Unlike pretax contributions, therefore, this money won't be taxed when it is withdrawn from the 401(k), although earnings on the money are subject to tax. Also, because this money was not initially sheltered from taxation, it generally may be withdrawn at any time.

Tax Talk

Vesting means entitlement to the money in a retirement plan, whether it's an employer-funded pension plan or employer contributions to a defined contribution plan such as a 401(k). When you are vested, you can take the money with you if you leave your job.

does—set criteria for when you can take the money and run. These criteria, based on years of service, are called *vesting*.

Federal regulations state that you must become vested in employer contributions under a specific schedule that is at least as favorable as one of two minimum standards. The first is gradual, over a period of three to seven years, and the second is all-at-once ("cliff") vesting after no more than five years on the job. You are always entitled to your own contributions, in full. A graduated vesting schedule might look like the following example.

Years of Service	Vested Percentage
3	20%
4	40%
5	60%
6	80%
7 or more	100%

Keep in mind that all the money you put in yourself remains yours at all times, with no vesting required.

Variations on a Theme

The 401(k) plan is the most popular and hence most widely known defined contribution plan. But 401(k) plans have been generally restricted to for-profit corporations. If you work for a nonprofit or for government, you may find one of the following variations:

➤ 403(b) plans are found in nonprofit institutions such as hospitals and school systems. Investment options are usually more limited than those found in 401(k) plans.

➤ 457 plans are the government version.

Although matching contributions have been rare in both 403(b) and 457 plans, both are moving closer to the 401(k) model.

The Ball Is in Your Court

One of the key distinguishing features of 401(k) plans is that you are in control. You decide how much to contribute, up to the ceilings permitted by your plan and by the government. You also decide how to invest the money.

In the early days of 401(k) plans, investment choices were often limited. Then Uncle Sam decided that employers who provided limited investment choices were responsible for what happened, for the success or failure of those investments. In other words, they could be sued if the 401(k) investments went sour and damaged retirement income prospects for employees.

The only way for employers to get out of this *fiduciary responsibility* is to provide at least three different investment options to employees. The choices must have significantly different characteristics of risk and reward. Your employer can't get off the responsibility hook by offering three different aggressive growth mutual funds. But it is perfectly okay to offer a menu consisting of a growth fund, an income fund, and a stable value fund.

Tax Talk

Fiduciary responsibility is the legal responsibility of investing money wisely for the benefit of the ultimate beneficiaries.

In fact, the Spectrem Group finds that more than 40 percent of all 401(k) participants have eight or more investment options available to them. The larger the company, the more investment options generally are offered. Even at smaller companies, however, you will generally find at least three choices. If you don't, it means that your employer has accepted the fiduciary responsibility of making wise investment choices for you.

On the A La Carte Menu

The most common investment options for 401(k) plans consist of an array of mutual funds. Some companies offer mutual funds that are also available to other investors; with these funds, you can easily track their performance in newspaper mutual fund tables. Other companies stick to funds that are not otherwise available, so it is difficult to monitor performance. Some offer self-directed accounts, where you can choose among any investment vehicle in the world at large.

Whether the mutual funds are generally available or not, you are likely to find both equity (stock) and income (bond) funds within your 401(k) plan. If your plan offers many choices, you will probably find several equity funds. For example, a recent survey of the 401(k) marketplace by William M. Mercer found *indexed* equity funds, balanced funds, and international equity funds in addition to growth equity funds.

Tax Talk

An **indexed** fund mirrors a general stock market index, such as the Standard & Poor's 500, making changes in the portfolio only when the underlying index makes a change. The managers of actively managed equity funds, by contrast, buy and sell among the whole array of market offerings in an effort to achieve the best results.

Tax Talk

Stable value options are cash equivalents that pay interest on a regular basis. **Guaranteed investment contracts** are issued by insurance companies; the interest rate is fixed for a specified period of years, but the underlying principal is not guaranteed.

You may also find *stable value* options on the 401(k) investment menu. Stable value options include money market mutual funds and *guaranteed investment contracts* (GICs).

Money market mutual funds are a convenient parking place for cash. In the outside world—outside your 401(k) plan, that is—a money market mutual fund is a convenient source of funds, both to pay large bills and to hold until you make an investment decision.

Within your 401(k), taking the cash is not generally an option (we'll talk about loans and hardship withdrawals in a minute), but you may want to use a money market fund either as a temporary parking place or as a stable value component of your retirement portfolio. Just don't keep very much money in this cash alternative, or you'll lose out on potential investment growth.

GICs were very popular among conservative 401(k) investors until two realizations dawned on those investors. The first was that the word "guarantee" in the label is somewhat misleading; it is possible to lose money on a GIC. Many people did lose money when issuing insurers went out of business. The second concern stemmed from the long upward rise in stock prices in the 1990s, as more 401(k) participants turned to equities for the potential of long-term growth.

Another option that is frequently available is employer stock. In fact, at some companies, matching contributions made by the employer are always invested in company stock.

While you may want to demonstrate your loyalty as a team player by investing your 401(k) assets in company stock—in fact, at some companies, you may not have much choice—it isn't necessarily a wise choice. Think about it. By investing retirement money in the same company providing your paycheck, you're placing all your bets on the same horse. If the company runs into trouble, both your current income and your future income will be on the line.

Making Your Choices

You make your investment choices when you first participate in the plan. You can also change those choices at regular intervals. At many of the largest companies, you can switch your investments on a daily basis, just by logging on to a computer. Not that you'd want to do so—it's better to choose investments for the long term, making adjustments only when necessary.

Tax Treats

If you and your spouse are both covered by 401(k) plans at work but can't afford to max out contributions to both plans, do a careful comparison to decide where to put most of your money. Consider these factors: Does one plan have a better employer match? If so, fund that plan first. Does one offer a better choice of investment options? Think about putting more money in that plan. Does one have earlier vesting, or allow loans where the other does not? Ditto. At the same time, don't lose sight of the fact that you each need retirement money in your own name. It may be like walking a tightrope, but keep your investment goals in mind, and you'll make the right choice.

So, before you decide which investments belong in your 401(k), give some thought to your long-range financial goals, your attitude toward risk, and your time horizon. Then develop an *asset allocation* strategy to help you meet your goals. In developing your personal strategy, look at the assets both inside and outside your 401(k) plan as part of a single investment portfolio.

The key to asset allocation is dividing the assets in your entire portfolio among various investment categories. The simplest division is among stocks, bonds, and cash equivalents such as certificates of deposit and money market funds. A more complex allocation might divide your stock holdings among large companies and small, aggressive and conservative funds, and domestic and international funds.

Whatever your initial choice, the portfolio must be periodically reviewed and rebalanced to maintain the desired percentages. Otherwise, as stock prices rise, you might find that 80 percent of your portfolio is represented by stocks instead of the 60 percent you planned. The imbalance could put your retirement security at risk. Rebalancing means that you will sell some of the winners and put your profits to work in an area that may do better at another time.

If you are many years from retirement, consider tipping your investments heavily toward the side of equities. Stocks have historically outperformed every other investment. Stock prices can go down,

Tax Talk

Asset allocation is the strategy of balancing investments among different instruments to minimize risk and maximize potential return.

of course, but with time on your side, you can afford to ride out market ups and downs. As you get closer to retirement, however, you may want to adjust the mix in your entire portfolio, including your 401(k) plan.

The nice thing about putting equities in a tax-sheltered plan is that buying and selling does not generate immediate taxes. The flip side of this equation is that taxes are not eliminated, just deferred. When you eventually take the money out, it will all be taxed as ordinary income and won't receive favorable capital gains treatment. (Stock issued by the company you work for is subject to special tax treatment; see Chapter 14, "Hold On to Your Gains.")

For this reason, especially because capital gains rates are at their lowest level in some years (see Chapter 22, "There's No Free Lunch"), some advisers suggest keeping the bulk of equity investments in taxable accounts. On the other hand, allowing appreciating assets to grow without the drag of taxes can give you much more money in the long run. You may want to discuss this question with your investment or tax adviser to find the solution most appropriate for you.

How are 401(k) plan assets invested? A study conducted jointly by the Employee Benefit Research Institute and the Investment Company Institute found the following breakdown:

Asset	Percent
Equity funds	44.0
Employer stock	19.1
Guaranteed investment contracts	15.1
Balanced funds	7.8
Bond funds	6.8
Money market funds	5.4
Other stable value funds	0.8
Other investments	1.0

Reprinted with permission of the Investment Company Institute (www.ici.org)

Who Pays the Freight?

There is one ongoing problem with 401(k) plans: They tend to be expensive, and more and more often, you pay the bills. In 1995, just 7 percent of all plans made participants pick up much of the cost. By 1997, according to Spectrem Group, that percentage was 24 percent.

Fees and expenses can significantly hinder the growth in your account and, in the end, reduce your retirement income. An example provided by the Pension and Welfare Benefits Administration of the U.S. Department of Labor tells it loud and clear.

Let's say that you have 35 years until retirement and a current 401(k) account balance of $25,000. If returns on investments in your account over the next 35 years average 7 percent and fees and expenses reduce your average return by 0.5 percent, you will wind up with $227,000 at retirement—even with no further contributions to your account. But if fees and expenses are 1.5 percent, just 1 percent more, your account balance will grow to only $163,000. That 1 percent difference in cost reduces your account balance at retirement by 28 percent.

So, it pays to pay attention—even though it may not be easy to get the information, and even though there may not be much you can do to keep costs down.

According to PWBA, 401(k) plan fees and expenses generally fall into three categories:

➤ Plan administration fees, for the day-to-day operation of the plan—record keeping, accounting, legal services, and so on. Administrative services are sometimes covered by investment fees deducted directly from investment returns. If they are charged separately, they may be paid by the employer or charged directly against plan assets. When paid directly by the plan, they may be allocated among individual accounts in proportion to account balances, or passed through as a flat fee against the participant's account.

➤ Investment fees are generally assessed as a percentage of assets invested, and although they may not be immediately evident, they directly affect your investment returns. Investment fees may include transaction costs (*loads*) connected with buying and selling mutual fund shares, and management fees (*actively managed* funds charge higher fees than *passively managed* funds, so you can exercise some control over costs by investing in index funds), and other fees involved in the day-to-day management of the investment.

➤ Individual service fees may be levied in connection with optional features offered under the plan and exercised by individual participants. If you elect to take a loan from your 401(k) funds (described later in this chapter in the section "Borrowing Your Own Money"), you might be charged a fee.

Tax Talk

A **load** is a sales commission earned by a stockbroker on the sale of mutual fund shares. Some loads are paid up-front, upon purchase, while others are paid when shares are sold. **Actively managed** funds are run by portfolio managers who buy and sell securities in an effort to achieve the best return for shareholders. **Passively managed** funds follow a market index and do not actively trade. As a result, they are less expensive to administer.

Is There a Problem Here?

A few years ago, there seemed to be a story every other day about some employer raiding the 401(k) piggy bank. The frequency may have been exaggerated, but there were certainly too many instances of employers—most often small employers who acted as their own administrators—misappropriating employee contributions to 401(k) plans. Perhaps the employer invested the money unwisely and it was lost. Maybe it was never invested at all. Sometimes there was outright theft.

The most common problem is a small employer's temporary need for cash. The employer may expect to repay the 401(k) plan quickly but find it impossible to do so.

Following numerous complaints—the Labor Department investigated hundreds in 1995 alone—the rules were changed. Your employer now must forward your contributions to the plan trustee within 15 business days after the month in which the money is deducted from your paycheck.

This tightening of the rules affords some protection, but you should still take steps to protect yourself. Here's how:

➤ Compare your pay stubs with your 401(k) statement; make sure that reported contribution amounts match up and that there are no clerical errors.

➤ Check your fund statements to make sure that your own contributions were invested along with scheduled company matching contributions.

➤ Be wary if your employer is a one-man band, both administering the plan and managing the investments. You're generally safer if an outside investment manager, or at least an outside payroll service, prepares paychecks and makes sure that contributions get to their proper destination.

Tax Tips

Because 401(k) plans have their origin in the federal tax code, you may expect some government insurance. Sorry. There is no government insurance on 401(k) plans as there is on traditional defined benefit pension plans.

Leaving Town

One of the neat things about 401(k) plans is that they are portable; you can take your own contributions (and your employer's contributions, once you are vested) with you if you leave. You don't have to wait for retirement. If you leave to take another job, the money is still yours. As long as you have reached age 55, you have the choice of taking the money in a lump sum distribution, rolling it over into an Individual Retirement Account for continued tax-deferred growth, or leaving it in place (assuming that your current plan permits this).

The best choice for most employees is generally rolling the money into an IRA. You'll find more details on all of these options in Chapter 14.

But what if you need the money sooner? Is your 401(k) money ever available to you in the event of emergency? Or, if it's not strictly an emergency, what about a real cash crunch?

Yes, you can generally tap your 401(k) funds. Although you shouldn't raid your retirement nest egg unless it's absolutely necessary, most plans permit loans, and many permit hardship withdrawals.

Borrowing Your Own Money

Most large corporations permit loans from their 401(k) plans. Overall, more than half of all plans, representing 70 percent of all plan participants, permit loans. This feature gives 401(k) plans a definite edge over Individual Retirement Accounts, which do not permit loans.

The most you can borrow is half of your account balance, up to a maximum of $50,000. Some plans impose lower ceilings, and most plans restrict loans to major purposes such as buying a house, paying for college, or meeting a medical emergency.

The interest rate on your loan is usually 1 to 2 percentage points above the current prime rate (that's the rate available to a bank's best customers). You may also be charged a servicing fee for the administrative hassle your company faces in making the loan.

Repayment will generally be through payroll deduction, with your payments going right back into your 401(k) plan. That means that you're paying interest to yourself. A lot of people view this as a virtually free loan, but don't fall into this trap. Your initial contributions were pretax, but the repayments are with after-tax dollars. That's fair. But remember this: When you eventually take the money out of your 401(k), it's going to be taxed again. So, for the privilege of taking a loan, you'll pay tax twice on the same dollars. Meanwhile, until the loan is repaid, you'll lose tax-sheltered growth on the money, creating a shortfall that may never be made up.

Tax Tips

If your employer follows joint-and-survivor rules on retirement distributions, you may be required to secure your spouse's consent to a loan from your 401(k). As is the case with traditional pension plans, if you're married, your spouse must be your primary beneficiary for your 401(k)—unless you both, in writing, elect another option.

Tax Traps

A 401(k) loan must generally be repaid within five years, although loans for the purchase of a home may run longer. But be careful: If you leave your job, you will have to repay the loan right away. If you can't, you've taken a distribution from the plan and will owe income tax on the full amount. If you're under age 59½, you'll also owe a 10 percent penalty tax on the distribution.

Hardship Withdrawals

The last-ditch alternative, if you need money desperately, is a hardship withdrawal from your 401(k) plan. Withdrawals are not a good idea, so they are a true desperation measure. You will have taken a distribution, so you will owe income tax and possibly a tax penalty. Depending on your tax bracket, that could mean a 35 percent to 40 percent bite right off the top. And, of course, you will lose all that tax-deferred compounding that was building a retirement nest egg.

But, let's face it. Things happen. If you are really up against it and have exhausted all your other financial resources (including loans from your 401[k] plan), a hardship withdrawal may be your only solution.

Many plans don't permit withdrawals at all. Those that do generally abide by IRS guidelines that permit the following four reasons for a hardship withdrawal:

➤ For unreimbursed medical expenses

➤ For college tuition

➤ For purchase of a primary residence

➤ To prevent eviction, or foreclosure on your mortgage

Employers can allow hardship withdrawals for other reasons—for a funeral, as an example, or to repair significant uninsured damage to your home—but because they face possible challenge from the IRS, many limit the choices to those the IRS has already approved.

What happens next? You'll owe income tax on the withdrawn amount, and you may owe a tax penalty as well. In addition, because you may not be able to afford the same level of future contributions to your 401(k) plan, your retirement nest egg may be seriously cracked, if not scrambled beyond repair. Don't withdraw 401(k) funds unless you absolutely must.

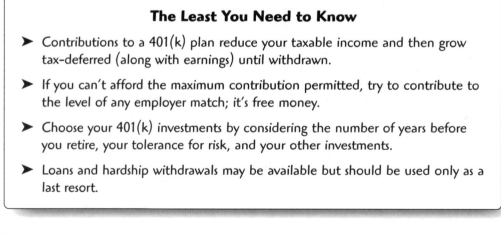

The Least You Need to Know

➤ Contributions to a 401(k) plan reduce your taxable income and then grow tax-deferred (along with earnings) until withdrawn.

➤ If you can't afford the maximum contribution permitted, try to contribute to the level of any employer match; it's free money.

➤ Choose your 401(k) investments by considering the number of years before you retire, your tolerance for risk, and your other investments.

➤ Loans and hardship withdrawals may be available but should be used only as a last resort.

Promises to Keep

In This Chapter

➤ Understanding how Social Security retirement benefits are the bedrock of retirement security

➤ Traditional pensions provide guaranteed retirement benefits—for those fortu-
nate enough to have them

➤ Deciding when to retire and how to take your pension benefits

➤ Learning that pension income is taxable

➤ Discovering that Social Security benefits may be taxable

Financial security in retirement has often been compared to a three-legged stool made
up of Social Security, a pension, and personal savings.

Despite massive publicity about future financial problems, Social Security is still the
bedrock of retirement security. Traditional employer-paid pensions, however, are beginning to resemble the dodo bird as they are increasingly replaced by 401(k) and
other employee-paid plans.

Personal savings are playing a larger role in building a retirement nest egg. But, if you
do have a traditional pension, you're in the catbird's seat. This chapter explains the
ins and outs of both Social Security and employer pensions, and shows you how to
make the most of both.

Uncle Sam Kicks In

Don't rely on Social Security benefits for your entire retirement income. The system isn't designed that way. Still, Social Security can provide a solid foundation for your retirement years, although you'll certainly want to supplement that income.

Retired workers currently receive an average of $804 a month in Social Security benefits—but that's the average for all retired workers. The maximum monthly benefit for someone retiring at age 65 in 2000 was $1,433. The neat thing about Social Security is that benefits are indexed to the cost of living and go up each year. Most pensions, by contrast, are fixed when payments begin.

Tax Treats

Wondering how much Social Security is in your future? Wonder no more. As of October 1, 1999, the Social Security Administration is mailing annual statements to every working American over the age of 25. The statement—which you should receive every year about three months before your birthday—includes a summary of how much you will receive at your normal retirement age as well as at earlier and later dates. It also shows the amount of monthly disability income you could expect if you became severely disabled, and how much your survivors will receive after your death. Don't want to wait? Call Social Security, at 1-800-772-1213, and request a statement at any time. Or, go online, at www.ssa.gov/mystatement.

Of course, Social Security is a contributory system. Throughout your working life, you pay taxes toward your eventual retirement benefits. Your employer pays an equal amount—unless you are self-employed, in which case you pay the whole thing, although a tax deduction eases a bit of the burden.

The tax changes from time to time. In 2000, you and your employer each pay 6.2 percent of your earnings, up to a ceiling of $76,200. An additional tax of 1.45 percent apiece on all earnings, with no upper limit, goes toward Medicare.

These taxes pay for more than retirement benefits. In addition to Medicare, the Social Security system offers survivors' benefits to your spouse and dependent children (up to a certain age) after your death. It will pay monthly disability income if you are severely disabled and unable to work.

You can retire and receive full Social Security benefits at age 65, although that age is gradually being pushed back for workers born after 1937 and will become age 67 for workers born in 1960 and thereafter. You can retire and receive benefits as early as age 62, although your benefits will be permanently reduced by 20 percent. You also can delay retirement to age 70 and receive increased benefits.

But you can spend your entire working life in a job covered by Social Security and still lose some benefits.

Win Some, Lose Some

Two wrinkles can cause you to lose some or all of your anticipated retirement income. The first is pension integration. The second is the earnings test.

Pension integration, as practiced by some private employers, reduces pension benefits by some or all of the Social Security retirement benefits the worker receives. The rationale is that the companies are recapturing the Social Security taxes they paid on behalf of employees. In some extreme cases, often with the lowest-paid workers, the practice has meant no pension at all.

It is now illegal for employers to wipe out more than half of a pension earned after 1989—but half can be a lot, if you're counting on the pension as retirement income. Furthermore, as much as 100 percent of a pension earned before 1989 can still evaporate under integration.

The earnings test is a Social Security regulation. Under this regulation, people under the age of 65 have Social Security retirement benefits reduced by any money they earn over specified amounts. After you reach age 65, you can earn as much as you like and still receive full Social Security benefits.

Tax Tips

You must apply for Social Security benefits; they aren't automatic. Contact Social Security at least three months before you plan to retire. Call toll-free, 1-800-772-1213, for information on how to proceed. Even if you plan to wait for Social Security retirement benefits, be sure to apply for Medicare before you reach age 65.

Tax Tips

If you and your spouse have both worked and contributed to Social Security, the lower-income spouse has a choice. If that's you, you can receive benefits based on your own individual work record; if it will be more, you can choose to receive half of your spouse's benefit. You will always get the higher of the two amounts, but you cannot get both.

Until recently, two age categories existed for the earnings test. People ages 62 through 64 lost—and still lose—$1 in benefits for every $2 earned in excess of $10,080. The amount is indexed to inflation and rises each year.

For those aged 65 through 69, the penalty was $1 in benefits for every $3 earned over $17,000. The amount was scheduled to increase according to a predetermined schedule reaching $25,000 in 2001 and $30,000 in 2002. But people over 65 can now receive full Social Security retirement benefits without regard to how much they earn. Thanks to a law passed in early 2000 and made retroactive to January 1, 2000, the earnings test on people 65 and over has been repealed.

Giving Back

The other downer is that, even though money was taxed going into the Social Security system, it may also be taxed coming out.

Social Security benefits used to be completely tax-free. No longer. Half of your benefits are now subject to income tax if you earn between $25,000 and $34,000 as a single taxpayer, or $32,000 to $44,000 as a married couple filing jointly. Fully 85 percent of your benefits are subject to income tax if you earn more than $34,000 as a single taxpayer or $44,000 as a married couple filing jointly.

For the purpose of this tax, income is defined as adjusted gross income (without Social Security benefits), plus tax-exempt income, plus half of the Social Security benefits. If the total exceeds the threshold amounts, the benefits are subject to tax.

Tax Traps

You thought tax-exempt interest was really tax-exempt? Guess again. Income that is otherwise tax-exempt is counted for purposes of determining whether your earnings put your Social Security retirement benefits into the taxable category.

You don't have to earn megabucks to have your Social Security benefits taxed. A married couple with a pension income of $18,000, an investment income of $25,000, and Social Security benefits of about $13,000 could wind up paying an additional $1,000 in income tax to Uncle Sam. And, because most states peg their income tax forms to the federal form, you could owe more in state income taxes as well—unless your state specifically exempts Social Security benefits from tax, as many do.

Moreover, because the threshold amounts are not indexed to inflation, more Social Security recipients each year find their benefits subject to tax.

Guaranteed Benefits

Pension income has long been the second leg of the retirement support system.

Traditional pensions come with a promise: Work for the same employer for the duration, and you'll receive a check each and every month after you retire. Of course, most of us no longer work for the same employer throughout our working lives. Many employers also no longer offer traditional employer-funded pension plans. If you're lucky enough to be covered under a traditional pension plan, here's what you need to know.

These employer-funded retirement plans are "defined benefit" plans, promising a guaranteed stream of income typically based on your age, earnings, and years of service. The guarantee means that you can find out, as you approach retirement, how much you will receive. Finding out means, in turn, that you can do some solid financial planning for your retirement years.

Defined benefit plans calculate benefits in several ways. The plan may offer an exact dollar amount. It may describe the promised pension as a percentage of salary and years of service—an example would be 1 percent of final pay times years of service. Or, it may describe the benefit in terms of a specific dollar amount and years of service—an example might be $30 per month at retirement for every year of service.

Tax Talk

Defined benefit plans are traditional pension plans, with benefits typically funded by the employer and based on length of service. The employer is responsible for investing the money and paying the benefits. By contrast, defined contribution plans such as today's popular 401(k) plans are funded primarily by employees and have benefits based on how much employees contribute and how wisely they invest.

When It's Yours, It's Yours

If your employer provides a pension plan, you generally must be allowed to become a participant no later than the start of the next plan year, or six months after you have reached age 21 and completed one year of service.

But participation doesn't mean that the money credited to your account actually belongs to you. The second part of the equation is vesting, the process by which you become entitled to your pension.

Tax Talk

Vesting refers to the amount of time you must work before earning a right to your pension that can't be taken away. When you are fully vested, your accrued benefit is yours—even if you leave the company before reaching retirement age.

Tax Tips

If you are covered by a defined benefit pension plan, your employer must give you a document called a Summary Plan Description (SPD) when you first become a participant in the plan, and again if major plan changes are adopted. Read the SPD. It tells you how service and benefits are calculated, when benefits become vested, when you will receive payment and in what form, and how to file a claim for benefits.

As I explained in discussing 401(k) plans in Chapter 10, "Building Your Nest Egg at Work," you are always fully entitled to money you have contributed to a pension plan and to investment earnings on those contributions, whether the plan is a defined benefit or defined contribution plan. When it comes to the money your employer puts in on your behalf, though, it's a different story.

If you're on the job at normal retirement age, you're generally entitled to your pension no matter how long you've been with the company. If you choose to take early retirement, however, companies have two choices when it comes to vesting. They can make you fully entitled to your pension all at once, when you have completed at least five years of service. Or, they can provide gradual vesting so that you are entitled to 20 percent of the accrued pension benefit after three years of work, 40 percent at four years, and so on, with full vesting after seven years. The following table shows the two vesting schedules.

Under some circumstances—an example is multiemployer plans under collective bargaining agreements—participants may need to complete 10 years of service to be vested.

The Employment Retirement Income Security Act of 1974, commonly called ERISA, requires that employers offer vesting schedules at least as generous as one of these:

Years of Service	Percentage of Accrued Benefit That Is Vested
Graded Vesting	
Less than 3	0%
At least 3 but less than 4	20%
At least 4 but less than 5	40%
At least 5 but less than 6	60%
At least 6 but less than 7	80%
At least 7	100%

Years of Service	Percentage of Accrued Benefit That Is Vested
Cliff Vesting	
Less than 5	0%
At least 5	100%

Uncle Sam Minds the Store

The first private pension plan in the United States was established in 1875, but it took almost 100 years before promised benefits were actually guaranteed. As a result of some shocking instances in which workers lost promised retirement benefits—in 1963, as an example, 4,000 Studebaker autoworkers lost their pensions—the Employee Retirement Income Security Act of 1974 (ERISA) was enacted to protect employees.

Employers must now follow strict ERISA guidelines in establishing and running traditional defined benefit pension plans. Just as important, ERISA established the Pension Benefit Guaranty Corporation (PBGC) to back up promised pensions with insurance.

Many corporate pension plans have more money than they need to pay promised benefits after a long run-up in stock prices such as we have had in recent years. But declining values can cause plans to be underfunded. Another threat arises from employer bankruptcy.

What happens to your pension if your employer goes out of business or the pension plan runs out of money? If your company pension plan is a defined benefit plan, you are protected by PBGC. If an employer has financial difficulties and cannot fund the pension plan, PBGC takes over and guarantees basic pension benefits to both current and future retirees.

If you think that you may be owed a benefit from a defunct pension plan, try to contact the pension plan administrator or the company where you earned the pension. If these efforts fail, check out the PBGC Web site at search.pbgc.gov, send an e-mail to missing@pbgc.gov, or write to the PBGC Pension Search Program, 1200 K Street NW, Suite 930, Washington, D.C. 20005-4026. Provide your name, address, daytime phone number, Social Security number, and date of birth—along with the name and address of the employer and dates of employment.

The maximum amount payable under PBGC's government-sponsored insurance program is adjusted annually and is permanently established for each pension plan at the time the plan terminated. For plans terminating in 1999, the maximum amount payable to any retiree at age 65 was just under $36,614, or about $3,051 a month. For someone retiring at 62, the maximum guarantee in 1999 was just under $29,000 a year, or $2,410 a month. These figures are based solely on the retiree's age, without survivor benefits.

Unfortunately, this guarantee sounds better than it is because PBGC has a large backlog of cases. But Congress is paying attention, and improvements may be in the works.

Tax Treats

With all the mergers on the corporate front these days, you need to keep track of a pension owed you from a prior job. Keep all the relevant documents. Notify the plan administrator if you move. And, if you hear about a merger, get in touch with the new company's benefits office and notify it that you're aware of how much you're owed. If you don't hear about a merger and first find out at retirement date that your prior employer no longer exists, you can take several steps. Ask the reference librarian in your local library to track down the current company name. Try the office of the Secretary of State in the state where you worked. Or, contact the U.S. Department of Labor's Pension and Welfare Benefits Administration at 202-219-8776 or online at www.dol.gov/dol/pwba.

Variations on a Theme

It may be fairly easy to understand the difference between defined benefit plans (guaranteed pensions provided by employers) and defined contribution plans (retirement plans funded by employees).

But nothing is ever simple in the wonderful world of tax shelters, and new ways to build retirement savings crop up regularly.

One of the new kids on the block is a cash balance offshoot of defined benefit plans. Not so new, but worth consideration, are the various *nonqualified plans* provided by companies in an effort to beef up retirement income for valued employees.

Cash Balance Plans

These hybrid plans have stirred considerable controversy—not when they are the first pension plan adopted by a company, but when a company switches from a traditional defined benefit plan to a cash balance plan.

Tax Talk

Nonqualified plans are retirement funding vehicles that do not enjoy tax-sheltered status. *Qualified plans* do offer tax deferral.

Traditional defined benefit pension plans reward long years of service with the same employer, often through a benefit formula pegged to the higher earnings of the last years on the job. Cash balance plans build value steadily throughout the years and offer a portable benefit that can be taken along when a worker changes jobs.

In the transition from one to the other, benefits for older workers are often temporarily frozen. Employees must then work for several more years to begin earning additional pension benefits. Sometimes they must work longer to get back to the same level of accrued benefits that they had before the switch.

Not surprisingly, older workers have complained. In some cases, they have complained so loudly that the company—IBM is a major example—changed its plans. And, because it is illegal for pension plans to discriminate against older workers, Congress may pass disclosure rules, the Equal Employment Opportunity Commission is investigating claims of discrimination, and the Internal Revenue Service is paying careful attention to conversion requests by employers.

Meanwhile, if you're young and mobile, a cash balance plan will probably suit you just fine. The employer funds the plan, just as with a traditional pension plan, and typically guarantees an investment return equivalent to the return on 30-year bonds issued by the U.S. Treasury. Additional profits, if any, are retained by the employer.

If you're over age 50 and have been with the same employer for many years, the switch to a cash balance plan may cause some grief—unless your employer eases the transition by increasing contributions for older workers or beefing up matching contributions to 401(k) plans. Better yet, your employer might let workers choose the old plan or the new.

If your company is making a switch in pension plans, ask for a detailed comparison of your personal benefits under the old plan and the new.

Nonqualified Plans

In an effort to motivate valued employees—often, but not always, highly compensated executives—companies may offer extra compensation in the form of nonqualified plans in addition to qualified tax-sheltered retirement plans.

One popular form of extra compensation involves incentive stock options. Options are simply the right to buy shares of the company's common stock at a stated price during a specific time period. Typically, the stock is purchased by the employee when its price is higher than it was at the time the option was given.

Tax Tips

Getting a divorce? Accrued pension benefits can be treated as a marital asset to be divided as part of a divorce settlement. But this won't be automatic. Talk to your lawyer if you are covered by a spouse's pension.

The difference between the two prices is taxable at favorable capital gain rates when the stock is sold—as long as it has been held for at least one year after the stock was purchased and two years after the option was granted.

Timing is critical when it comes to exercising options for maximum tax benefit—especially because stock options may make you susceptible to the alternative minimum tax discussed in Chapter 22, "There's No Free Lunch." Be sure to consult a tax adviser.

When It's Time to Go

The choice you must make with respect to Social Security is basically when to retire.

The choices you can make under a traditional pension arrangement are more extensive. They include when to retire, along with how to receive your benefits.

When to retire is a fairly straightforward calculation. If your company plan permits early retirement, benefits will probably be reduced. But you can find out just what those benefits will be and evaluate them in terms of your other sources of income.

Tax Treats

Retiring early may cost you much more in pension benefits than you realize. It isn't simply that benefits are reduced for early retirement. They are. But staying on, with steady increases in salary, means that your pension will be based on more years of service at a higher income. Because most traditional pensions are based on a formula consisting of final average salary and years of service, the difference can be significant.

How to receive your benefits may be a bit more complicated. Here you may find two choices: While a defined benefit plan must offer to pay an annuity for life (except where the value of the benefit is less than $5,000), some plans offer employees the option of taking the benefits in a lump sum.

If you do decide to take monthly checks—not a bad idea, if you want to be sure not to outlive your pension—you must decide whether those checks should be based on your own individual life expectancy or on the joint life expectancy of you and your spouse.

If the plan offers a lump sum payment instead of monthly checks, you may be tempted to accept. But think carefully before you say yes. At least one recent study indicates that most employees lose out when they elect a lump sum benefit over a lifetime pension. In any case, whether you'll come out ahead with a lump sum depends on your investment skills. You can beef up those skills, although there is never any guarantee of profits when you invest. But success also depends on two other factors that you can't control: the rate of inflation and stock market performance. Monthly checks, by contrast, are guaranteed to last a lifetime.

If you are married and take your pension in the form of monthly checks, those checks will be based on a "joint and survivor" arrangement—unless you both elect, in writing, to forgo this option.

The *joint and survivor* arrangement protects your spouse even before you retire because there will be automatic survivor benefits as long as you are partially or fully vested. However, your spouse will have to wait until the earliest date that you could have received retirement benefits under the plan.

With a joint and survivor pension, the worker accepts a reduced amount so that the surviving spouse can continue receiving pension benefits for life. In the typical arrangement, the worker's pension is about 90 percent of the amount it would be if it were guaranteed for a single lifetime, and the spouse continues to receive half of this amount after the worker's death. If you are willing to take a smaller pension, and if the company plan permits the arrangement, then your survivor could receive 75 percent or even 100 percent of your pension after your death.

Before you pass up the joint and survivor option in favor of a larger pension based solely on your own life expectancy, consider this: A pension based on an individual life will be larger, but it could leave your spouse with little or no income if you die prematurely. The joint and survivor rule was passed to protect spouses from just this eventuality.

On the other hand, your spouse may not need survivorship benefits if he or she is very ill and expected to predecease you or, more happily, if he or she has a good pension or enough income from other sources to provide a comfortable lifestyle.

To the Max

Insurance agents sometimes try to convince about-to-retire workers to take the larger individual pension and use the additional sum, over and above the joint and survivor pension, to buy life

Tax Talk

Joint and survivor pension benefits are paid over the lifetimes of the worker and the worker's surviving spouse. They are designed to protect surviving spouses who may have little other source of income.

insurance. They argue that the life insurance will more than make up for the missing pension when the worker dies. These arrangements are often called pension maximization, or pension max, for short.

Should you take the bait? Not unless you're young enough and healthy enough to buy life insurance at a reasonable price. If you wait until you're about to retire, even if you are in excellent health, your age will probably preclude getting a rate that is cost-effective.

Even then, there are other factors to consider. For example, pension max virtually never makes sense if your pension is indexed to inflation. It also doesn't make sense if your company plan restores full benefits if your spouse should predecease you. And forget about the life insurance option if post-retirement health insurance is tied to your pension; taking single-life benefits would leave your surviving spouse without health insurance.

Taxing Times

Pension benefits are taxable. If you don't arrange to have income tax withheld from each check, you must pay quarterly estimates. Mark your calendar to make those estimated payments before the 15th of April, June, September, and January—and don't forget to make the payments, or you will face tax penalties.

Tax Tips

Social Security and some or all of your pension income may be exempt from state income taxes in some states. Ask your tax adviser before you retire about your state tax obligations.

But there's one worry you can forget about. Retirees came out way ahead a few years ago when states were forbidden to tax retirement income earned in the state but received by someone who has moved away. Until this ruling, several states—California was a leader—chased pension recipients who had moved to other states, in an attempt to collect state income taxes.

Don't forget that Social Security benefits also may be subject to tax, if your income exceeds the specified levels described earlier in this chapter.

The Least You Need to Know

➤ Social Security benefits can begin any time from age 62 to age 70; "normal" retirement age is gradually rising from age 65 to age 67.

➤ Social Security benefits, formerly tax-free, are now partially subject to income tax for married couples with income of more than $32,000 a year, and for single taxpayers with income exceeding $25,000.

➤ Traditional employer-paid pensions provide guaranteed benefits, but how much you'll receive depends on when you retire and whether you take a lump sum, monthly checks based on your individual life expectancy, or a survivorship pension for your spouse.

➤ Pension benefits are guaranteed by the Pension Benefit Guaranty Corporation when a corporation goes out of business or terminates its pension plan.

➤ Pension benefits are taxable, although states may no longer levy income tax on benefits earned by retirees who have moved out of state.

Chapter 12

On Your Own (IRA) Account

In This Chapter

➤ Discovering the new eligibility rules that mean most people can contribute to an IRA

➤ Finding that your spouse can have an IRA even if you are covered by a retirement plan at work

➤ Learning that early withdrawals can now be made for many reasons, without tax penalties

➤ Determining whether a Roth IRA suits you better than a traditional IRA

➤ Deciding where to put your IRA money: It's trickier than it appears

Individual Retirement Accounts have been a staple of retirement planning—and tax-deferred savings—for many years. With annual contributions that are deductible (for many people) and income tax on earnings deferred until the money is withdrawn, IRAs have been attractive indeed. But the rules keep changing. Just when you think you know how to make the most of an IRA, Uncle Sam changes the game plan and you have to readjust your thinking.

About the only thing that has stayed constant since 1981 is the $2,000 ceiling on annual contributions. But Congress is tinkering here, too, and you may soon find that you can put more away each year in an IRA. Stay tuned. Meanwhile, now that IRAs come in three flavors, you must decide which IRA is best for you. You also must decide how to invest your annual IRA contributions. This chapter tells you what you need to know.

Yes, You Can

When IRAs were first introduced in 1974, contributions were limited to $1,500—and those contributions were deductible only for workers not covered by an employer-sponsored retirement plan. The big boost in IRA popularity came in 1981, when new laws decreed that every income-earning American could put away $2,000 a year and deduct that $2,000 from federal income tax. Just how popular were the new IRAs? In 1982, IRA contributions soared to $28.3 billion, up from an average of $3.2 billion a year during the period from 1975 to 1981.

Then in 1986, Congress tightened the rules, and contributions dropped by half. The new rules introduced income ceilings for workers covered by any sort of retirement plan at work. Those ceilings were so low that many people simply stopped making IRA contributions. (There is a nondeductible option—more later—but many people gave up on the whole idea.)

Tax Tips

You can make your IRA contribution for the year right up until the tax filing date for that year's return. For the 2000 tax year, the filing date is April 16, 2001 (because the 15th is a Sunday). Extending federal tax filing to August 15 or October 15 does not extend the deadline for IRA contributions. In any case, your IRA will grow much faster if you make your contribution as early each year as possible.

Now the rules have changed again. We're not quite back to the days when anyone and everyone could open a deductible IRA, but income limitations have been greatly eased. At the same time, penalties have been lifted on many early IRA withdrawals, and new forms of IRA have been introduced.

For the 1997 tax year, the last year under the old rules, you could make fully tax-deductible contributions to an IRA only if you were not covered by an employer-sponsored retirement plan or, if you were covered at work, if you earned under $25,000 as a single taxpayer or $40,000 as a married couple filing jointly. A stay-at-home spouse could not make a deductible contribution to an IRA if the income-earning spouse was covered by a retirement plan at work. The only exception was a "spousal IRA," with a total contribution for both spouses of $2,250 a year.

Under the new rules, income ceilings for deductible IRAs are rising steadily for the next few years. For the 1999 tax year (tax returns filed in 2000), contributions were fully deductible for single taxpayers earning up to $31,000, and for married couples earning up to $51,000. By 2005, single filers will be able to make fully deductible contributions at income of up to $50,000. By 2007, married couples filing jointly will be able to make fully deductible contributions at income of up to $80,000. Partially deductible contributions can be made at somewhat higher levels of adjusted gross income. The following table shows the ceiling amounts.

Here's how much you can earn and make a tax-deductible contribution of $2,000 to an IRA, even if you are covered by a retirement plan at work. Contributions are phased out at the second figure in each column.

Tax Years Beginning	Single Taxpayers	Married Taxpayers Filing Jointly
1998	$30,000–$40,000	$50,000–$60,000
1999	$31,000–41,000	$51,000–61,000
2000	$32,000–42,000	$52,000–62,000
2001	$33,000–43,000	$53,000–63,000
2002	$34,000–44,000	$54,000–64,000
2003	$40,000–50,000	$60,000–70,000
2004	$45,000–55,000	$65,000–75,000
2005	$50,000–60,000	$70,000–80,000
2006	$50,000–60,000	$75,000–85,000
2007 and thereafter	$50,000–60,000	$80,000–100,000

Source: 1997 Tax Legislation: Law, Explanation and Analysis, CCH Incorporated

As an example, a single taxpayer with adjusted gross income of $30,000 can take a full deduction for her $2,000 contribution to an IRA, regardless of whether she is covered by an employer-sponsored retirement plan at work. In 1997, when the ceiling was $25,000, the deduction would have been limited to $1,000.

Better yet, the 1997 legislation separated spouses—at least for the purpose of determining IRA eligibility. Until the Taxpayer Relief Act took effect, starting with the 1998 tax year, the most a non-earning spouse could contribute to an IRA was $250 a year. That's not much when it comes to building a retirement nest egg.

Now, in a giant leap forward, a homemaker can make a fully deductible $2,000 contribution to an IRA, regardless of whether the spouse is covered by a retirement plan at work. What's more, the income ceiling for these contributions is $150,000 per family, phasing out at $160,000.

Let's say that you and your spouse have an adjusted gross income of $125,000 for the year, and

Tax Tips

Deductions for IRA contributions can be taken even if you don't itemize deductions on your income tax return. Unlike most other deductions, they reduce your adjusted gross income, not just your taxable income. This has two nifty results: First, you'll pay less tax because your income is lower. Second, it's easier to take itemized deductions for things such as medical expenses that must exceed a percentage of adjusted gross income.

one of you is covered by a 401(k) plan at work. The covered worker cannot make a deductible IRA contribution because your income is too high. But the nonearning spouse neatly fits the category of couples earning under $150,000 and can make a deductible contribution of up to $2,000 to an IRA.

Penalty-Free Zone

Because the money is meant for retirement, traditional IRAs enjoy tax-favored status—contributions are often deductible, and taxes on earnings are always deferred until the money is withdrawn. That's why early withdrawals—originally defined as those made any time before age 59½, unless you were totally disabled—were frowned upon, with frowns reinforced by a 10 percent tax penalty. The only exceptions to the age 59½ rule were death and disability.

Tax Tips

The Internal Revenue Service offers many free publications that can help you sort out tax law as it applies to you. The publications are available online at www.irs.ustreas.gov or by calling 1-800-829-3676. See Publication 590, for example, for detailed information on IRAs.

Today it's a different story, as more and more penalty-free withdrawals have been sanctioned by law.

You've always been able to take money out of an IRA without penalty once you reach age 59½. But you can now do so at any age as long as you take a series of substantially equal periodic payments over either your own life expectancy or the joint life expectancy of you and your beneficiary. This provision gives great leeway for people who may need to tap their IRAs early.

In addition to being able to take money out if you become disabled or if you take the money in substantially equal payments, now you can also take money out of your IRA at any time, subject to income tax but not to tax penalty, under these circumstances:

➤ If the money is used for medical expenses in excess of 7.5 percent of your adjusted gross income. (You don't have to itemize deductions for this purpose.)

➤ If the money is used to pay for health insurance premiums while you are out of work.

➤ If the money is used for higher education for any member of your family.

➤ If up to $10,000 is used for the purchase of a main home by a first-time home-buyer. (That buyer can be any member of your family.)

As a result, IRAs have become far more flexible. Remember, though, that IRA money should still be saved for retirement unless you absolutely have no other source of cash to meet an emergency.

Tax Treats

Want to give your youngsters a head start toward saving for the future? Give them money matching their own earnings, so that they can contribute to an Individual Retirement Account. You can even employ the kids in your own business, as long as they perform actual work. Just be sure to keep careful records if your children work for you, showing how many hours were worked and how much was earned. (Note: While a traditional IRA works for this purpose, a Roth IRA is even better; see the next section for details.)

New Kid on the Block

The 1997 tax legislation did more than increase the income ceilings for tax-deductible contributions to traditional IRAs. It introduced the new Roth IRA, a super retirement savings vehicle for those who qualify.

Unlike the traditional IRA, contributions to a Roth are never tax-deductible. The flip side of losing a deduction today, however, is that withdrawals from a Roth are tax-free as long as the account has been in place for at least five years and you are at least age 59½. Withdrawals are also tax-free if you die, if you become disabled, or, in amounts up to $10,000, if you are purchasing a first home. Better yet, your own contributions may be withdrawn at any time with no tax obligation.

Tax Traps

Traditional IRAs are protected in many states against the claims of creditors. The same may not be true of Roth IRAs. Before you open a Roth or convert an existing IRA to a Roth, check on your state's laws concerning asset protection.

Tax-free withdrawals are a real boon to retirement savers—especially savers with incomes too high to qualify for a traditional deductible IRA. In order to make contributions of $2,000 a year to a Roth IRA, you must have adjusted gross income of less than $95,000 for a single taxpayer, or $150,000 for married taxpayers filing jointly. Contributions of smaller amounts may be made at up to $110,000 for singles and $160,000 for married couples.

Tax Treats

Distributions of earnings from a Roth IRA after the five-year holding period but before reaching age 59½ are generally subject to both tax and the 10 percent tax penalty. There is no penalty, although income tax will be due, if payments are spread over your life expectancy or if the money is withdrawn to pay for medical expenses exceeding 7.5 percent of adjusted gross income, medical insurance premiums paid while you are unemployed, and higher education. Making a Roth taxable by using it for these purposes undercuts the tax-free advantage of the Roth.

You should know two other significant facts about the Roth IRA. First, unlike the traditional IRA, you can continue to make contributions to a Roth IRA after you reach age 70½ as long as you still have earned income. Second, you don't have to take the money out at any specific age; you can leave it to accumulate for your family. (Chapter 14, "Hold On to Your Gains," has more details on taking money out of retirement plans.)

The Roth also offers an additional advantage to higher-income taxpayers who expect to be making IRA withdrawals while receiving Social Security retirement benefits. Tax-free withdrawals from a Roth, unlike taxable withdrawals from a traditional IRA, won't count as income in determining whether Social Security benefits are taxable.

To Roth or Not to Roth

But a Roth IRA isn't the right choice for everyone. Assuming that you're eligible for both a Roth IRA and a traditional deductible IRA, how do you decide?

The determining factor may be your tax bracket now compared to your tax bracket in retirement. This may be hard to tell, especially if you're a long way from retirement. You may expect to enjoy a life of leisure and later decide to keep working, thereby upping your tax bracket. Or Congress may raise or lower taxes before you retire. Crystal balls are notoriously unreliable. However, if you expect to pay federal income tax at a lower rate in retirement than you do now, a current deduction for a contribution to a traditional IRA may provide more of a tax break.

Note, too, that a deduction reduces the out-of-pocket cost of making your annual IRA contribution. For taxpayers in the 28 percent federal income tax bracket, a deductible

$2,000 contribution actually costs $1,440. If your state has an income tax, and if it allows you to take a deduction for the IRA contribution, you'll save still more. An 8 percent state income tax, as an example, saves $160 on a $2,000 IRA contribution.

On the other hand, for workers with many years before retirement rolls around, tax-free accumulations within a Roth can build to a tidy sum. In fact, many advisers believe that, for new contributions to an IRA, there's no question at all: You'll come out ahead with a Roth rather than a traditional IRA, as long as you meet the eligibility requirements.

Switching Gears

If your adjusted gross income does not exceed $100,000 for the year (married or single), you can jump-start a Roth IRA and permanently shelter further growth from taxes by converting a traditional IRA to a Roth. This may be a good move for people with many years left in which to make additional contributions.

Conversion is an even better move if you won't need the IRA money in retirement and would like to leave it to your family. Because you're not required to take money out of a Roth at any particular time, as you are with a traditional IRA, you can leave it in place and let it continue to grow. In fact, Roth IRAs are being treated as a sophisticated estate-planning strategy by taxpayers with a high net worth and their advisers.

If you're uncertain about whether to convert an existing IRA to a Roth IRA, consider your current tax bracket, your anticipated tax bracket in retirement, and the rate of return you expect to receive on your IRA. You can simplify your decision by plugging into one of the online Web sites that can perform the calculations for you. One good choice is the site run by the mutual fund company T. Rowe Price, at www.troweprice.com.

You can convert a traditional IRA to a Roth IRA by simply notifying the institution holding your IRA that you want to do so. There's no need to establish a new account, although it's a good idea to follow up and make sure that the appropriate paperwork has been completed. You can also convert part of an existing IRA into a Roth IRA, although doing so means that you will need a new Roth IRA account.

When you convert to a Roth IRA, you are actually taking the money out of your traditional IRA. That means you must pay income tax on the full amount. You'll come out way ahead if you can pay those taxes out of a source other than the IRA itself. In fact, paying the tax from the IRA may result in an early withdrawal penalty—because the money isn't being put directly into another IRA—if you are under age 59½. Whatever your age, however, there is no tax penalty on money converted from a traditional IRA to a Roth IRA. And, once the taxes are paid, additional accumulations are completely tax-free.

Tax Tips

A one-year tax break was built into the Roth law. Taxpayers who converted to a Roth IRA during 1998 could spread the tax bill over four years. To create your own tax break, though, just convert a portion of your traditional IRA each year for a few years. That way, you'll owe income tax for each year only on the amount actually withdrawn.

Tax Talk

Recharacterization is Internal Revenue Service jargon for changing the status of an IRA. It applies in two situations: Reversing an annual contribution, in either direction, between a Roth IRA and a traditional IRA; and undoing a conversion from a traditional IRA to a Roth IRA.

If you convert a traditional IRA to a Roth IRA and then change your mind, you're not stuck with the decision. The law allows you to "recharacterize" your IRA to change its designation from Roth back to traditional.

You might want to undo a Roth conversion if you thought you were coming in under the $100,000 income ceiling and then exceeded the limit. If you don't undo the conversion under these circumstances, you could be in big tax trouble. First, depending on your age, you could be hit with tax penalties because the money you took out of the IRA becomes an early withdrawal instead of a conversion. Second, because you closed the traditional IRA to make the conversion and the Roth IRA is invalid, you're left without any IRA at all.

Alternatively, you might want to make a switch if you converted a traditional IRA and then, because your IRA was invested in stocks and the stock market lost a chunk of its value, your IRA lost value, too. Let's say that your IRA was worth $100,000 at the time of conversion. You owe income tax on that $100,000, even if the IRA is worth only $70,000 by the end of the year because stock prices dropped. If you undo the conversion—*recharacterize* your IRA, in IRS jargon—you can avoid the tax on the money you don't actually have.

It's helpful if you decide to correct a mistake before the end of the tax year. But it is possible to do so into the next year, up until the date that you file your federal income tax return for the preceding year. That's typically April 15, but extensions may give you until August 15 or even October 15. Talk to your tax adviser if you wish to undo a Roth conversion after April 15 to be sure that you can still do so.

Another Option

If you aren't eligible for either a traditional IRA or a Roth IRA, are you completely out of luck? No. You can still use a nondeductible IRA to build a retirement nest egg. You can contribute up to $2,000 a year. (Note that no matter how many IRAs you may have and which type you adopt, total annual contributions cannot exceed $2,000.)

Although the contribution won't be tax-deductible, your own after-tax contributions will be tax-free when withdrawn. All the earnings in the IRA are sheltered from taxes until withdrawn. Even though income tax will then be due on the earnings, deferring the tax bill has great advantages. For a taxpayer in the 28 percent tax bracket earning 7 percent on the IRA, the tax-deferred yield is equivalent to a taxable yield of 9.7 percent.

But should you use a nondeductible IRA? Maybe not—or at least you should give serious thought to the wisdom of doing so.

That's because tax deferral may be outweighed by other factors. For one thing, you'll still face IRA restrictions, including tax penalties for early withdrawal. So don't consider a nondeductible IRA if you know you'll need the money in the near future.

Another potential pitfall is changing tax rates. If tax rates are higher when you retire, you lose any advantage in deferring the tax. Although Congress talks about cutting taxes, current tax rates are actually lower than at many periods in our history. There's no reason to be confident that they will not be higher in the future.

But perhaps the strongest argument against the nondeductible IRA, for many taxpayers, is the paperwork headaches they generate. For every year that you have a nondeductible IRA, you must fill out IRS Form 8606 to keep track of contributions. You must file the form each year, even if you do not have to file a tax return for the year, and you must keep all the forms over the years to determine how withdrawals will be taxed when you eventually start to take money out of your IRA. Any nondeductible contributions will not be taxed upon withdrawal, but deductible contributions plus all the earnings in your IRAs are subject to income tax.

It gets worse. You might think that you could drain one IRA and then another, just to keep the bookkeeping simple. But the Internal Revenue Service insists that you take proportionate amounts from deductible and nondeductible IRAs with each withdrawal. So, as an example, if you have $100,000 in all your IRA accounts combined, made up of $25,000 in nondeductible IRA contributions and the rest in a combination of earnings on those contributions plus a deductible IRA, you'll owe taxes on 75 percent of the first withdrawal. As the amount of money in the IRA changes each year, so will the proportion of the money that is taxed.

Mess up the paperwork—or don't keep the documentation you need for what could be 20 or 30 years—and the IRS will assume that your entire withdrawal is taxable.

If you can achieve a comparable yield in other investments, you may be better off without an IRA if the only one you can have is nondeductible. Tax-free municipal bonds, bond funds, or an annuity might be a better choice. On the other hand, a lot depends on your time horizon. Can you sustain yields over time? The following table indicates how much better an IRA looks over time. The following are the assumptions:

➤ All investments earn 8 percent (before taxes).

➤ All investors are taxed at the 28 percent federal rate.

➤ The IRA funds are withdrawn in a lump sum and taxed at 28 percent.

Taxable Investments vs. Nondeductible and Deductible IRAs

Years	Taxable Investment	Nondeductible IRA	Deductible IRA
5	$11,867	$11,924	$12,446
10	$27,568	$28,130	$30,248
20	$75,831	$82,369	$92,402
30	$160,326	$192,978	$221,069
40	$308,252	$425,285	$489,195

Source: "New IRA Opportunities," CCH Incorporated, 1998

Stashing the Cash

One thing to remember: An Individual Retirement Account is not an investment. It is a tax-sheltered container for investments. Within your IRA, you can invest your annual contributions in a variety of ways. The following table shows the choices investors made in 1998. Coins don't show up on the table because they're a recent addition to the IRA menu.

Among your choices are these:

➤ Money market deposit accounts or certificates of deposit at banks

➤ Money market mutual funds

➤ Individual stocks or bonds

➤ Stock or bond mutual funds

➤ Annuities

➤ Gold, silver, and platinum coins issued by federal and state governments

The following table describes where people invested their IRA money in 1998. The percentages add to more than 100 percent because many people have more than one IRA and because IRAs can be invested in more than one type of investment vehicle.

	Traditional IRAs	Roth IRAs
Bank money market deposit accounts or CDs	30%	11%
Individual stocks	32%	26%
Individual bonds	14%	5%
Variable annuities	14%	12%
Fixed annuities	11%	3%
Mutual funds	64%	71%
Stock funds	54%	59%
Bond funds	19%	18%
Hybrid funds	19%	27%
Money market	19%	22%
Other	2%	4%

Reprinted by permission of the Investment Company Institute (www.ici.org)

The key to making IRA investment decisions is the same as making any investment decisions: Evaluate your entire portfolio, both tax-sheltered and taxable, in light of your investment objectives, your time horizon, and your tolerance for risk. Then adopt an asset allocation strategy, a mix of investments that will balance risk with potential reward.

But the first step, as you open an IRA, is choosing the institution to hold your account. IRA custodians include banks, brokerage firms, mutual funds, financial planners, and insurance companies. To some extent, the custodian you select will dictate the investments that are available.

The following table shows where traditional and Roth IRAs were opened in 1998, as a percentage of households owning each type of IRA. The percentages add to more than 100 percent because many people have more than one IRA.

	Traditional IRAs	Roth IRAs
Full-service brokerage	33%	27%
Discount brokerage	6%	13%
Insurance company	15%	17%
Independent financial planning firm	18%	22%
Bank or savings institution	44%	21%
Mutual fund company	22%	21%
Other	3%	0%

Reprinted with permission of the Investment Company Institute (www.ici.org)

Growth or Income

You may want to think about whether to concentrate the investments within your IRA on growth or on income.

Tax Tips

Account management fees on IRAs tend to be low; most mutual funds, as an example, charge under $50 a year. But the fees are deductible if you pay them by separate check and if you itemize deductions on your federal income tax return. They are not deductible if they are taken directly from the account.

Opinions differ as to which strategy is best. Because money in an IRA is sheltered from income tax, you don't pay income tax on interest and dividends, and you don't owe capital gains tax on profitable transactions—until you take the money out. Then it is subject to income tax, and because there is no favorable capital gains tax rate for profits earned within an IRA, all of it is taxed at higher regular income tax rates.

Because you lose the benefit of lower capital gains tax rates on transactions within an IRA, some advisers suggest investing for growth in taxable accounts instead. On the other hand, investing in stocks inside your IRA means that you can buy and sell as appropriate to your investment strategy without worrying about paying the capital gains tax on each transaction.

Which to do? Consider your investment temperament and overall investment strategy. If you tend to buy and hold for the long term, as an example, you could take advantage of lower long-term capital gains tax rates by holding growth investments outside your IRA.

But if you are an active investor, making frequent trades without holding stocks or funds long enough to qualify for lower long-term rates (more than one year), you might as well invest for growth within the IRA.

Avoid IRA Mistakes

As you decide where to put your IRA money, avoid these mistakes:

➤ Opening too many accounts. You'll complicate your record-keeping, and you'll probably have annual account management fees on each one.

➤ Putting tax-exempt investments such as annuities or municipal bonds in an IRA. Your IRA is already sheltered from taxes, and you can't shelter the same money twice. Why carry an umbrella when you're wearing a rain slicker?

➤ Being too conservative in your investments—or lazy about where you invest. Sure, it's easy to simply take out a certificate of deposit each time you make an IRA contribution. But achieving a higher return on your investment can make a big difference in the amount of money you have at retirement. With $12,000 in an IRA earning 7 percent, as an example, you'll have $46,436 in 20 years. If you earn 9 percent on that same $12,000, you'll wind up with $67,253.

➤ Ignoring an institution's IRA rules. Tax law may say that you can withdraw IRA money after age 59½ without penalty, for example, but a bank may still levy its own penalty for taking money out of a certificate of deposit before it matures.

➤ Choosing investments that are tough to convert to cash, especially if you're nearing the age when you must start making withdrawals from your IRA. In the 1980s, many investors were sold limited partnerships for their IRAs; limited partnerships (see Chapter 21, "Blue Plate Specials") are hard to value and can be harder to sell.

Individual Retirement Accounts are a boon to retirement savers, especially those who are not covered under retirement plans at work. IRAs are easy to open—you can do so through just about any bank, stockbroker, or mutual fund. But managing an IRA wisely is a bit more complicated.

The Least You Need to Know

➤ Income ceilings for tax-deductible IRAs are rising steadily.

➤ Tax penalties have been eliminated on many early IRA withdrawals.

➤ The Roth IRA, with tax-free withdrawals, is an excellent retirement and estate-planning tool for eligible taxpayers.

➤ Many different investment vehicles can be used to fund an IRA.

Chapter 13

You're on Your Own

In This Chapter

➤ Providing your own retirement benefits if you're self-employed

➤ Choosing between defined contribution and defined benefit types of plans

➤ Providing benefits for employees

➤ Being careful about financial responsibility for employee investment decisions

---

Self-employment has many rewards, but fringe benefits are not among them. If you work for yourself—and only for yourself—you're on your own when it comes to providing retirement income.

Fortunately, you have a number of tax-sheltered retirement plans at your disposal. They come with different rules and regulations, but they all offer the opportunity for both current tax relief through deductible contributions and ongoing tax relief through deferral of tax on earnings.

This chapter walks you through your choices, whether you are a one-person enterprise or a small business with a number of employees.

Be Your Own Sugar Daddy

If you're self-employed, whether on your own or with employees, chances are that you're plowing every penny back into the business. But you need to plan for eventual retirement as well. First, it will be here before you know it. Second, contributing money to a *qualified* retirement plan is one of the best ways to shelter dollars from taxation. And—a factor not to be ignored—growing businesses find that tax-sheltered retirement plans are one of the best ways to attract and motivate employees.

Several tax-sheltered plans are available to the self-employed. Which one you should choose depends on the following factors:

➤ **How much you earn**—Some plans let you shelter larger chunks of income from tax and may be more appropriate for the entrepreneur with an established full-time business.

➤ **Whether you have employees or expect to go it alone indefinitely**—With some plans, you must provide retirement benefits for employees if you provide them for yourself.

➤ **Whether you prefer a defined contribution or a defined benefit plan**—Most retirement plans for the self-employed are defined contribution plans, where you can put aside a specific proportion of income each year. But high-earning self-employed individuals may prefer a defined benefit plan, where larger contributions may be made to fund a preset retirement benefit.

In general, most of the plans follow the same rules as those governing Individual Retirement Accounts.

In order to be deductible, contributions must be based on earned income, not investment income, and must meet contribution ceilings for the particular plan. Taxes on earnings are deferred until the money is withdrawn. Money may be withdrawn without penalty at age 59½ and must be withdrawn starting at age 70½. But there are variations, and one plan may suit your needs better than another.

The three plans to consider when you have no employees are the Keogh Plans, the SIMPLE, and the SEP.

The Old Standby

Keogh Plans have long been the gold standard in retirement plans for the self-employed. Named for U.S. Representative Eugene Keogh, who devised the plans

> **Tax Talk**
>
> **Qualified** retirement plans meet criteria set by the Internal Revenue Service and are therefore sheltered from tax.

> **Tax Tips**
>
> You don't have to be self-employed full-time to shelter income from tax in a retirement plan. If you earn any money as an independent—whether by tutoring in the evening hours or sitting on a corporate board of directors—you can open a retirement plan and make annual contributions based on your self-employment income. This is true even if you are also covered by an employer-sponsored retirement plan at work.

and shepherded the legislation through Congress, they are also called HR-10 plans.

Most Keoghs are defined contribution plans—profit sharing, money purchase, or a combination of the two.

With a profit-sharing Keogh, you can contribute up to 15 percent (actually 13.04 percent) of your net income each year, to a maximum of $30,000. (Although the law says $30,000, the actual cap is currently $25,500 because the total annual compensation on which deductible retirement contributions can be based is now $170,000. Fifteen percent of $170,000 is $25,500.)

If your income is erratic, the neat thing with a profit-sharing Keogh is that the contributions are based on profits and are therefore optional. You don't have to contribute in any year (even if you do make money) if you choose not to do so.

Money purchase Keogh Plans are for people who know they can put money away year after year. You must select a percentage of net self-employment income, up to 25 percent (actually 20 percent; see the accompanying "Tax Traps" sidebar) and then be consistent about making the contributions each year, up to the maximum annual ceiling of $30,000. If you fail to make an annual contribution, the IRS can impose an excise tax.

With a combination or paired plan, using both money purchase and profit sharing, you can hedge your bets for maximum contributions (up to a total of 20 percent) and maximum flexibility. Using a paired plan, you might commit 13 percent of net income to a profit-sharing plan with the balance as a fixed contribution to a money purchase plan.

It's easy to open a defined contribution Keogh because most banks, brokerage firms, and mutual funds have standard prototype plans and documents. In choosing a custodian for your retirement plan, find out what investments are available (although most financial institutions now offer a complete range of investments) and inquire about fees that may be levied on your account.

Tax Traps

Keogh contribution levels must be taken with a grain of salt because "net income," for this purpose, is defined as income after expenses, half your self-employment (Social Security) tax, and the contribution itself are subtracted from your total income. So, where a 25 percent contribution is permitted, the actual contribution is about 20 percent. Where a 15 percent contribution is specified, the actual amount is just over 13 percent. Be careful; contributing too much will lead to tax penalties.

Tax Tips

The annual fee you pay to maintain your Keogh account is tax-deductible—but only if you pay for it with a separate check rather than letting it be deducted from the account.

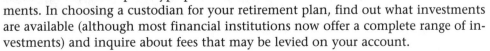

Tax Tips

Zero-coupon corporate bonds can work well in a tax-sheltered retirement account. Zeroes do not pay periodic interest (they return their entire yield at maturity), but they are taxed on phantom income along the way. Within a qualified retirement plan, however, there is no tax to pay.

With a Keogh Plan (of any kind), you can continue to make annual contributions as long as you have earned income. You have to start making withdrawals at age 70½, as with other qualified plans, but you do not have to stop making contributions. (With an Individual Retirement Account, by contrast, contributions come to an end at age 70½, even if you are still employed.)

But there is one big potential nuisance with a Keogh: Once assets in the plan reach $100,000, annual federal tax returns must be filed. No tax is actually paid, but Form 5500 must be filed. Alternative plans such as the SEP-IRA and the SIMPLE-IRA do not require tax filings; see the description of these plans later in this chapter, under "New and Improved."

It's also important to plan ahead because a Keogh must be opened before the end of the calendar year, although contributions can then be made up to your tax filing date in the following years.

High-End Perk

For older self-employed professionals and entrepreneurs earning big bucks, the defined benefit Keogh Plan permits socking away the most money of all in the shortest period of time. You establish a target benefit at the outset (up to a ceiling of approximately $135,000 a year, adjusted periodically for inflation) and then make contributions to provide that benefit at your designated retirement age. There is no dollar ceiling on the contributions as there is in other retirement plans, so if you have adequate income from other sources, you may be able to put away most of your self-employment income.

You'll need an accountant and an actuary at the outset, when you establish the defined benefit Keogh. Then you'll need actuarial help on an ongoing basis to determine the level of annual contributions, to file the necessary tax returns, and to make sure that your plan is in compliance with changing IRS regulations. Expect to spend as much as several thousand dollars a year for professional advice, although the fees are deductible as a business expense. The payoff is much larger tax deductions. Don't take shortcuts, or your plan may be disqualified.

Defined benefit Keogh Plans make the most sense for people over age 50. But don't wait until you're within 10 years of retirement to get started because Congress has set limits on contributions for the first 10 years. Only 10 percent of the target benefit can be funded in the first year, or a maximum of $13,500.

The intent was to discourage people from setting up a plan, funding it immediately, taking a major tax deduction, and then closing the plan. But the result has been less attractive retirement plans and a lessening of interest in defined benefit plans among pension consultants.

Calling It Quits

But what if you already have a defined benefit plan? If so, you've reaped sizable benefits over the years. When it's time to retire, however, you may face unanticipated complications.

With most retirement plans for the self-employed, there's little paperwork and no problem when it's time to say goodbye to work and embrace retirement. Simply notify the plan custodian and begin taking withdrawals, being sure to take at least the minimum required amount based on your life expectancy once you are over age 70½.

Defined benefit Keogh Plans are a little different. Because defined benefit plans are the same as corporate pension plans in the eyes of the IRS, a single misstep can bring harsh taxes and penalties.

Corporate pension plans don't run into the same problems because they don't close down when participants retire. They keep rolling on. Your one-person plan can't continue; it retires when you do.

To close down your defined benefit Keogh Plan, you must adopt a resolution to terminate the plan. If you have employees, you must also file a termination notice with the Pension Benefit Guaranty Corporation and notify the employees that the plan is being terminated.

Then file Form 5310 with the IRS, to find out if your plan is in compliance with regulations. You aren't required to file this form if you don't have employees but, if you don't secure the ruling, the IRS could come back later and disqualify the plan. If it does, you'll owe back taxes and probably penalties as well.

You'll also need to file a final tax return showing the balance in the plan as zero. You can accomplish this and continue to defer taxes on earnings by rolling the balance in your Keogh Plan into a rollover IRA.

Tax Traps

If you have too much money in your defined benefit Keogh, taxes can wipe out close to 90 percent of the extra amount. How much is too much? Enough to generate yearly retirement benefits larger than the IRS allows. At this writing, that's about $135,000, which would take accumulated assets of about $1.7 million for someone age 65. It sounds like a lot, but market run-ups in the recent bull market left many self-employed professionals with overfunded plans. While you're still working, adjust contributions to keep assets in line.

Tax Traps

Are you a self-employed individual with a defined benefit Keogh plan? Be careful when it's time to retire and terminate your plan. Defined benefit Keoghs are now subject to many of the same rules as corporate pension plans—so, if you're married and want to roll your plan into an IRA, be sure to have your spouse sign a written consent. If not, you'll wind up with a taxable distribution.

Tax Tips

What happens to your retirement plan if self-employment isn't all it's cracked up to be, and you go back to work? In most instances, you can simply freeze your plan, making no further contributions, and leave it in place until you are at least age 59½ and can withdraw the money without a tax penalty.

New and Improved

For a long time, Keogh Plans were the only game in town. Now, however, they are just one of several options. For many people, they may be the least attractive option.

The big drawback is the paperwork. Keogh Plans are more complicated to administer than newly available retirement options. In addition, if you have employees—or expect to add staff as your business grows—you'll have to fund their retirement benefits along with your own under a Keogh arrangement.

The two contenders for most popular retirement plan today are both based on the Individual Retirement Account. They are the SEP-IRA and the SIMPLE-IRA.

SEP-IRAs

A SEP plan is very much like a standard IRA except that, instead of the maximum $2,000-a-year contribution, you may contribute up to 13.04 percent of net self-employment income or a maximum of $30,000. As with the profit-sharing Keogh Plan, although the law says $30,000, the actual cap is currently $25,500. That's because the total annual compensation on which deductible retirement contributions can be based is now $170,000. Fifteen percent of $170,000 is $25,500.

"Net self-employment income," again, is defined as self-employment income minus 50 percent of your self-employment tax and the SEP contribution.

An SEP is easy to establish, with standard prototype plans available at most financial institutions. With a SEP, no annual tax filings are required and contributions can vary from year to year. In addition, a SEP is the only retirement plan that can be initially established right up until the date you file your federal income tax return for the preceding year.

SIMPLE Plans

SIMPLE plans—the acronym stands for Savings Incentive Match Plan for Employees—can be based on an IRA or a 401(k) model. Either way, the maximum annual contribution is $6,000, although you can contribute an "employer match" for yourself of 3 percent of your income, up to another $6,000, for a total of $12,000.

The good thing about SIMPLE plans is that the $170,000 ceiling on income doesn't apply. The not-so-good thing is that it takes $200,000 of income to be able to contribute the additional $6,000. If you earn $50,000 in self-employment income, your employer match, at 3 percent, comes to just $1,500.

A SIMPLE plan is easy to set up and run, and it may be the best bet if you have relatively little self-employment income from a part-time enterprise. Contributions aren't mandatory, so you can always skip a year if money is tight.

Contributions to a SIMPLE plan are limited by the amount of your income, not by a percentage of income as with a Keogh or a SEP. This provision may permit you to contribute more to a SIMPLE under some circumstances, although it still takes net self-employment income of $200,000 to produce a $6,000 matching contribution.

Helping the Help

When your business grows and you have employees, the retirement plan decision becomes a bit more complicated. The plan that suits you as a one-person shop may not be appropriate once employees are involved.

Tax Tips

For more information, see the IRS's free Publication 560, "Retirement Plans for Small Business." It is available by calling 1-800-829-3676 or online at www.irs.ustreas.gov/prod/forms.

Tax Tips

Contributing money to your self-employment retirement plan is just the first step. Investing the money so that it will grow is an essential second step. You may invest in almost anything (except precious metals, art, or your own business), but you should probably stick to mutual funds or, via a self-directed account, publicly traded securities.

Your first choice is between a defined contribution plan and a defined benefit plan. With defined contribution plans, employees make contributions, and separate accounts are maintained for each employee. With defined benefit plans, employer funding is generally the rule; money may be pooled and investments integrated until each employee retires.

Tax Traps

Steer clear of tax-free municipal bonds in retirement accounts. Income tax is deferred on earnings in a retirement plan, but withdrawals are taxed. So, by placing tax-free bonds inside the tax shelter of a retirement account, you will be converting tax-free income into taxable income. Not a wise move.

If you choose a defined contribution plan, you must also make a choice between a money purchase plan and a profit-sharing plan. But whatever plan you choose, it must be nondiscriminatory—that is, you cannot contribute a higher percentage of income for yourself (or other executives) than you do for all employees.

If you have a Keogh Plan, as an example, you must include in your plan any employees who are age 21 or older, who work for you full-time (at least 1,000 hours per year), and who have been with you for at least one year (two years, if you offer immediate vesting). Because Keoghs are qualified pension plans, you also will make the contributions on behalf of your employees.

When employees are covered, a Keogh Plan is just like any other pension plan and must meet guidelines established in federal law.

With a SEP-IRA, you avoid some of the administrative headaches (including tax filing) of a Keogh. But you must make contributions for every employee who has reached age 21 and who has worked for you in three of the five preceding years, even if that work is part-time. The contributions you make for your employees may be no more than 15 percent of pay or $25,500, whichever is less. The contributions you make are tax-deductible.

One drawback is that vesting is automatically immediate; you might open an account for an employee and find that employee in line behind you, waiting to withdraw the money.

Your contributions to a SEP on behalf of employees are discretionary but must be made in proportion to compensation, with each employee receiving the same percent of pay. The nice thing about a SEP is its administrative simplicity; contributions are deposited directly into IRAs for the employees, and the employees make their own investment decisions. You have no responsibility for those decisions.

SIMPLE plans are designed for businesses with up to 100 workers, where there is no other retirement plan. The maximum annual pretax contribution that each employee can make is $6,000. In addition, you must make a dollar-for-dollar matching contribution in one of two ways: Either a maximum of 3 percent of pay for each employee who chooses to participate in the plan, or a flat 2 percent of pay for every employee, whether or not the employee participates.

In fact, "whether or not the employee participates" is a key phrase. According to the tax research firm of CCH Incorporated, the SIMPLE has a unique feature. Unlike any other retirement plan, you must offer your SIMPLE plan to all eligible employees, but you can still set up the plan even if none of the employees chooses to participate.

The legislation authorizing SIMPLE plans permitted them to be either SIMPLE IRAs or SIMPLE 401(k)s. In fact, the 401(k) format proved to be fairly cumbersome and few, if any, sponsors are making it available.

SIMPLE IRA plans eliminate some of the hassles associated with other retirement plans but have some wrinkles of their own. You may choose the financial institution to receive contributions, but employees then have a right to transfer to a SIMPLE IRA at another institution without cost or penalty. Or, you may let employees choose the financial institution at the outset, but they must then relinquish the right to make a cost-free transfer.

All contributions are immediately vested in the employees, but there is a two-year waiting period before contributions can be transferred to another IRA (other than a SIMPLE IRA) without tax penalties. In this instance, the tax penalty for premature distribution is 25 percent instead of the usual 10 percent.

Tax Tips

Are you technologically savvy? You can save money on administrative costs in connection with a 401(k) plan by choosing an online option. One candidate is Fidelity Investment's e401(k), designed for small businesses and based on administration through the Internet. The e401(k) was introduced in late 1999, with anticipated costs 25 percent less than standard 401(k) plans for small business.

Introducing a 401(k)

Although the salary reduction plans known as 401(k) plans are most common among large corporations, they may also work for small companies. The trick is finding a vendor willing to write a plan for a handful of employees. There are a few out there—including the Principal Financial Group, T. Rowe Price, ADP, and Paychex—but you'll have to weigh the administrative costs and paperwork against the benefits for the number of employees you have.

If you expect your business to continue growing, however, it may make abundant sense to introduce a 401(k) plan early on. The very presence of these defined contribution plans is a powerful attraction for employees.

When you offer a 401(k) plan, employees may contribute pretax dollars up to a maximum amount that changes from time to time. At this writing, it is $10,500. You may choose to match employee contributions, but you are not required to do so.

You're on the Hook

If you offer a 401(k) plan to your employees, you must decide whether you will make the investment decisions or pass the buck.

If you make the investment decisions, you will be responsible for how they turn out—and you may let yourself in for a lawsuit from a disgruntled employee who thinks you should have done better.

If you want employees to make their own decisions, you must offer at least three different investment options. "Different" means having significantly different characteristics of risk and reward. For most employers, this means offering at least one each of a stable value fund (money market funds or similar cash equivalents), a stock fund, and a bond fund. It also means allowing employees to make changes in their investment mix at least as often as quarterly.

The easiest approach for small employers is to find a vendor offering an all-in-one package of investment options plus plan administration. Look for a vendor with many fund choices, but insist on flexibility in your agreement so that you can seek out other funds if performance falls short in a given category.

In selecting a retirement plan for yourself—and, even more important, in selecting a plan for employees—be sure to get professional advice. The following table provides a brief overview of your retirement options. Your accountant or other financial adviser can help you select the most appropriate plan, and then help you monitor performance on an ongoing basis.

Retirement Options for the Self-Employed

	Funding
KEOUGH	
Profit sharing	Employer, discretionary
Money purchase	Employer, mandatory
Defined benefit	Employer
SEP-IRA	Employer, discretionary
SIMPLE-IRA	Employer and/or employee Must be no other plan
401(k)	Employee and/or employer

	Annual Contributions	Coverage Requirements
KEOUGH		
Profit sharing	15% of net income to maximum $25,500	Must be offered to all full-time employees 21 or older, employed at least one year

	Annual Contributions	Coverage Requirements
KEOUGH		
Money purchase	25% of net income to maximum $30,000	Same as above
Defined benefit	To fund target benefit	Same as above
SEP-IRA	Up to 15% of pay; maximum $25,500	All employees 21 or older employed (even part-time) three of last five years
SIMPLE-IRA	Employee: Up to $6,000. Employer: Match employee contribution to 3% of salary, or 2% of every employee's compensation	All employees who earned at least $5,000 in previous two years
401(k)	Employee: Up to $10,500; Employer: May match a portion	Same as Keogh

One of the big drawbacks to self-employment is the lack of benefits that employees often take for granted. As an independent, you must provide your own benefits. One of the retirement plans outlined in this chapter should meet your needs.

The Least You Need to Know

➤ Don't overlook planning for retirement in your focus on building your business.

➤ You can fund a retirement plan with part-time or moonlighting self-employment income even if you are also covered by a retirement plan at work.

➤ If you are a one-person business, with no employees, you can choose from a menu including Keogh Plans, SEP-IRAs, and SIMPLE-IRAs.

➤ If you have employees, you can use an SEP plan, a SIMPLE plan, or a 401(k).

Chapter 14

Hold On to Your Gains

In This Chapter

➤ Knowing the critical retirement dates of ages 55, 59½, and 70½

➤ Choosing your beneficiary, which dictates tax savings on retirement money

➤ Preserving retirement savings with rollovers

➤ Leaving an individual retirement account to charity for tax benefits

There are clear tax benefits to putting money away for retirement. There can be even more tax advantages to taking the money out—if you plan carefully and if you follow the rules.

Whether you will have access to accumulated 401(k) funds, tap a Keogh, or make withdrawals from an individual retirement account, good planning can minimize taxes and preserve your assets.

This chapter walks you through what may be some of the most complicated tax rules in the Internal Revenue Service code, the rules governing distributions from retirement plans. We'll look first at what to do as you manage your own tax-sheltered retirement funds, and then address the issue of preserving an IRA that you may inherit.

You're the Boss

It's easy to feel ringed around with restrictions when it comes to taking money out of your retirement plan. But you do have a lot to say about when and how you withdraw the money.

Some of the decisions you will face include these:

➤ When to take the money, retired or not

➤ How to determine payouts from an IRA or a Keogh Plan

➤ Whether to roll a lump sum distribution into an IRA and keep the tax deferral working

➤ Who to name as your beneficiary

Don't throw up your hands and walk away. These decisions are critically important. They will determine how much you will eventually get out of your retirement plan—and how much your family will have after you are gone.

Moreover, the absence of a decision is a decision all by itself. In other words, if you can't make up your mind among the various options, you'll be letting your retirement plan decide. And its choices could wind up being the worst possible decisions for your family.

Birthday Rules

How did age 65 become the magic age for retirement? Believe it or not, it all dates back to Chancellor Otto von Bismarck and the first retirement plan introduced in Germany in the nineteenth century. Because the average person then died well before age 65, Bismarck figured that he could look good by introducing a retirement plan—and save lots of money by making the retirement age 65.

When Social Security was introduced in the United States in the 1930s, it picked up the notion of age 65 as the "normal" age for retirement. From our government's point of view, it probably also made sense to adopt a retirement age that most people wouldn't reach.

Today, however, most people do reach age 65. As the following table shows, life expectancy increased dramatically during the twentieth century, although it wasn't until 1950 that the average baby boy could expect to reach age 65.

Average Life Expectancy at Birth in the United States

Year	Male	Female	Average
1900	46.3	48.3	47.3
1920	53.6	54.6	54.1

Year	Male	Female	Average
1930	58.1	61.6	59.7
1940	60.8	65.2	62.9
1950	65.6	71.1	68.2
1960	66.6	73.1	69.7
1970	67.1	74.7	70.8
1980	70.0	77.4	73,7
1990	71.8	78.8	75.4
1995	72.5	78.9	75.8

Now that life expectancy is considerably longer, the Social Security system is confronting a possible shortfall of funds. So, the "normal" retirement age for Social Security, the age at which full benefits can be received, is gradually moving upward for those born after 1937. For people born in 1960 and later, full benefits will be payable at age 67.

Meanwhile, most corporate retirement plans picked up on the same date and made 65 the age to "pass Go and collect the $200."

You can start collecting Social Security benefits as early as age 62, although, if you do, your benefits will be permanently reduced to 80 percent of the amount you would have received at your normal retirement age. You can also choose to wait as late as age 70 and collect a larger benefit.

But the actual average age of retirement in the United States is 62. What does this trend toward early retirement mean in terms of collecting retirement benefits besides Social Security? Many corporate retirement plans allow early retirement, although this is strictly up to the employer.

When to Retire

Before you decide when to start fulfilling your retirement dreams, take a good hard look at your sources of retirement income. Some money won't be available at all until you hit certain key birthdays. Other money may be available, but only at the cost of a tax penalty.

Here are some key birthdays to note:

➤ At 55, you may become eligible for a traditional corporate pension plan, although benefits are likely to be reduced for early retirement. At 55, if you leave your job, you can take money from a 401(k) plan without a tax penalty for early withdrawal.

➤ At 59½, you may tap retirement funds without incurring a 10 percent tax penalty—and without having to meet the IRA special exceptions about using money for education, health insurance (when unemployed), or the purchase of a first house.

➤ From 62 to 65, you can take early retirement benefits from Social Security at a reduced rate. At 65, for people born through 1937, you can receive full Social Security benefits. At 70, if you decide to wait until then, you can receive larger benefits.

➤ At 70½—or, more precisely, on the April 1 following the year in which you reach age 70½—you must start taking distributions from an IRA.

As you can see, 65—the birthday most often associated with retirement—is just one date in a long string of important birthdays.

Roll Over and Stay Alive

With 401(k) plans based on your own contributions, the money is yours. If you leave your job in the year in which you reach age 55 or thereafter, whether you are taking another position or retiring from the work force, you can take the money and run.

You actually have three choices: You can take the cash, leave it in place (if permitted by the current plan), or use it to fund a rollover IRA.

Before you pick up a check and dream about a red Ferrari, consider the tax consequences.

You may avoid the tax penalty if you're old enough, but income tax is always due on a lump sum distribution. What's more, your employer is required to withhold 20 percent of the distribution for income tax. Worst of all, you will give up years of tax-deferred growth in your retirement nest egg.

If you leave the money in place, it will continue to grow tax-deferred. But your investment choices may be limited once you leave the job. Some 401(k) plans give those who've left the same investment options as those who stay, but many do not, so this may not be your best choice. Another disadvantage is that most company plans pay a lump sum upon death. If this is the case, your beneficiaries will have to pay an immediate—and probably sizable—income tax. They also will lose the benefit of continuing tax deferral over their own lifetimes; that benefit is available only from an IRA.

The best choice, for most people, is moving the money to a rollover IRA. Moving it to a rollover IRA preserves tax deferral and allows for continued growth without the drag of tax payments.

Tax Treats

The numbers are impressive. If you take a lump sum distribution of $22,000, you'll have $15,840 after federal income taxes at 28 percent. You'll wind up with even less if you must pay state and local income taxes. If the money is rolled into an IRA where it grows at 8 percent for the next 30 years, you would wind up with more than $225,000!

Moving the money directly, in a transfer from your employer to the IRA custodian, eliminates the need for tax withholding. Otherwise, if you take the money and then put it into a rollover IRA, 20 percent will be withheld for taxes. If you make up the 20 percent within 60 days so that you roll over the entire amount, you will get the withheld tax back—but not until the following year, after you file your federal income tax return. If you don't make up the 20 percent withheld by your employer, it will be treated as a taxable distribution.

Rollover Rules

The first rule for a rollover IRA is this: Don't touch the money. If it passes through your hands, even briefly, taxes will be withheld.

The second rule is this: Keep the 401(k) distribution separate, as a rollover IRA. You are allowed to deposit it into an existing IRA or add new annual contributions to a rollover IRA, and doing so could minimize paperwork. But keeping the money separate keeps it flexible. If you take another job, and you've kept the rollover IRA separate from any other IRAs you may have, you will be able to roll it into the new employer's 401(k) plan. There's always time to consolidate IRAs after you retire.

Can you roll a 401(k) distribution into a Roth IRA instead of the traditional IRA, to take advantage of its permanently tax-free status? Yes, but not directly. You must first roll the money into a

Tax Tips

If you're taking a lump sum from an employer plan, flexibility rules. You don't have to make a choice between taking it all in cash or rolling it all over to an IRA. You can spend some of it, paying income tax and any tax penalty, while rolling the rest of it into an IRA to continue tax-deferred growth.

traditional IRA. Then, if your adjusted gross income is not more than $100,000, you can convert the traditional IRA to a Roth IRA.

Company Stock Has Square Wheels

Although it's generally a wise tax move to roll a lump sum distribution into an IRA, you may want to think twice before doing so if your 401(k) holds many shares of highly appreciated company stock. In this case, you can benefit from a special tax break—but only by not rolling the stock into an IRA.

If you include the stock in an IRA (a traditional IRA, not a Roth IRA), you'll eventually pay tax at your ordinary income tax rate. At this writing, the federal income tax rate can be as high as 39.6 percent. Instead, if you withdraw the stock from the retirement plan and place it in a regular taxable brokerage account, you'll pay income tax at the time of the transfer—but only on the original cost of the shares to the plan, not on the current market value.

Tax Talk

Net unrealized appreciation (NUA) is the growth in value of company stock held in a retirement plan from the time of its purchase by the plan until you take it out. Thanks to a special tax break, the tax on NUA is deferred until you sell the stock.

The tax on the difference—what the Internal Revenue Service calls *net unrealized appreciation*—can be deferred until you sell the stock. Then, to cap the tax benefits with a maraschino cherry, you'll pay no more than the maximum 20 percent long-term capital gains rate on the appreciation before the date of distribution. This long-term capital gains rate is yours even if you sell the stock the day after the distribution. However, if you hold on to the stock and sell it later, regular tax rules apply to any appreciation from the date of distribution to the date of sale.

Your Own (IRA) Account

You can withdraw money from your IRA without tax penalty once you reach age 59½—even earlier, if you meet the special rules discussed earlier. You must start to take the money out of a traditional IRA by the April 1 after the year in which you reach age 70½. This is your required beginning date, or RBD. (There is no required beginning date for Roth IRAs because, as noted in Chapter 12, "On Your Own [IRA] Account," you can leave the money in place forever.)

The only flexibility in the RBD is that you may take your first distribution any time up to the April 1 after the year in which you reach age 70½. Because the second distribution must be taken before the end of the calendar year, waiting could mean winding up with two distributions in one year. If this adversely affects your income tax bill, you may want to make the first withdrawal in the preceding year.

In addition to marking the beginning date for IRA distributions, the RBD is the final deadline for two other critical decisions.

First, you must name a beneficiary or beneficiaries for your IRA. You can change the beneficiary later, but the life expectancy of the designated beneficiary in place at the time you reach age 70½ will determine how payments are made—and taxes deferred—throughout your lifetime.

Second, you must decide which method of distribution to use. You have a choice between reducing your life expectancy by one each year, or recalculating your life expectancy for each distribution. The following sections describe both decisions in more detail.

Tax Treats

If you have sizable sums in an IRA and want to name two or more beneficiaries of different ages, most advisers suggest splitting the IRA into separate IRAs and naming one beneficiary on each. That's because, with a single IRA, the oldest beneficiary dictates the distribution schedule. A recent IRS private letter ruling lets multiple beneficiaries base withdrawals on their individual life expectancies. But the ruling applied only to an IRA owner dying before the required beginning date for distributions. Because this isn't an event you want to count on, many advisers suggest that it's still wise to split IRAs and name separate beneficiaries.

Name That Beneficiary!

The following are some key points to remember about beneficiary designations:

First, you must name your beneficiary on the IRA documents. Doing so in your will doesn't count.

If you fail to name a designated beneficiary on the IRA documents—and a secondary or *contingent* beneficiary, in case the primary beneficiary dies before you do—the proceeds of your IRA may go to your spouse, but only if your IRA custodian follows this procedure. With many IRA sponsors, the proceeds will go into your estate when you die.

Tax Talk

Contingent could be translated as "just in case." A contingent beneficiary—on an IRA, a life insurance policy, or any other financial instrument—is the individual who will receive the proceeds if the primary beneficiary dies before you do.

Tax Tips

Although you don't need to have a beneficiary in place before you reach age 70½, why wait? Name one now. You can always make a change later. But if you die prematurely, without a designated beneficiary, your family may suffer financial as well as emotional loss.

Shifting the IRA to your estate may seem as if it would make the transition easy for your family. In fact, it's the worst possible outcome. When a designated beneficiary inherits an IRA, tax deferral can be extended for years. When an IRA goes into an estate, it must be liquidated almost immediately, and income tax must be paid on the proceeds. IRA proceeds count as part of a taxable estate; if income taxes are added to estate taxes, 80 percent or more of the IRA could be lost to taxes.

If you're married, you'll probably want to name your spouse as your primary beneficiary. A spouse has the most flexibility when it comes to dealing with an inherited IRA.

Only spouses, for example, are allowed to roll over an inherited IRA into their own names and extend tax-deferred growth by stretching payments over their own life expectancy. Only spouses can name new beneficiaries and, if those beneficiaries are younger, extend payouts over still more years. (A recent private ruling by the IRS allows nonspouse beneficiaries to name new beneficiaries, but the financial institution holding your IRA must allow this.)

But you might not be married. Or, if your spouse has sufficient assets, you may want to leave your IRA to your children or grandchildren.

You can name a grandchild as beneficiary, but the Internal Revenue Service won't let you take maximum advantage of the age differential. For purposes of determining how much you must withdraw from your IRA during your lifetime, joint life expectancy is calculated as if the beneficiary is no more than 10 years younger than you are.

After your death, however, the 10-year rule doesn't apply. Distributions can then be made over the actual remaining life expectancy of you and your beneficiary. This could mean decades of ongoing tax deferral.

Distribution Choices

Between the ages of 59½ and 70½, you can take any sum of money out of your IRA without tax penalty. Starting after age 70½, when you have reached your required beginning date, the law is clear: You must make minimum withdrawals based on your life expectancy.

You may always take more than the minimum required distribution. But if you take less money than you are required to take in any one year, based on IRS tables, you face a tax penalty of 50 percent. That's half of the difference between the amount you took and the amount you were required to take.

While the life expectancy used to calculate your minimum required distributions must follow IRS tables, it is not a cut-and-dried number. You have a choice between two ways of calculating your life expectancy (and your joint life expectancy, if you are married and your spouse is your beneficiary).

The first way—the one your financial institution will probably use if you don't let them know you want the other one—involves recalculating your remaining life expectancy each year.

This recalculation method has some major advantages. Because life expectancy doesn't actually decrease by a full year for each calendar year, it lowers the amount you must take each year. For example, IRS tables show that a man of 70 has a life expectancy of 16 years. According to the same tables, a man of 71 has a life expectancy of 15.3 years.

So, using recalculation allows more money to remain in the IRA and grow tax-deferred. It also means that you can never outlive your IRA.

The second is a *term certain* method in which your life expectancy is figured out just once, at the time of the first withdrawal. Then one full year is subtracted in each succeeding year so that the entire IRA is distributed by the end of the term.

If you live longer than the IRS tables anticipate, you could outlive your IRA under this method of calculating life expectancy for the purpose of distributions. Nonetheless, term certain may be a better choice for many people. That's because the

Tax Traps

You could be sure that you named a beneficiary for your IRA, but stop right now and find out if that designation is up-to-date—and if it is still on file. Many financial institutions have merged in recent years. Some are simply sloppy about keeping records. If they don't have a beneficiary designation on file for you, the money will go into your estate and lose any further opportunities for tax-deferred growth.

Tax Traps

The law may allow a wide variety of options in naming beneficiaries and choosing distribution methods for your retirement money. But financial institutions are not required to offer every option the law permits. You may have to shop around to find an IRA sponsor willing to offer the strategy that will save taxes for your family.

Tax Talk

Term certain is another way of describing a fixed term. For IRA distributions, the fixed term is based on life expectancy at the required beginning date.

Tax Tips

You may have several IRAs, opened with different institutions or to achieve different investment objectives. Unless you have different beneficiaries, however, consolidating accounts at retirement will make it much easier to manage your retirement income. It will also simplify paperwork if you can reduce the number of monthly statements you receive.

term remains fixed even at your death, giving your beneficiary the option of continuing to take distributions on the same schedule. With the recalculation method, distributions must be accelerated when the beneficiary dies.

There's a third choice that can work well if you are naming a younger spouse as your beneficiary, although it may not be available at all financial institutions. This is a hybrid method, in which you hedge your bets by using the recalculation method for yourself and the term certain method for your spouse.

Using the recalculation method for your own distributions means that you can't outlive your IRA. It also means that, if your spouse dies first, you won't be forced into an early distribution. At the same time, if your spouse lives longer, he or she can roll over the IRA, name new beneficiaries, and establish a new distribution schedule based on longer life expectancies.

The hybrid method can also be applied in reverse, with the term certain method for you and the recalculation method for your spouse. Either way, you could lose the bet if you and your spouse die prematurely and in the wrong sequence, because this will result in a shorter payout period.

If the hybrid method appeals to you, be aware that the calculations are complex and that you may need professional assistance. You may also need to seek out a financial institution that will permit this distribution method. Despite the extra effort, it may be worth considering this option—but only, in the view of many advisers, if you have sizable sums in your IRA and expect to outlive the life expectancy tables.

If you want either the fixed term or a hybrid method, you must elect it in writing before your required beginning date.

Today and Tomorrow

There's one more thing you need to know about beneficiary designations and distributions: Your beneficiaries must follow different rules about distributions from your IRA, depending on whether you die before or after your required beginning date (RBD).

If you die in the saddle, before you reach your required beginning date of age 70½, a spousal beneficiary has several choices:

➤ Roll the IRA into a new IRA with new beneficiary designations, and wait until the spouse reaches age 70½ to begin making withdrawals; this is usually the best choice.

➤ (1) Begin distributions by December 31 of the year the IRA owner would have reached age 70½, or (2) December 31 of the year following the year of the IRA owner's death, whichever is later. These distributions are based on the beneficiary's life expectancy.

➤ Take all the money by the end of the fifth year following the year of the IRA owner's death.

A nonspouse beneficiary has only two options:

➤ Take the money over the beneficiary's life expectancy, starting by the end of the year following your death.

➤ Take all the money by the end of the fifth year following the year of your death.

If you die on or after your RBD, the beneficiary designation you made before that date will dictate distributions. In this situation, a spouse can choose between these two alternatives:

➤ Continue to take distributions on the schedule you started.

➤ Roll the IRA into a new IRA, name a new beneficiary, and begin distributions by the spouse's required beginning date, based on a combination of the spouse's and the new beneficiary's life expectancy.

In the same situation, where you die on or after your RBD, a nonspouse beneficiary must start taking distributions by the end of the calendar year following your death. If you named a much younger beneficiary and had to abide by the maximum 10-year difference in your ages in calculating your own distributions during your lifetime, the beneficiary can go back to the original joint life expectancy in calculating distributions after your death.

On the Receiving End

If you've inherited an IRA, the welcome news may soon be tempered by some harsh reality. Unfortunately, many of the financial institutions acting as IRA custodians have no idea how to interpret the complex laws relating to inherited IRAs, have no forms for the purpose, and—worst of all—give advice that is just plain wrong.

Horror stories abound. Look at the following examples from the files of Ed Slott, a Rockville Centre, New York accountant and the publisher of the monthly newsletter,

Ed Slott's IRA Advisor. You can learn from them not only what to do when you inherit an IRA, but what to tell your family now to avoid problems for your heirs.

➤ A 41-year-old woman inherits a $500,000 IRA from her 68-year-old father. An accountant says she must take all the money within five years after her father's death. She does as he says—and not only pays more than $325,000 in income tax on an IRA that had grown to about $700,000, but she also misses out on 40 years of additional tax deferral. The accountant was just plain wrong. Because her father died before he reached age 70½ and his required beginning date, the woman could have elected to spread the distributions over her own life expectancy. If you want to extend tax-deferred growth by spreading distributions from an inherited IRA over your own life expectancy—remember, you can always take more if you need it—you must take the first distribution by December 31 of the year following the year of the death. Let the institution know, in writing, that you are electing to take distributions over your own life expectancy, and ask them to acknowledge receipt.

➤ Another woman inherits an IRA from her mother. The attorney handling her mother's estate suggests that she open a rollover IRA and retitle it in her own name. Wrong again, on two counts. First, only a spouse can roll an inherited IRA into his or her own name. Second, unless you are the spouse of the IRA owner, putting your own name on the inherited IRA will make it a taxable distribution. If you inherit an IRA from anyone but a spouse, you must keep the original owner's name on the IRA. The correct label would be some version of this: "IRA of (name of original owner), deceased (with the date), for the benefit of (your name) as beneficiary." And, if you inherit your spouse's IRA as a young widow or widower, you may not want to automatically roll it all over into your own IRA. Once you do, any withdrawals before you reach age 59½ will be subject to a 10 percent tax penalty. Instead, you could leave it in place and make withdrawals as a beneficiary.

➤ A man inherits his mother's $1.1 million IRA. Although her estate paid $450,000 in federal estate taxes on the IRA, no one told the man that the $450,000 could be deducted from income taxes.

If you inherit an IRA on which federal estate taxes have been paid, tell your advisers about this deduction. They may not know, and their ignorance could cost you a bundle.

With all due respect to accountants and other financial advisers, the laws and regulations surrounding distributions from IRAs are incredibly complex. Both Congress and the Internal Revenue Service have outdone themselves here. In addition, IRAs have been around just about long enough for the first big wave of inheritances to be getting under way.

As financial institutions and advisers confront the issue, both should become more familiar with the rules. Some have already started to revise their in-house policies to permit beneficiaries to extend distribution schedules.

Meanwhile, if you inherit a sizable IRA, it pays to seek an adviser specializing in this area.

An adviser may suggest drafting your own beneficiary designation form, to be sure that your wishes are carried out. Many institutions have simple forms, with a single line for the beneficiary designation. At the very least, you need space to name a backup or contingent beneficiary.

If you have several children you want to name as equal beneficiaries, you may need space to spell out exactly what happens if one of them predeceases you. If you fail to do this, the institution may divide the IRA between your two surviving children even if you wanted the other child's share to go to her children.

A tailor-made form can solve such potential problems—but be sure to get a signed acknowledgement from the institution that the form is on file and will be honored.

Doing Well by Doing Good

If you plan to leave money to a favorite charity in your will, consider naming the charity as beneficiary of an IRA. Doing so will save a bundle because retirement money is taxable to human beneficiaries but is not taxable to a charity.

Let's say that you leave an IRA worth $10,000 to a favorite niece and $10,000 to your alma mater. The gifts may seem equivalent, but they are not. Tax will be owed on the bequest to your niece, but not on the bequest to the college. Family comes out ahead, in terms of net after-tax results, if the IRA goes to the college and the cash to your niece.

But be careful. Don't name a charity and a person as joint beneficiaries on the same IRA. Because the shortest life expectancy governs the distribution schedule, and a charity has no life expectancy, the money will have to be distributed right away. It won't matter to the charity, which is tax-free. But it could matter a lot to the human beneficiary, who will lose a lot to taxes.

More information on estate planning with IRAs is in Chapter 24, "You Can't Take It with You."

The Least You Need to Know

➤ Your 65th birthday may be the least important milestone in retirement planning; for maximum tax benefits, pay special attention to 55, 59½, and 70½.

➤ Distributions from a 401(k) can—and probably should—be rolled over into an IRA, with the exception of appreciated employer stock.

➤ By age 70½, you must name a beneficiary for your IRA, determine which life expectancy calculation to use, and start taking distributions.

➤ Significant differences govern the way a spousal beneficiary and a nonspouse beneficiary can take distributions from your IRA after you are gone.

➤ Get expert advice. Laws surrounding IRAs are complex, and many financial advisers do not specialize in this area.

The Ins and Outs of Annuities

If putting away all you can in tax-qualified retirement plans on and off the job—including a 401(k) plan and an individual retirement account—still leaves you worried about having enough income for a comfortable retirement, an annuity may fill the bill.

But annuities are one of the most complicated financial instruments ever invented. They're hard to understand—and, to make matters worse, they're often oversold. Before you take the bait, read this chapter.

The Game Plan

Annuities are contracts issued by life insurance companies, but they are the flip side of life insurance. Where life insurance provides money for your survivors, an annuity can provide lifetime income for you.

Annuities have distinct advantages:

➤ Unlike tax-qualified retirement plans such as 401(k) plans and IRAs, there is no ceiling on contributions; you can put as much money as you like into an annuity.

➤ Unlike tax-qualified retirement plans, contributions to an annuity can be made from any source; they are not restricted to earned income.

➤ Earnings within an annuity grow tax-deferred; they are not subject to income tax until they are withdrawn.

➤ There is no "required beginning date," as there is with qualified plans; you can delay the start of distributions as long as you like.

➤ No annual income tax filings are required.

➤ In some states, although not in all, assets in an annuity are protected from creditors.

➤ Annuities are very flexible instruments; they may be immediate or deferred, fixed or variable.

➤ Perhaps most important, when you purchase an annuity, you are purchasing a guarantee of lifetime income.

But annuities also have some built-in disadvantages, which should be weighed carefully before you decide to buy. You'll find more detail later in this chapter, but consider these points, for example:

➤ Unlike most tax-qualified plans, contributions are never tax-deductible.

➤ Annuities are designed for the long term, and many have hefty surrender penalties in the early years; never buy an annuity (other than one without a surrender penalty or an immediate annuity; more later) with money you may need soon.

➤ Withdrawals are taxed as ordinary income, as they are in tax-qualified plans, so there is no capital gains advantage when underlying investments are sold.

➤ Also as in tax-qualified plans, withdrawals before age 59½ are subject to a 10 percent tax penalty.

➤ Fees associated with variable annuities are often very high.

➤ If you die owning an annuity, just as if you die with assets in an IRA, the amount will be subject to both income and estate tax; there is no *step-up* in value on assets in an annuity.

Before you decide whether an annuity fits in your financial plans, consider the various types of annuities.

Now or Later

Annuities can be immediate or deferred. An immediate annuity, as the name implies, is bought with a lump sum and distributions start within a year of purchase. Because annuities generally are purchased to build tax-deferred savings for retirement, immediate annuities run a distant second to deferred annuities on the popularity scale.

But an immediate annuity can be a useful choice if you've received a windfall in the form of an inheritance, a lump sum distribution from a retirement plan, a bonus, or profits from the sale of a home or business. Investing the money in an immediate annuity can provide guaranteed income for life without the headaches of managing the investment yourself. Even better, it offers the advantage of a guarantee that you can't outlive the income.

Tax Talk

A **step-up** in value means that inherited assets are valued for tax purposes at the date of the owner's death instead of at their original purchase price. The step-up can save considerable tax dollars, but it does not apply to annuities or to individual retirement accounts.

When you purchase an immediate annuity, you decide whether you want to receive payments monthly, quarterly, semiannually, or annually. Most people buying an immediate annuity want monthly income, but it's nice to have other options.

Most immediate annuities are fixed annuities, with payments staying the same for the entire distribution period. Some companies, however, are now offering immediate variable annuities, basing the payments on the performance of an underlying mutual fund or funds. The variable option may offer a better chance of keeping up with inflation over the years.

A deferred annuity—by far the more popular form—is purchased with a lump sum or installment payments with distributions starting sometime in the future. Just when distributions start is up to you. Some contracts and some state laws specify age 85, but in no case will you be required to start distributions at age 70½, as is required under tax-qualified plans.

A deferred annuity offers tax-deferred growth. During the accumulation phase, interest and dividends within the annuity are not subject to income tax. Earnings are subject to ordinary income tax when distributions are made during the payout phase, but the idea is that you may then be in a lower tax bracket. If you expect to be in the same or a higher income tax bracket after you retire, you may want to think twice about whether an annuity is a good idea.

Deferred annuities may be fixed or variable.

Fixing the Future

When you buy a fixed annuity, immediate or deferred, you are promised a fixed return on your money. Typically, the insurance company will guarantee an introductory rate for a period of time up to five years, and then determine a new rate on each renewal period. Many contracts contain a "bailout" provision, though, so that if rates drop below a specified minimum level, you can transfer to another company without incurring surrender charges.

Tax Tips

Be sure to pick a stable, top-rated insurer. You may not receive distributions until many years in the future, and you want the company to be around. In addition, when you buy a fixed annuity, your money becomes part of the insurer's general account and is subject to attack by its creditors.

A fixed interest rate appeals to many conservative investors—and it does give you the certainty of knowing how much you will have. Because the insurance company knows the interest rate at each renewal, it can tell you how much money you will have in your account at the end of the period.

But fixed-rate investments inevitably lose ground to inflation and should never make up the largest part of your investment mix. If you buy a fixed-rate annuity, be sure to strike a balance by investing for growth through mutual funds or individual stocks.

Surrender charges are part of just about every annuity contract, fixed and variable, and it's important to understand that when you invest in an annuity, you are effectively locking up your money for a number of years. Surrender charges may be as high as 7 percent in the first year, gradually declining to 0 after seven years.

Some companies apply surrender charges only to the initial investment. Others also apply it to any additional contributions. Be sure that you understand the terms of any annuity contract you enter into.

A Mixed Bag

An offshoot of the conventional fixed annuity is the indexed annuity. Indexed, or equity-indexed annuities, combine the potential return of the stock market with limits on the risk of losing money in market declines. But don't confuse this hybrid product with the true variable annuity described in the next section.

An equity-indexed annuity ties its performance to a market index while guaranteeing a minimum interest rate and the return of principal. You do not select the investments, as you do with variable annuities, and the insurance company does not actually invest in the stock market.

Although equity-indexed annuities may produce better returns than traditional fixed annuities, they also have some built-in constraints on performance. The accounting firm of Ernst & Young explains:

➤ Although dividends make up at least half of the average total return in the stock market over the last 70-plus years, dividends aren't counted in equity-indexed annuities. Instead, the return is linked only to price appreciation.

➤ Even without dividends, equity-indexed annuities typically don't match the entire return of the index. The match may be anywhere from 55 percent to 90 percent. The result: If the index appreciates 10 percent and the match is 75 percent, the rate credited to the account would be 7.5 percent.

➤ Some equity-indexed annuities come with an interest rate cap that limits potential returns.

Playing the Odds

With the booming stock market of recent years, fixed annuities have lost a lot of appeal and variable annuities have taken the lead in popularity. New investments in variable annuities grew from $12 billion in 1990 to $98.8 billion in 1998 and were expected to exceed $118 billion for 1999, partly as a result of enthusiastic sales promotion and partly because of the product's real advantages.

Variable annuities offer many of the same features as fixed annuities—tax deferral, unlimited contributions, no required beginning date—plus the potential for greater returns based on the performance of underlying investments that you select.

A variable annuity combines insurance features such as a guaranteed death benefit with a selection of underlying investments called *subaccounts*. How much your annuity will eventually pay depends on the performance of the subaccounts you choose. As an added advantage, you can switch investments between subaccounts without incurring any tax obligation. (That's the case for now, at least. A proposal by President Clinton in 1999 would have made such transfers taxable events. The proposal didn't go anywhere, but such things have a way of coming back.)

Tax Talk

Subaccounts in a variable annuity are mutual funds, either funds designed specifically for the insurance company or versions of existing mutual funds. Although they may have fund names you recognize, however, they are not the same funds.

Tax Talk

A **prospectus** is the legal document setting forth the terms of an investment offering. The prospectus for a mutual fund describes the fund's objectives and the securities it holds. It also provides financial information.

Tax Traps

Some variable annuities come with a fixed option so that you can blend the variable component with a guaranteed return on a portion of the account. Most variable annuities offer fixed-income funds as subaccount options. But it's generally a mistake to use either the fixed option or fixed-income funds for more than a small portion of an annuity. The only way to overcome the high costs associated with variable annuities is to go for growth.

Choosing Investments

Your choices of subaccounts are similar to the choices in mutual funds outside an annuity. You'll find subaccounts for aggressive growth, growth, income, and so on. You may even find the same subaccounts in annuities offered by different insurers. There's also a trend toward so-called "multimanager products" offering subaccounts from various fund managers within a single annuity package.

Whether the underlying funds come from one fund manager or several, each subaccount must be described in a prospectus within the *prospectus* for the annuity as a whole.

The growing number of subaccounts adds to the difficulty in reading and understanding an annuity prospectus. The product is so difficult to comprehend, in its special blend of investment-plus-insurance, that the SEC has delayed enforcing its rule that prospectuses must be written in plain English. Nonetheless, many insurers are working to make annuity language accessible.

Sales Gimmicks

Variable annuities may be popular, but they're frequently criticized for their high fees and the high-pressure sales tactics that too often result.

In response to the criticism, insurers have introduced some bells and whistles to improve the basic variable annuity product.

While most variable annuities offer a guaranteed death benefit to protect your principal, some have extended the guarantee to protect against a market downturn. The feature varies from policy to policy but typically offers a choice among three options: the portfolio value at the time of death, the original amount invested plus 5 percent, or the high point of the portfolio at a specified time. The guarantee may cost from 0.1 percent to 0.5 percent of the assets in the account each year.

Is the guarantee worthwhile? Most analysts say no. For one thing, the market would have to be down sharply before the guarantee is worth much. For another, you would have to die. The added benefits don't apply during life and, as you recall, annuities were originally designed to provide retirement income.

In another departure from the classic annuity, at least two companies have introduced annuities that include a long-term care feature. This may be worthwhile, but compare the cost against the cost for a standalone long-term care insurance policy.

Loads and Fees

One of the biggest drawbacks to purchasing a variable annuity can be the cost. There are some new low-cost products on the market, but most variable annuities still come with hefty fees.

Two types of fees are charged as a percentage of assets. The first, annual insurance charges, covers the following:

➤ Administrative costs, or the insurer's cost of doing business

➤ Mortality and expense risk, known as M&E, paying for guaranteed lifetime income and the guaranteed death benefit

➤ Commissions, where annuities are sold by financial intermediaries, of from 4 percent to 8 percent of your first-year premium

➤ Distribution fees, on no-load annuities sold directly to consumers, of no more than 1 percent a year

Annual insurance charges recently averaged 1.27 percent a year. The second asset-based charge is an investment management fee. According to the National Association for Variable Annuities (NAVA), the fee ranges from 0.5 percent to 1.0 percent per year, depending on the type of subaccounts chosen. The recent average amount was 0.77 percent a year.

In addition, there may be an annual contract charge of $30 to $40 a year. Some contracts charge

Tax Traps

In the highly competitive marketplace for variable annuities, some companies are offering a sign-up "bonus" in the form of 3 percent or 4 percent of your contribution immediately added to the account value at the time of purchase. The trade-off is typically higher fees. The SEC is looking suspiciously at the sales practices surrounding these bonus arrangements and had begun to investigate in early 2000, on the grounds that many of the products were both costly and poor performers. Don't go for a gimmick without checking out the underlying product.

an additional fee if contract owners make what the insurer considers too many transfers among subaccounts.

And, of course, there are the surrender charges mentioned earlier. Surrender charges can hit hard if you need your money before they phase out. But hope may be at hand. Fidelity Investments announced early in 2000 that it would join some low-cost providers and drop its surrender charges for both new and existing policyholders. Perhaps other annuity providers will follow suit.

Expenses are spelled out in the prospectus. They may also be found in newspaper tables, such as those in *The Wall Street Journal,* reporting on annuity funds' performance and fees.

The fees can add up to a lot. Asset-based charges on variable annuities currently average a bit more than 2 percent a year. Annual expense ratios on mutual funds average less than 1.5 percent a year. So, you may prefer to invest directly in mutual funds rather than in comparable funds within a variable annuity.

With asset-based charges plus contract charges and possible surrender charges, it definitely costs more to invest in subaccounts through a variable annuity than to invest in mutual funds directly—unless you choose one of the low-cost annuities listed in the accompanying Tax Treat. But there may be two offsetting factors. First, NAVA claims that the subaccounts within an annuity carry lower fees than publicly traded mutual funds so that the total expense isn't that much higher. Second, with an annuity, you are buying a guarantee of lifetime income.

To Buy or Not to Buy

An annuity can supplement the retirement income you can build through tax-qualified plans and can give you the peace of mind of guaranteed income. But don't buy an annuity unless you have done the following:

> ➤ Have already contributed the maximum amount to tax-qualified plans, especially those where contributions are deductible and earnings are tax-deferred.

> ➤ Have a long time before you will need the money. This is especially true with variable annuities, where it can take many years to overcome the drag on performance of high costs. According to many studies, you will lose money if you take money out of a variable annuity before 10 to 15 years have elapsed. You certainly don't want to take it out before you reach age 59½ because you will face a 10 percent tax penalty.

> ➤ Expect to be in a lower tax bracket after retirement. Because distributions from annuities are taxed as ordinary income, high-bracket taxpayers may be better off investing outside an annuity where they can take advantage of lower capital gains tax rates. (Of course, taxes are a moving target. If capital gains rates are higher in the future as they have been in the past—or if the insurance industry

succeeds in lobbying efforts to obtain capital gains status for distributions—annuities will be more attractive.)

➤ Expect to use annuity distributions as retirement income. Insurance consultant Peter Katt, writing in the *AAII Journal*, points out that annuities are a poor choice for leaving money to heirs because of the tax consequences stemming from no step-up in value at death.

➤ Think you might at some point file for bankruptcy and live in a state where annuities are protected from creditors. Your lawyer, the local Bar Association, or your state's Attorney's General office should be able to provide this information about your state.

If you fit one or more of these categories and want to buy an annuity, you can find various products through insurance companies, stockbrokers, and mutual fund families. Before you buy, compare costs and features. Pay attention to surrender charges; several new low-cost annuities don't have any surrender charges. Also pay special attention to the variety and performance of subaccounts in each annuity, and be sure to choose an annuity with a wide choice of underlying funds.

Take the Money and Run

When you purchase an immediate annuity, and when you start to take annuitized payments from a deferred annuity, you must choose among various payment options. Typically, these include the following options:

➤ A life annuity, with payments made as long as you live, guarantees that you can't outlive your income. The downside of this option is that payments stop when you die, even if that is the day after you receive your first payment. Your heirs will receive nothing, and all your accumulated nest egg will go to pay annuitants who live longer than average.

➤ A "term certain" (sometimes called "period certain") annuity promises payments for the period you elect. Term certain payments are typically available for periods of 5 to 30 years. If you elect a 10-year certain period, for example, payments are made to you for 10 years and then stop. If you die sooner, your named beneficiary or beneficiaries will continue receiving payments for the balance of the 10-year term.

➤ A "life annuity with period certain" guarantees payments for life with payments for no less than the specified period.

➤ A joint-and-survivor option gives you and your spouse lifetime income. It's also possible to elect a joint-and-survivor annuity with a term certain feature.

Annuity distributions are based on life expectancy, so the older you are when payments begin, the more you will get. (For a joint-and-survivor payment option, the life expectancies of both of you will be considered.) But annuity distributions are also based on gender; because women live longer and are likely to collect for a longer period of time, their monthly checks are smaller.

To Annuitize or Not to Annuitize

The point of an annuity, typically, is to provide regular income. That's what you do when you "annuitize" a lump sum; you convert it into regular periodic payments. (In fact, as part of putting their prospectuses into plain English, some companies are dropping the jargon word "annuitize" and calling the process "converting savings into income.")

Tax Traps

When you buy a variable annuity, you're probably most interested in fund choices, fund performance, and tax deferral. But look ahead to when you'll be taking distributions, and be sure that you understand how those distributions will be taxed. If you're in a high tax bracket in retirement, you'll notice the impact.

But you may have other, better choices. Annuitization is unpopular in some quarters because once you make your choice, you're locked in and can't make a change. Instead, you can arrange systematic withdrawal of funds and change the amounts from time to time. Under this arrangement, your heirs get any money left in the account when you die. The downside is that there is no guarantee of lifetime income, as there is when you annuitize, so you could outlive your income. (There are also tax consequences for each choice; see the next section, "Tax and Consequences.")

In addition, under some contracts, you can take up to one year's interest on the policy anniversary date without surrender charges. Under many contracts, you can take out up to 10 percent of the accumulated value without surrender charges; some companies are increasing the amount to 15 percent. If you are under age 59½, however, you will have to pay a 10 percent tax penalty.

If you want or need the money—for example, if you bought an annuity to fund a grandchild's college education or decide that you want to take a trip around the world—you can surrender the contract and take a lump sum payment. Or, during the years before you start regular payments (the "accumulation phase" of an annuity), you can take a partial withdrawal and leave the rest of the money in place to fund later retirement income.

Tax and Consequences

Taking the money, as I indicated at the outset, leads to one of the major disadvantages of annuities: the tax you'll owe. Here's what you can expect.

While you own an annuity, and before distributions start, everything is hunky-dory. Taxes are deferred during the accumulation period—that is, they are deferred while you are alive and accumulating assets within your annuity.

If you die during the accumulation period, the annuity will be part of your taxable estate. What's more, your beneficiary will have to pay income tax on the amount in excess of your original contribution. If you put $100,000 toward a deferred annuity that is worth $225,000 when you die, $125,000 will be immediately taxable as ordinary income. Remember, there is no step-up in value at death on assets in an annuity.

If you live beyond the accumulation period, and start collecting regular payments (annuitization) on your deferred annuity, each payment is made up of both principal and interest. The interest portion is taxed as ordinary income—even if part of it is made up of capital gains on the underlying investments in a variable annuity. Remember what I said earlier: There is no advantageous capital gains treatment of profits within an annuity (and, to be fair, on profits within an individual retirement account as well). But dividing each payment between taxable and nontaxable amounts may be the better deal.

If you take a partial withdrawal or systematic withdrawals—in other words, if you take money out at any point without annuitizing the distributions—the entire amount is treated as earnings (until the earnings are used up and you're tapping principal) and is therefore taxable. In addition, if you are under age 59½, you will run afoul of the IRS rules against premature withdrawals, and you will owe a 10 percent tax penalty.

An annuity is best purchased if you plan to use the money during retirement. It is not a good vehicle for leaving money to your family. If you die owning an annuity, the proceeds are subject to estate tax (see Chapter 24, "You Can't Take It with You") and will be subject to income tax as well. Life insurance proceeds, by contrast, are counted in your taxable estate but are not subject to income tax.

If you own a fixed annuity and are unhappy with the interest rate, or a variable annuity whose subaccounts are performing poorly, you can make a tax-free switch into another annuity. Such transfers are known as a "1035 exchange," for the applicable provision of the tax code. Although you won't pay tax on a 1035 exchange, you may owe a surrender charge to the original issuer if you make the exchange during the surrender period. You may also start a surrender period all over again on the new contract.

Tax Tips

There are exceptions to the 10 percent tax penalty on premature withdrawals. You may take the money earlier, paying income tax but no penalty, if you are disabled, if you set up a series of substantially equal periodic payments based on your life expectancy, or if you take an immediate annuity.

The Least You Need to Know

➤ Fixed annuities appeal to conservative investors, but their guaranteed returns lose ground to inflation.

➤ Variable annuities, with their investment choice, offer the potential for greater returns.

➤ If you buy a variable annuity, select growth investments to offset high fees.

➤ Use an annuity to supplement retirement income if you have fully funded tax-qualified plans, have a long time before you will need the money, and expect to use it to provide retirement income.

Part 5

Put Your Money to Work

Here we get to the nitty-gritty of investing your money in ways that make tax sense.

The chapters in this part zero in on money market mutual funds, tax-free municipal bonds, Uncle Sam's Treasury obligations, and special investment options ranging from real estate investment trusts to unit investment trusts. You'll find information on the pros and cons of investing in individual securities versus joining forces in mutual funds. And you'll find a guide through the maze of tax laws and regulations governing investing.

Chapter 16

Everyone into the (Money Market) Pool

In This Chapter

➤ Using money market mutual funds as a cash management tool generally offering higher interest rates than bank accounts

➤ Investing via money market mutual funds in short-term, highly liquid government and corporate obligations

➤ Understanding that money market mutual funds are not insured but are considered very safe

➤ Choosing taxable or tax-free money market mutual funds to suit your tax bracket

Americans know that getting together produces results. We used to apply the adage "many hands make light work" to things like barn-raisings and quilting bees. Today we pool our money to make investments and to save for the future.

Up until 1972, when the first money market mutual fund was introduced, we relied on savings accounts and certificates of deposit for our savings. By late 1999, money market mutual funds accounted for about one-quarter of all the money in mutual funds, for a total of $1.577 trillion of total mutual fund assets. Retail money funds—those owned by individuals rather than institutions—held a total of $919.82 billion.

Savings accounts and certificates of deposit continue to attract savers. But the money market is a powerful draw. This chapter explains the ins and outs of pooled savings.

Skip the Savings Account

Until money market mutual funds were introduced in 1972, the *money market* was available only to investors with more than $100,000 to invest. This meant mostly institutions, along with some wealthy individuals. Money market mutual funds allowed all of us to get in on the act by pooling our investment dollars and buying shares in an entity—the fund—that could invest in the money market. You can invest in a money market mutual fund for as little as $1,000 (a few funds require even less) and then make additional investments in smaller amounts.

Tax Talk

The **money market** consists of large-denomination short-term securities, including Treasury bills, commercial paper, and jumbo certificates of deposit.

Money market mutual funds were the first mutual funds to offer a constant price per share; it's the yield that varies, not the price, which is designed to stay at $1 per share. Money market funds were also the first to offer check-writing privileges and instant liquidity. In fact, money market mutual funds are generally dedicated to providing the highest possible yield consistent with preserving capital and ensuring liquidity.

From 1972 until 1982, money market mutual funds had no competition. They were the only game in town for the small saver who wanted a better yield. Then, in 1982, federal restrictions on bank interest rates were lifted and banks introduced money market deposit accounts.

What's the difference between a money market mutual fund and a money market deposit account? Try these on for size:

➤ Bank money market deposits are federally insured up to $100,000. Money market mutual funds are not insured, although they are regulated by the Securities and Exchange Commissions and are considered very safe. No investor has ever lost money in a money market mutual fund, although a few funds have been bailed out by their parent companies when investments soured. If you can't stomach risk, stick with a bank money market deposit account—or a money market mutual fund investing solely in Treasury obligations of the U.S. government.

➤ In exchange for deposit insurance on a bank money market deposit account, you generally have to give up some yield. Banks typically pay less interest on their accounts, in part because banks have higher operating costs. Money market mutual funds don't have brick-and-mortar structures to build and operate, and they typically pay higher rates of interest.

➤ All your money in a money market mutual fund earns interest at the same rate, with the yield computed daily. This is generally true even if your balance falls below the minimum required to open the account. Banks, on the other hand, often have fixed rates, which change from time to time. Bank rates may also be tiered in a "stair-step" fashion in which higher interest rates are paid on higher balances. Some banks and thrifts also charge fees for maintaining the account.

➤ Most money market mutual funds permit unlimited check-writing, although each check may have to be written for at least $500. Banks don't usually specify the size of an individual check drawn on a money market deposit account, but they are required by law to limit transactions other than cash withdrawals to six a month, including three by check.

All in the Family

Money market mutual funds can be either taxable or tax-free. Both offer safety of principal, current income, and *liquidity*.

Both taxable and tax-free money market funds offer definite advantages when it comes to managing your cash:

Tax Talk

Liquidity means that an asset can be quickly and easily sold without concerns about price. The shares of money market mutual funds are always priced at $1 and are highly liquid. You'll never lose money when you convert shares to cash.

➤ Most money market funds are "no-load" funds, with no sales charge or commission. Like all mutual funds, however, they do have management expenses. When high, these expenses can drastically reduce yield. (The section "Costs Count," later in this chapter, provides more detail on fund expenses.)

➤ Most money market funds offer check-writing privileges. Many funds, but not all, set a per-check minimum of $500. This isn't a terrible hardship, though, because it lets you pay your major bills (such as a mortgage or insurance premiums) directly from the money fund while periodically writing a check to your checking account to have money available for smaller expenses. A few money market funds actually have no check-writing minimums; if one of these suits your purposes, you can use it as your sole checking account.

➤ Many money market funds are part of a "family" of funds that includes a variety of stock and bond funds managed by the same company. With telephone switching privileges, it's easy to move your money from one fund to another. The convenience of this "family" element may be one of the most important reasons for selecting a money market mutual fund. If you like the funds of a particular fund family, or if you do all your investing through one stockbrokerage firm, using that family's or that firm's money fund can make investing a cinch.

➤ Distributions are typically reinvested in the money market mutual fund, but you may also choose to take some or all distributions in cash or to reinvest them in another mutual fund in the same family.

Tax Traps

Selling shares of a money market fund in order to switch into a stock or bond fund doesn't have any tax consequences because the shares of a money market fund are always pegged at exactly $1. Selling shares of a stock or bond fund—even if you are doing so to make a purchase within the same fund family and no money actually reaches your pocket—may incur a gain or loss and will have to be reported on your income tax return.

Using a Money Fund

Money market funds should not be viewed as investments, but as a substitute for cash. When you are investing for a long-term objective, you need growth and you can't achieve growth in a money fund. You should use a money fund the way you should use a bank account, as a place for short-term savings. Consider these uses:

➤ As a higher-yielding alternative to a checking account

➤ As a parking place for cash while you consider investment alternatives after you win the lottery, come into an inheritance, or sell a house

➤ As a safe place for money you will need within a few months for a specific need, such as a down payment on a house or a college tuition bill

➤ As an emergency reserve holding the three to six months' living expenses you might need to tide you over in a pinch

No Guarantees Here

Just how risky are money market mutual funds?

As I said before, the money you have in a money market mutual fund is not protected by federal deposit insurance. But the risk of losing money is very small because money funds manage risk through the short maturity dates on the securities in their portfolios, through diversification, and through concentrating on high-quality investments with complete liquidity.

Low risk isn't no risk. In several well-publicized instances, an investment within a fund portfolio bit the dust and threatened the $1-per-share net asset value that money funds strive to maintain. In each case the fund sponsor provided money to make up the shortfall, and the $1-per-share price held firm. It is possible that the buck could be broken in the future, but if it did happen, the net asset value would still probably hold at 98 or 99 cents.

Your money is protected because money funds are strictly regulated. For example, under current rules, no more than 5 percent of a taxable money fund's assets may be invested in the securities of a single issuer—unless that issuer is the federal government. In addition, the maximum average maturity of securities within the portfolio is 90 days. Most money funds stick to shorter maturities. At this writing, the average maturity in a taxable fund is 54 days and in a tax-free fund is 49 days.

So, you're unlikely to lose principal invested in a money fund. A more serious risk is that money market fund returns will not protect you against inflation or provide growth to meet future needs. But this is a risk only if you use a money fund as an investment. As I noted earlier, money funds are more properly used as a place for short-term savings and an emergency cushion.

No Peas in a Pod

All money market mutual funds are alike in their basic composition, holding short-term securities and keeping a stable dollar-per-share price. But money market mutual funds also differ in some significant ways.

Three major categories of money market mutual funds offer investors a choice:

➤ General-purpose funds invest mainly in the unsecured short-term corporate debt known as commercial paper. They may also invest in other short-term instruments such as repurchase agreements ("repos") and jumbo certificates of deposit. Their yields reflect short-term interest rates in the financial markets. Dividends on general-purpose funds are taxable.

➤ Government funds invest in U.S. Treasury issues and, in some instances, in other U.S. agency obligations as well. Dividends on Treasury-only funds are subject to federal income tax but are generally tax-free on the state level. Dividends on funds that include other agency obligations may be partially taxable; your fund will let you know how to report dividends for state tax purposes.

➤ Tax-exempt funds buy short-term municipal securities. There are national tax-free funds, where dividends are free of federal income tax and, to the extent that individual securities within the portfolio are issued by your state, may be free of state income tax as well. Double tax-free funds also are available in about half of the states. These invest solely in securities issued by a particular state and are therefore free of both federal and state income tax for residents of that state. Here yields reflect supply and demand in short-term debt obligations issued by states and municipalities.

Which type of fund should you buy? If you are very conservative, you may want to stick to a Treasury-only or government fund. They pay a little less than general-purpose funds, but the lag in yield is okay if it will let you sleep better at night.

195

If you are in a high federal income tax bracket—and especially if you live in a high-tax state—you may want to concentrate on tax-exempt money funds. As an example of the spread in yields between taxable and tax-exempt yields, taxable funds recently returned an average of just under 5 percent (the seven-day compound yield), while tax-free funds returned an average of 2.83 percent. Refer back to Chapter 2, "Pay Now, Pay Later, Pay Not at All," to check equivalent taxable and tax-exempt yields to see which will work best for you in your tax bracket.

But don't blindly insist on sticking with tax-free funds, in the belief that you are putting one over on Uncle Sam. If a taxable fund would produce more after-tax income, the only one you're fooling is yourself. As a rough rule of thumb, taxpayers in the 15 percent and 28 percent tax brackets will come out ahead with taxable funds, while taxpayers in the top two brackets of 36 percent and 39.6 percent do better with tax-frees. If you're in between, at the 33 percent bracket, you must look at your own specific tax situation to make the determination.

Tax Traps

Some tax-free money funds invest in securities that may in fact be taxable. If you might be subject to the Alternative Minimum Tax (see Chapter 22, "There's No Free Lunch"), you may want to steer clear of these funds.

Even if you'll do better with tax-frees, it may be foolhardy to insist on a money market fund holding only tax-free securities issued by your state. Single-state funds are less diversified and therefore slightly more risky. Also, while it is true that a single-state money market fund may let you skip both federal and state income taxes on dividends, a national tax-free fund may actually offer a higher yield. That's because, in some states with high income taxes, there may not be enough high-quality bonds to meet demand.

The Devil Is in the Details

Always compare yields before you invest. But don't chase yields by moving from fund to fund—the difference is generally so slight that it doesn't pay. In any case, yields are not the only consideration. Read the fund's prospectus to find out the following:

➤ What investment restrictions apply? Money funds are not allowed to have more than 5 percent of holdings in any single issue or to invest more than 5 percent of the fund's assets in commercial paper that is below top-grade. Most funds are even more conservative, so you may want to check out a particular fund's practices.

➤ What is the minimum initial investment? Most money funds require $1,000 to $2,500 to start, but other funds have lower and higher minimums.

➤ What is the average maturity of the fund's holdings? Money funds must keep the maximum average maturity of securities within the portfolio to 90 days, but most funds use shorter maturities. Shorter maturities reduce risk. Here's something else to remember: When interest rates are dropping, longer maturities preserve higher yields. When rates are rising, shorter maturities move up faster.

➤ What is the minimum amount for a check drawn on the fund? The most common minimum amount is $500, but if you can find a fund with no minimum—there are a few—you can dispense with a checking account and use the money fund to pay all your bills.

➤ What services can you expect? Will you receive an unlimited number of checks that you can use for redemptions? Can you request redemption of shares by telephone, to be wired to your bank account? Are there any restrictions on the number of times you can move money from fund to fund within a fund family?

➤ If you're using a money market mutual fund at a stockbrokerage firm, is there a "sweep" feature to automatically move interest and dividends on other investments into the interest-paying money market mutual fund? If so, how often is the transfer made? If your investments generate sizable interest and dividends, you'll want frequent transfers.

Costs Count

The single most important factor affecting money fund yield is expenses. Funds that keep costs down produce higher yields for shareholders. It's as simple as that.

Expenses include operating expenses and management fees, and are expressed as an *expense ratio*. The median expense ratio for taxable funds is currently about 0.70 percent. Stay away from money funds charging much more.

You should also try to stay away from funds charging so-called 12(b)1 fees, named after the regulation permitting them, that pass marketing expenses on to shareholders. With a 12(b)1 fee, existing shareholders pay the cost of the fund's expenditures to attract new shareholders.

In the highly competitive money market mutual fund marketplace, at least half of all funds are waiving all or part of their expenses at this writing in an effort to attract new shareholders. Be careful. Yields on these funds can be attractive, but fund management can end the waiver at any time. If you're not paying attention, you may not realize that expenses have gone up and yields have gone down.

Tax Talk

The **expense ratio** expresses fund operating expenses and management fees as a percentage of total investment. The amount is taken out of the fund's current income and therefore reduces yield.

The prospectus must spell out fund fees, and it must include a hypothetical example showing expenses over various time periods.

How to Invest in the Money Market

You can invest in a money market mutual fund just as you would invest in any mutual fund—by buying direct through a fund family or buying through a brokerage firm.

Which is right for you? It depends on what kind of investor you are. If you buy mutual funds and make your buying decisions on your own, go with a money market mutual fund in one of the fund families you use. If you invest through a stockbroker or financial planner, it will probably be most convenient to use a money fund offered through that firm.

You can also arrange for automatic investment in a money market mutual fund. Many employers will do direct deposit of your paycheck to the account or fund of your choice. Or, you can arrange automatic transfers of deposits from your bank account to your money market fund.

The Least You Need to Know

➤ Money market mutual funds are dedicated to paying the highest possible interest rate while preserving capital and making your money immediately available.

➤ Money market mutual funds generally offer higher yields than bank money market deposit accounts.

➤ For the highest after-tax returns, high-bracket taxpayers should choose a tax-free money market fund, while low-bracket taxpayers are often better off with a taxable money market fund.

➤ Funds charging higher-than-average expense ratios generally return lower yields.

Chapter 17

Muni Madness

In This Chapter

➤ Buying a bond means lending money and the issuer promises to pay you back

➤ Discovering that most bonds pay interest twice yearly and the principal on maturity

➤ Understanding the generally tax-free nature of municipal bonds

➤ Using ratings to measure bond safety

Are you getting ready to go seriously tax-free? As you've seen throughout this book, there are many ways to shelter your hard-earned dollars from income tax. But municipal bonds are truly the definition of tax-free.

If you buy a muni bond issued in your state, in most cases it will be free of both federal and state income tax. Every penny you earn will be yours to keep. Of course, you generally won't earn as many pennies as you would in a taxable investment, so you must look at your tax bracket to see whether taxable or tax-free investments will put you ahead in the tax game.

You may already invest in the stock market, but bonds are nothing like stocks. This chapter unwraps the mysteries of municipal bonds and lets you see where you fit in. Chapter 18, "Making the Most of Bonds," tells you how to maximize your use of bonds in your personal investment portfolio.

The Ins and Outs of Bonds

Bonds differ from stocks in many ways. When you buy shares of stock, you are becoming a part owner of the issuing corporation. You will share in the profits and losses sustained by the corporation. When you buy a bond, you are becoming a creditor of the issuer. As a creditor, if a corporation encounters financial difficulties, you are generally entitled to repayment before shareholders.

A bond is nothing more or less than an IOU. When you buy a bond, you are lending money to the issuing corporation or government entity. In return, the issuer promises to return your principal at the bond's *maturity date* and pay you interest along the way.

Bond maturities generally range from 1 to 30 years and are often grouped as follows:

➤ Short-term bonds have maturities of up to 4 years.

➤ Intermediate-term bonds have maturities of 5 to 12 years.

➤ Long-term bonds have maturities of 12 or more years.

Bonds can provide regular income—in fact, they're often called fixed-income securities. Bonds are also very safe; if you hold them to maturity, you will get your principal back. But bond prices do fluctuate. If you decide to sell bonds before maturity, you may get more or less than you paid for them.

The way in which periodic payments are made is also different for bonds than for stocks. Dividends are paid to the investors who own shares of common stock on the record date, even if those investors bought the shares just the day before. But interest is paid to investors in bonds only for the period of time that the bonds are actually owned. When you buy a bond, accrued interest is included in the purchase price so that the seller receives interest to the date of sale.

In another area, information about stock prices is readily available. Just look at the stock market tables in the newspaper. Information about specific bond issues is much harder to obtain. Because there are more than 20,000 municipal bond issuers, more than 50,000 municipal bonds issued each year, and more than 1.5 million individual municipal bonds outstanding, bond tables list only a representative sampling and information about specific local issues may be scarce.

Tax Talk

A bond's **maturity date** is the future date on which the principal will be repaid.

It may also be difficult to understand exactly what you are paying for a particular bond. Buying bonds—and understanding pricing—will be discussed in detail in Chapter 18.

But it's important to note right at the outset that bonds are very sensitive to two related economic factors: inflation fears and interest rates. Even though consumer prices have risen only modestly for several years, a hint that inflation is picking up momentum has an immediate negative impact on bond prices. An actual rise in interest rates also causes an immediate decline in bond prices. When the Federal Reserve Board raised key interest rates in 1999 in an effort to cool the super-charged economy and stave off inflation, bond prices tumbled.

Tax Treats

Why do prices of bonds fall when the federal government releases statistics showing a strong drop in unemployment or a major rise in housing starts? Such positive economic news is received warily by the bond community because strong growth can lead to infla-tion, which, in turn, often leads to higher interest rates and erodes the value of bonds. Investors with long memories recall 1994 fears of an inflationary spurt from 3 percent to 4 or 5 percent; the fear contributed to a 20 percent drop in the price of long-term bonds.

Bond Basics

Bonds are generally issued in units of $1,000, although you usually have to make a minimum purchase of at least $5,000. Unless you can afford to invest considerably more, however—to achieve diversification among several bond issues of different types and maturities—you might be better off buying bonds through a bond mutual fund, as described in Chapter 20, "Ganging Up with Mutual Funds."

When you buy an individual bond, the interest, expressed as a percentage of the principal amount, is usually fixed until maturity and is paid twice a year. As an ex-ample, a $1,000 bond yielding 7 percent will pay investors $70 a year in two semi-annual payments of $35. The interest payments used to be made when an investor clipped coupons attached to a bond and turned them in; today bonds don't come with coupons (although yield may still be expressed as a coupon), and interest pay-ments are mailed.

Tax-Free Specifics

Municipal bonds—the tax-free instruments we're focusing on here—are debt obliga-tions issued by states, cities, and counties to pay for public projects such as highways, hospitals, and schools.

Tax Tips

Don't put tax-free municipal bonds in tax-deferred investments such as an Individual Retirement Account or a variable annuity. There's no advantage to doing so because IRAs and annuities are already tax-deferred. And there's a big disadvantage because all the money you eventually take out of a traditional IRA or an annuity will be taxed as ordinary income.

Tax Tips

A $1,000 bond costs $1,000—except when it costs $900 or $1,100. Unless you buy a bond when it is first issued, you will probably pay more or less than face value. Such bonds are either "premium" or "discount" bonds, and receive special tax treatment. The year-end information return you receive from your broker for tax purposes will indicate taxable amounts, but you should consult a tax adviser.

Two main types of municipal bonds are general obligation bonds and revenue bonds:

➤ General obligation bonds are considered safest because they are backed by the full faith and credit—the taxing power—of the issuer. A state might issue general obligation bonds to build or upgrade sewage plants.

➤ Revenue bonds are a tad riskier—and generally pay a little more in interest to compensate for the risk—because they are backed only by revenues from the particular project. An example would be tolls from a highway or bridge project.

Most revenue bonds pay off. But every once in a while, there is a fiasco. Investors with long memories may recall the bonds issued by the Washington Public Power Supply System to build two nuclear power plants. Analysts called the bonds a good investment. But the power plants were never built, and the bonds went into default. Similar situations have occurred with some small municipal issues designed to finance nursing homes or manufacturing plants. The issuance of such "private-activity" bonds has been restricted by recent federal law; when these bonds are available, their interest may be taxable.

Understanding Yield

Here's rule number 1 when it comes to bonds:

> Interest rates and bond prices have an inverse relationship; they move in opposite directions. Bond prices rise when interest rates fall and decline when interest rates rise.

An example will illustrate why this occurs. Let's say that you purchase a new 10-year $1,000 bond paying 7 percent. Interest rates rise, and now an investor can buy a new $1,000 bond paying 8 percent. In order for your bond to yield 8 percent, its price drops to about $875. That's how much you would get if you sold your 7 percent bond in an 8 percent interest rate environment. It has become a discount bond.

Conversely, let's say that interest rates decline so that a new $1,000 bond pays only 6 percent. This makes your 7 percent bond more valuable, so its price rises to about $1,166. It has become a premium bond. Refer to Chapter 18 for a more detailed description of premium and discount bonds.

None of this matters if you hold bonds to maturity—and if you succeed in reinvesting each semiannual payment at the same interest rate. If you sell early, however, prevailing interest rates affect how much you can expect to receive.

These are some other things you need to know about yield on bonds:

➤ In evaluating bonds, look at both current yield and yield to maturity. Current yield is the interest income divided by the bond's current price. Yield to maturity is the amount you will earn if you hold the bond until it matures and reinvest each interest payment at the same interest rate. On a newly issued bond, held to maturity, the yield is fixed. On an older bond, bought at a premium or a discount, the yield will vary with the price.

➤ Typically, the longer the maturity of a bond, the higher the interest rate. But long-term bonds are riskier than shorter-term bonds. If interest rates rise by 1 percent, the price of a bond with a 2-year maturity would typically lose about 2 percent of its value, while the price of a 30-year bond would fall about 12 percent. You have more to gain—and to lose—by holding longer-term bonds. The following table shows the approximate impact on the price of a bond yielding 8 percent when interest rates rise or fall by 1 percent.

Maturity	Rates Fall by 1 Percent Prices Fall By:	Rates Rise by 1 Percent Prices Rise By:
1 year	+1.0%	–0.9%
5 years	+4.2%	–4.0%
10 years	+7.1%	–6.5%
20 years	+10.7%	–9.2%
30 years	+12.5%	–10.3%

➤ The safer the bond, the lower the yield you can expect. Ultra-safe U.S. Treasury obligations typically carry lower rates, while higher-risk revenue bonds offer higher yields to offset the risk.

➤ Some bonds are subject to call, or early redemption by their issuers. Bonds with call features may offer a higher return to compensate for the possibility that the bonds may be redeemed prior to maturity. If you buy a bond with a *call feature*, look at yield in terms of current yield, yield to maturity, and yield to call date. (Some bond analysts refer to the yield to call date as the "yield to worst" because it reflects what happens to your income when bonds are redeemed early.)

Tax Talk

A **call feature** is a provision permitting the issuer of a bond to pay it off early. The **total return** is the change in value of an investment over the entire time you own the investment, including reinvestment of all dividends and capital appreciation.

Tax Tips

Zero coupon bonds may sound exotic, but you know the concept from Uncle Sam's familiar EE-bonds (remember Chapter 7, "Uncle Sam's IOUs"). Here, too, you buy at a discount and receive the face value, including all the interest, when the bonds are redeemed at maturity.

➤ In the end, what really matters is not yield but *total return*. Total return consists of the interest payments you receive while holding the bond plus (or minus) the profit (or loss) you take when you sell (if you don't hold until maturity). It represents all the money you make by investing in this particular bond. Yield may be close to total return on a short-term bond but may be very different on a long-term bond. In a bond with a 20- or 30-year maturity, total return is affected by how much you can earn on reinvested interest payments. In turn, how much you can earn is affected by prevailing interest rates.

When Zero Is the Answer

Zero coupon bonds are a special breed. Ordinary bonds are issued at their face value, and investors receive interest payments twice a year. "Zeros" don't pay interest along the way. Instead, the bond is sold at a steep discount from its face value. The difference between the price you pay for the bond and the full face value that you receive at maturity is your interest, compounded over the life of the bond.

In an example provided by the Bond Market Association, you might pay approximately $6,757 for a 20-year municipal zero coupon bond with a face amount of $20,000. When the bond matures, you receive the full face value of $20,000, with $13,253 representing accumulated compound interest at a 5.5 percent rate of return.

Caution: The interest that you don't receive each year on a taxable zero coupon bond must still be reported as income on your annual income tax returns. This phantom income is not a problem if you buy corporate zeros in a tax-sheltered retirement account—and it's not a problem if you buy tax-free municipal zeros.

Tax-free zero coupon bonds can be a wise investment if you can buy and hold them until maturity. Although most zeros carry maturities ranging from 8 to 20 years, zeros are available with maturities from 1 to 40 years. But zeros are very volatile investments; their prices fluctuate dramatically, and you could lose a lot of money if you sell them early.

The best bet is to buy bonds with maturity dates pegged to when you will need the money. Let's say that your preschooler will be ready for college in 15 years; you could buy a zero that will mature just before the first tuition payment is due. Consider "stripped" Treasuries for maximum safety; strips are an investment created when a brokerage firm separates a Treasury bond into a series of certificates sold at a discount. Consider zero coupon municipal bonds if you can find highly rated general obligation bonds issued within your state.

Risk Isn't a Four-Letter Word

When you think of risk, you probably think of the likelihood of losing money on an investment because its price goes down. But when it comes to bonds, there are specific primary risk factors to consider.

Tax Traps

Municipal bonds are not always tax-free. They are not tax-free if you own bonds, either individually or as part of a mutual fund, that are not issued by the state in which you live. And they are not tax-free if you own private-activity municipal bonds and are subject to the federal Alternative Minimum Tax. See Chapter 22, "There's No Free Lunch," for more information.

Credit risk refers to the quality of the issuer and the possibility that the issuer may not be able to make required interest or principal payments. Treasury bonds are the safest because they are backed by the full faith and credit of the federal government. Most municipal bonds are very safe as well, although some municipal issuers have run into financial trouble.

Market risk refers to the possibility that interest rates in general will rise after you have purchased your bond. When interest rates rise, as we've seen, bond prices decline. There's no need to worry about market risk on bonds you will hold to maturity because you are guaranteed full return of principal. If you sell bonds early, however, you could receive less than you expect if interest rates have gone up since your purchase.

Reinvestment risk is the risk that you won't be able to reinvest your semiannual interest payments at a comparable interest rate. This risk also applies to the face value of the bond at maturity.

Although there are never any guarantees in the world of investing, credit risk and market risk can be reduced by buying only top-rated bonds.

Alphabet Soup

A bond is a bond is a bond—but not all bonds are created equal. Credit ratings issued by independent rating agencies help you assess the quality of a bond before you invest. More precisely, ratings evaluate the bond issuer's financial strength and its ability both to repay the principal at maturity and to make periodic interest payments over the life of the bond.

Credit rating agencies analyze the soundness of the bond issuer, its history of repayment, the economic outlook for the issuer, and the revenues backing the bond. Ratings then reflect each agency's best judgment as to the issuer's ability to meet interest payments and repay the principal.

Each agency has its own system, and the agencies may not agree on the rating of any one bond. In general, however, the ratings look like school report cards. The more "A's," the better the bond. The following table shows the bond ratings of three major credit rating agencies. Although each agency has eight or more grades it assigns to bonds, the top four grades are generally considered "investment grade," with the rest below investment grade or downright speculative. As an individual investor, you are generally best off with bonds in the top three categories.

These are bond ratings by two rating agencies:

	Moody's	Standard & Poor's
Investment grade	Aaa	AAA
	Aa	AA
	A	A
	Baa	BBB
Below investment grade	Ba	BB
	B	B
	Caa	CCC
	Ca	CC

Any bond with a rating below Ca or CC is typically either in default or in imminent danger of default.

What Ratings Mean

Note that a good rating does not guarantee that you will make money on your investment or even that you can get your principal back on demand. You can still lose money if you sell your bonds when interest rates have risen and bond values have consequently dropped. In fact, ratings don't provide much information about volatility and market performance. For more information, ask your broker for the rating agency's research report on the bond issuer. Reports back up the rating with reasons and often indicate whether the agency believes that the issuer's creditworthiness will improve or deteriorate.

Note, too, that you may check a bond's rating before you invest, but that rating can change over time. A bond can be downgraded at any time if the rating agency decides that the issuer is no longer as creditworthy. A rating can also be upgraded. In evaluating any bond issue, you may want to check not just the current rating, but also the rating history.

Safety First

U.S. Treasury securities always have the highest possible triple-A rating. So do insured bonds. Insurance is provided by several independent organizations. Approximately half of all municipal bonds carry insurance, although it's important to note that insurance ensures liquidity but does not guarantee the issuer's creditworthiness. If an issuer does run into financial trouble, the insurance guarantees that investors receive interest and principal payments without delay.

The cost of insurance can lower yields slightly, but the lower yield may be worth accepting if it helps you sleep soundly at night. As an example, the price and liquidity of uninsured bonds associated with Orange County, California, were hit hard when the county filed for bankruptcy in December 1994. But bonds insured by MBIA, one of the major insurance companies in the muni market, retained their triple-A rating and held their market value better than their uninsured counterparts.

A third way to achieve safety in municipal bond investing is to seek out *pre-refunded* bonds. These bonds are super-safe because the municipality has set aside an escrow fund, typically consisting of U.S. Treasuries, to back up the payment of interest and principal. Pre-refunded municipals are generally short-term bonds of 10 years or less, with yields close to those of similar triple-A bonds.

Another way to minimize risk—a way that applies across the board in all investments—is to diversify. Don't stick to municipal bonds issued in a single state, even for double or triple tax exemption, if that means exposing yourself to concentrated risk. Don't buy individual bonds at all unless you have at least $100,000 to invest—some advisers suggest

Tax Traps

Can you rely on ratings? Bond ratings are based on the agencies' best estimates of issuers' creditworthiness. But critics have complained that politics may sometimes play a role in the ratings of municipal bonds, as elected officials seek the most favorable rating possible.

Tax Talk

A **pre-refunded** bond is created when a municipality takes advantage of a decline in interest rates to refinance older bonds, but must wait until a designated future call date to actually retire the older bonds. Meanwhile, the proceeds of new bonds are used to buy Treasuries to back up the older bonds.

that $250,000 is even better—so that you can buy several bond issues at $25,000 apiece. If you have less to invest, you can achieve diversification and obtain professional management by buying municipal bonds through a mutual fund; see Chapter 20 for details.

The Least You Need to Know

➤ Bonds pay semiannual interest and return the principal amount at maturity.

➤ Owning municipal bonds can produce steady tax-free income.

➤ Zero coupon bonds, purchased at a discount, can provide money at a targeted maturity date.

➤ The safest tax-free bonds are short-term triple-A obligations.

➤ Bond prices fall when interest rates rise, and rise when interest rates drop.

➤ You are guaranteed return of principal if you hold bonds to maturity; selling early may produce a profit or a loss.

Chapter 18

Making the Most of Bonds

In This Chapter

➤ Learning that bonds have a place in your portfolio

➤ Buying bonds individually or through a mutual fund

➤ Tailoring the maturity dates of individual bonds to meet your needs

➤ Finding that transaction costs are often hidden

Now that we've introduced tax-free bonds and you've decided they belong in your portfolio, it's time for a closer look.

This chapter introduces asset allocation, a strategy for combining investment vehicles into a personal portfolio. It then describes the way bonds—specifically, tax-free bonds—may fit in your investment portfolio. It also explains the pros and cons of buying bonds individually against buying shares of bond mutual funds. You'll find out where and how to buy individual municipal bonds—and how hard it is to find out how much you're paying when you buy or sell.

A Place for Bonds

Bonds play a role in most diversified investment portfolios. Diversification simply means holding a variety of investment types as a way of minimizing risk. The theory is that because they react differently to economic stimuli, some investments do well when others do not. Holding a variety of investments can therefore level your exposure to risk.

But mindlessly buying one from column A and two from column B is not a good way to achieve diversification. *Asset allocation* is a more structured way of determining the mix of an investment portfolio. When you follow an asset allocation strategy, you determine an initial mix of investments designed to meet your objectives within your tolerance for risk, and then rebalance your portfolio periodically to keep the proportions of the original mix.

The asset allocation strategy is described in Chapter 10, "Building Your Nest Egg at Work," as it applies to investments in a 401(k) plan. As you develop your investment portfolio, however, you should view your entire portfolio—inside and outside your retirement plans—as a unified whole.

Allocating Your Assets

The simplest asset allocation model divides assets among stocks, bonds, and cash. More sophisticated models divide stocks among domestic and international, growth and value, large companies and small. Similarly, bonds might be divided among taxable and tax-free, short-term and long-term, domestic and international.

Whatever mix you initially choose, it should be reviewed periodically and should be adjusted in line with your current life stage and investment time horizon. Where a young single in a low tax bracket might be heavily invested in aggressive growth stock with a leavening of taxable corporate bonds for stability, a high-bracket individual nearing retirement might want a mixture of growth stocks and tax-free bonds.

Whatever mix you start out with also should be reviewed and rebalanced either at regular intervals (every year or two) or whenever one asset has clearly outdistanced another. Let's say that you started out with a mix of 55 percent in stocks and 35 percent in bonds, with the remainder in the cash equivalent of a money market mutual fund. Then the explosive growth of the stock market increased the value of your stocks so that they now make up 65 percent of your portfolio. Selling some of your winners and using the profits to bring the allocation back into balance helps to keep risk under control. It also sets the stage for a shift in investment performance, when today's winners stagnate or lose ground and today's losers become winners.

If you are interested in steady income and guaranteed return of principal at maturity, then bonds may have a place in your asset allocation. If you want tax-free income—and you are in a tax bracket where tax-free income is an advantage—then municipal bonds belong in your portfolio.

Taxable and Tax-Free

As a general rule of thumb, you can forget about tax-free bonds if you are in the lowest federal income tax bracket of 15 percent, and you should definitely consider them only if you are in either the 36 or the 39.6 percent federal tax brackets. In the middle—at 28 or 31 percent for federal taxes—you should calculate the after-tax yield on each investment to see which works best for you.

The following table gives the equivalent yields of taxable and tax-free bonds at various federal income tax brackets. As an example, someone in the 28 percent federal tax bracket would have to invest in a taxable bond yielding at least 8.3 percent in order to equal or exceed the 6.0 percent yield on a tax-free municipal bond. But the table shows only federal tax rates. Don't forget to include state income tax in your calculations; a California resident in the 33 percent federal tax bracket and an 8 percent state bracket has an effective tax bracket of 41 percent.

Tax-Exempt Yields and Their Taxable Equivalents

Tax-Exempt Yield	Taxable Equivalent Yield (%) at Federal Tax Rates				
	15%	28%	31%	36%	39.6%
3.0%	3.53	4.17	4.35	4.69	4.97
3.5%	4.12	4.86	5.07	5.47	5.79
4.0%	4.71	5.56	5.80	6.25	6.62
4.5%	5.29	6.25	6.52	7.03	7.45
5.0%	5.88	6.94	7.25	7.81	8.28
5.5%	6.47	7.64	7.97	8.59	9.11
6.0%	7.06	8.33	8.70	9.38	9.93
6.5%	7.65	9.03	9.42	10.16	10.76
7.0%	8.24	9.72	10.14	10.94	11.59

Here's another way to determine whether tax-free bonds make sense for you. To find equivalent yields of taxable and tax-free investments, divide the tax-free rate by the "reciprocal" of your tax bracket. (The reciprocal is the number you get by subtracting your tax bracket from 100.) For example, if a municipal bond is yielding 6 percent and you are in the 28 percent tax bracket, dividing 6 by 72 (the reciprocal of 28) shows that you would have to receive 8.3 percent in a taxable issue to be competitive. You can do the same thing in reverse—multiply a taxable yield by the reciprocal of your tax bracket—to get the tax-free equivalent. If you're not sure of your tax bracket (the incomes for each bracket change each year), ask your stockbroker for an equivalency table, like the one in the previous table, based on current tax rates.

To Pool or Not to Pool

Now that you've decided to buy municipal bonds, should you buy individual issues or shares of a mutual fund? There are advantages and disadvantages to each approach.

A mutual fund may be appropriate for you in these circumstances:

➤ You want professional management along with built-in diversification.

➤ You don't want to do your own research and purchase individual bonds.

➤ You are willing to pay annual management fees.

➤ You appreciate receiving monthly interest checks—or the opportunity to automatically reinvest the interest.

➤ You appreciate the flexibility of being able to sell at any time. While there's no guarantee that fund shares will be worth more when you sell than when you buy (or as much), you won't face the hefty costs that you'll face if you sell an individual bond before maturity.

The ins and outs of mutual fund investing are discussed in more detail in Chapter 20, "Ganging Up with Mutual Funds."

Buying Singletons

Mutual funds may deserve a place in your investment mix, but individual bonds may be appropriate for you instead of or in addition to mutual funds in these circumstances:

➤ You know that you will need the principal back at a specific date (and not before)—for making a college payment, as an example, or starting retirement on the right foot. You can't select a maturity date with a bond fund, only with individual bonds.

➤ You have a reliable financial adviser—or are willing to do some research and select individual bonds.

➤ You are willing to pay the trading costs associated with buying and selling individual bonds, costs that are higher for small investors.

➤ You have enough money to diversify a bond portfolio. It takes at least $50,000—some advisers suggest as much as $250,000—to minimize risk by purchasing several different bond issues.

Once you've decided to include tax-free municipals in your investment mix, the next decision concerns bond maturity.

Matching Maturities

As I've indicated, a major advantage associated with individual bonds is being able to match the bond's maturity to your need for cash. But this doesn't necessarily mean that someone who is retiring in 20 years should stick to 20-year bonds. Tying up money for 20 years carries substantial risk. If interest rates rise in the interim, the value of your bonds will fall.

Maturity is one measure of risk. *Duration,* a calculation of cash flow during the life of a bond, is another. Bond analysts use duration to measure bond price volatility. Higher duration means greater risk.

Long-term bonds are risk-free only when you hold them to maturity. But what if you have a sudden need for cash? If it's hard to project your financial needs five years down the road, how can you be certain about 20 years?

Buying a long-term bond, knowing that you will probably sell it early, is every bit as risky as taking a flyer on a speculative stock. This is true even though you may achieve higher yields by accepting longer maturities. Consider this: Investors were happy to accept 4 percent yields on long-term bonds in the 1960s. A decade later, when long-term bonds were paying 6 percent, investors who had bought 30-year bonds at 4 percent still had 20 years to go.

There's a better solution to achieve long-term financial objectives with bonds. It's called "laddering," which is discussed in the next section.

Building a Ladder

You've probably heard of a stock-buying strategy called *dollar cost averaging.* This entails putting a specific amount of money into stock purchases at regular intervals, thereby buying more shares when prices are low and fewer shares when prices are high so that you average the purchase cost over time.

You can adopt a similar strategy to reduce the reinvestment risk in owning bonds. To create a ladder of bonds, you buy a series of bonds designed to reach maturity at one-year intervals. For example, to build a 10-year ladder, you could buy 10 bonds with maturities ranging from 1 to 10 years. Every time one of the bonds matures, the resulting cash can be reinvested to stretch the cycle still further. Or, if you need the money, you'll have it available without having to sell bonds early and risk capital loss.

Tax Talk

Duration, a term used by bond analysts, can be as important as maturity. Duration is a more precise measure of risk because it considers periodic interest payments as well as the final return of principal. In most cases, a bond's duration is shorter than its scheduled maturity. This can be misleading with callable bonds—and does not apply at all with zero-coupon bonds, where both interest and principal are paid at maturity.

Tax Talk

Dollar cost averaging is the strategy of making regular fixed-dollar investments, buying more shares when prices are lower and fewer when prices are higher, thereby reducing the average cost of shares over time.

213

Tax Tips

Never buy a bond—or anything else—from a cold-calling stranger. You want solid reliable information before buying municipal bonds, and you need to deal with an individual and firm that you can trust.

Tax Tips

Watch out for call features on bonds you're using to construct a ladder. If any of your bonds can be called early, they will distort anticipated results from laddering.

In addition to achieving a constant cash flow and reducing the risk entailed with reinvesting the proceeds of all your bond holdings at one point in the interest-rate cycle, laddering also tends to average out the effect of price changes over time.

Something Old, Something New

To find the maturity dates you need, you may have to buy older bonds available on the secondary market.

New issues are preferable, when you can find them. They are less expensive to buy because fees are generally absorbed by the issuer. They are usually priced at or close to their face value, with identical prices and yields offered by all the brokers entitled to make the original offer.

The offering circular or prospectus on a new bond issue should include information about the issuer's creditworthiness, along with the repayment schedule and sources of funds for repayment. The prospectus is sometimes available only days before the bond offering, but your broker should be able to provide you with the information in advance.

But there may not be a new issue available that meets your needs. If one is announced, your brokerage firm may not be part of the underwriting group and may not have it available, or the issue may be snapped up by institutional investors before individuals have a chance. So, you may have to turn to the secondary market where older issues are bought and sold.

The pricing of older bonds is a lot more complicated. First, prices fluctuate with supply and demand, which, in turn, is tied to interest rates. Remember the inverse ratio of interest rates and bond prices. When interest rates drop after a bond is issued, its price will rise so that it sells at a premium. The reverse is also true: When interest rates rise, prices decline so that a bond will sell at a discount.

In an example provided by the Vanguard Group, a bond with a face value of $1,000 and a coupon rate of 8.25 percent might sell for $1,085 when prevailing interest rates are around 6.25 percent. This makes its current yield 7.6 percent (based on $82.50 in annual interest divided by the $1,085 current market value). But—and it's an important but—when the bond is redeemed at maturity, exactly $1,000 in face value is paid and the $85 premium paid for the bond is lost. The result: The bond has a yield to maturity of 6.25 percent—exactly what a bond yields if it is selling at its face value and an interest rate of 6.25 percent. The following table illustrates the pricing and yield of premium and discount bonds. Three bonds—each different, yet the same:

	Premium Bond	Par Bond	Discount Bond
Coupon rate (%)	8.25	6.25	5.25
Face value ($)	1,000	1,000	1,000
Current value ($)	1,085	1,000	958
Annual interest ($)	82.50	62.50	52.50
Current yield (%)	7.60	6.25	5.48
Yield to maturity (%)	6.25	6.25	6.25

Source: The Vanguard Group

Price Points

Buying older bonds is tricky. Despite recent steps by the Securities and Exchange Commission to clarify pricing, it's still extremely difficult for individual investors to find prices and to understand the costs involved in bond transactions.

Let's look again at the differences between stocks and bonds. Trading information on every one of the approximately 9,000 stocks listed on the major exchanges is available every day in newspaper stock tables. The same is not true of bonds—at least in part because it might take 90 pages or more to list every one of the 1.5 million individual municipal bonds. And that's just municipals, not to mention corporate bonds.

The stock market is an organized exchange. Trades are reported every day, and the cost of trading is clear. The bond market has been likened to a bazaar, in which traders first buy bonds and then resell them to institutional and retail customers at prices set by the traders. Large institutional customers have clout and can often negotiate lower prices. Retail customers—that means you—are often at the mercy of the traders. In some cases, this means paying what the market will bear. And you, as the buyer, won't even know.

On a stock transaction, the commission paid to the broker is clearly stated on the confirmation slip. On a bond transaction, costs are hidden, buried in the price and yield shown on the confirmation slip. Bond confirmation slips may actually have a "0" in the space for commission, leading unwary investors to believe that there is no transaction cost. Nothing could be further from the truth.

The cost of buying bonds is expressed as a *markup,* the difference between what the broker pays for the bond and the higher price charged to you as a customer. The markup (or markdown, on a sale) on any specific transaction is a well-kept secret. The Municipal Securities Rulemaking Board requires that dealers "must buy and sell a

Tax Talk

The **markup** is the dealer's profit on a bond transaction. The markup is often higher on long-term bonds, where spreads between buying and selling prices are larger. Some dealers may push long-term bonds because they will make more money on the transaction. Determine your desired maturity before you go shopping for bonds, and don't be talked into an investment that isn't right.

municipal security at a fair and reasonable price." The National Association of Securities Dealers requires that markups be "fair." But neither regulatory agency sets actual dollar or percentage limits on markups, and these can range from less than 1 percent to more than 3 percent. Unscrupulous dealers have charged much more. The real problem is that you'll probably never know the markup when you buy or sell bonds.

The pricing problem is compounded by the scarcity of specific issues of municipal bonds. Bond dealers buy up bonds and keep a supply in their inventory. You may be urged to buy a bond from the inventory. Doing so will keep your costs down, but you have to be sure that the bond suits your needs. If your broker must go outside the firm inventory to find bonds for you from another firm, the markup will have to cover price differentials for both firms.

You can try to comparison-shop by checking on the price of a specific bond at different dealers. This can be frustrating, however, because municipal bonds are so thinly traded that a specific issue is often not widely available.

In any case, you should be aware that there can be significant differences between how much you must pay for a bond and what you would get if you were selling the exact same bond. Before you buy, ask the dealer the current difference between the "ask price" (how much you'll pay) and the "bid price" (how much the broker will pay to buy it back). If you plan to hold the bond to maturity, the selling price won't matter—but you never know.

So, what did the SEC do to clarify pricing? Not as much as many investors would like. After several years of consideration, the SEC decided to watch disclosure developments in the municipal market. Two developments to date are these:

➤ Bond issuers must now release annual financial reports to update the information accompanying new bond issues. The information is available at central data banks. Individual investors probably won't have direct access to the reports, but analysts believe that their availability may make prices in the secondary market more realistic.

➤ Trading data is now available for any bond that trades four or more times on the previous trading day. This is a big advance over the previous situation, where there was no compilation of trading data. But it doesn't mean much in the thinly traded municipal market where very few issues trade with any frequency.

Where and How to Buy

Buying municipal bonds is much more difficult than buying stocks or corporate bonds. Although a great many municipal bonds are issued each year, it can be hard to locate a particular issue.

When you're in the market for bonds, the first step is establishing a relationship with a reputable bond dealer. You can work with a stockbrokerage firm, although you should ask for a bond specialist, or you can work directly with a firm that specializes in bonds. The point is that few financial representatives can be truly knowledgeable about both stocks and bonds. You want to work with someone who knows bonds, knows your needs, and will work with you to find the right bond issues for your portfolio.

Don't set your heart on a specific issue. Instead, tell the bond dealer what you're looking for in the way of yield, tax status, and maturity date. The dealer should be able to offer several options. Be prepared to act quickly if a new issue becomes available; new munis sell out quickly, and you won't have much time to consider the offer.

Tax Traps

The federal government has won its case against several Wall Street firms accused of "yield burning," or reaping profits by inflating municipal bond prices and forcing down yields. The multiyear crackdown was expected to produce about $150 million in settlements. But be careful. Where firms have not settled, the Internal Revenue Service may revoke the tax-free status of the bonds—and subject the bond owners to back taxes and interest.

Tax Treats

Mysterious pricing in the bond market may give way to open trading on the Internet within the next few years. Tentative steps have already been taken, although, so far, most apply only to institutional investors. The city of Pittsburgh conducted a successful sale of general obligation bonds at a site called MuniAuction. The Bond Market Association's Web site, www.investinginbonds.com, provides valuable information on the bond market and reports transactions of actively traded munis—although the reports cover about 1,000 issues out of 1.4 million outstanding. Another site, www.bondsonline.com, offers pricing information on bonds. Some Wall Street firms also are beginning to offer at least some municipal bonds online.

Reading the Tables

Although few of the approximately 1.5 million individual municipal bonds outstanding are traded each day—most investors buy and hold to maturity—and even fewer are listed in newspaper tables, representative prices can provide a benchmark for evaluation.

In an example provided by the Bond Market Association, a newspaper listing might look like this:

Issue	Coupon	Maturity	Price	Yield to Maturity
Nebraska Public Power District	5.00	1-1-28	97	5.20

This municipal bond issue has an interest (coupon) rate of 5 percent and matures on January 1, 2028. The most recent price is $97; because prevailing interest rates are higher than 5 percent on similar tax-free bonds, the buyer can pay less than face value and will earn 5.2 percent as a yield to maturity.

What to Look For

Here's a handy checklist for evaluating tax-free bonds. Before you buy, look at the following:

➤ Credit quality, as measured by the rating assigned by Standard & Poor's or Moody's. Triple-A bonds, as discussed in Chapter 17, "Muni Madness," are generally the safest bet.

➤ Yield to maturity and—don't forget—yield to call. Many municipal bonds can be called early, although there may be call protection for the first 10 years. After that, the bonds can be redeemed by the issuer; this usually happens only if interest rates have dropped so that new bonds can be issued at lower cost. If your bonds are called, you will have to reinvest your money at the lower prevailing rates; to compensate for this possibility, callable munis usually yield slightly more than their noncallable cousins.

➤ Liquidity, a measure of how easy it will be to sell your bond before maturity. Local issues, while desirable because of their tax-free nature, may be difficult and costly to sell.

What to Do When Things Go Wrong

If you have a dispute with a bond dealer about the purchase of municipal bonds, first try to resolve it with the dealer or firm management. If the dispute is not resolved, put the details of your complaint in writing and try these avenues of complaint:

➤ The National Association of Securities Dealers, 1735 K Street NW, Washington, D.C. 20006. Write to NASD, Attn: Surveillance Department, to file a complaint about unfair or illegal practices. Write NASD, Attn: Dispute Resolution, for information about arbitration.

➤ The Securities and Exchange Commission, 450 Fifth Street NW, Washington, D.C. 20549.

When It's Time to Sell

One of the big advantages of buying individual bonds, as we've noted earlier, is that you can buy bonds with maturity dates pegged to when you'll need the money, and then hold them until they mature.

But that doesn't mean that you should blindly hold on to bonds indefinitely. You may find that your financial situation changes and you need the money. Try to avoid a forced sale of bonds, if possible—perhaps by laddering maturities—because selling older bonds can be expensive. Transaction costs and the market spread can seriously diminish your return.

Sometimes, even if you don't need the money, it makes sense to sell. For example, there's a tax benefit to selling a bond that has declined in value and putting the money into another similar, but not identical, bond. The technique is called "swapping," and it's just that: You swap one bond for another, taking a loss on the bond that has dropped in price. You can then turn the loss to good use by letting it offset gains on other investments, thereby reducing your federal income tax obligation.

Swaps don't always work, but 1999 was a good example of a year when swaps were frequently a spectacular success. Interest rates were rising late in the year, so bond prices declined. At the same time, the bull market in stocks had given many investors large taxable gains. Moving the loss on bonds from paper to actual could provide a means of reducing the tax bite on the stock side.

In an example provided by the brokerage firm of Tucker Anthony, suppose that you owned a bond issued by the Long Island Power Authority in October 1998, with a maturity date of 2015, a price of $97.47, and a yield of 4.85 percent. By late 1999, the bond was selling at $90.44 and was yielding 5.55 percent. If you had purchased $50,000 in face value of these bonds, you would have a paper loss of $3,500.

Tax Tips

Watch out for what the Internal Revenue Service calls the "wash-sale" rules. A swap is deemed a wash sale if you buy essentially identical securities within 30 days before or after the sale. If to claim a tax loss you swap one bond for a virtually identical bond, the loss will be disallowed. But the loss will be added to the cost of the new bond, raising its cost basis for tax purposes.

You could leave it alone and continue holding the bonds until maturity, when the full principal would be paid. Or, you could sell the bonds, applying the loss against any capital gains for the year. If you have no gains, the loss can be applied to offset up to $3,000 of ordinary income, with the rest carried over to future years. Tax law dealing with investments is discussed in more detail in Chapter 22, "There's No Free Lunch."

The key to a swapping strategy, however, is that you then buy replacement bonds to maintain your original investment objectives. The new bonds should be similar but not identical to the original bonds. Buying back the originals would result in your loss being nondeductible. Switching to a similar bond from another issuer, or even to a bond from the same issuer with different interest rates and maturity dates, is okay—and may even permit you to upgrade quality or increase income.

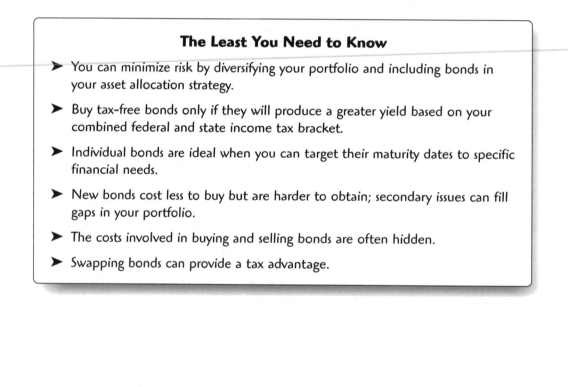

The Least You Need to Know

➤ You can minimize risk by diversifying your portfolio and including bonds in your asset allocation strategy.

➤ Buy tax-free bonds only if they will produce a greater yield based on your combined federal and state income tax bracket.

➤ Individual bonds are ideal when you can target their maturity dates to specific financial needs.

➤ New bonds cost less to buy but are harder to obtain; secondary issues can fill gaps in your portfolio.

➤ The costs involved in buying and selling bonds are often hidden.

➤ Swapping bonds can provide a tax advantage.

Uncle Sam Treasures You

If you want safe and sure income along with some tax benefits, consider lending money to Uncle Sam either directly through Treasury issues or indirectly through various agency obligations. Both can be purchased individually or through mutual funds.

This chapter describes the various Treasury obligations, including the new kid on the block in the form of inflation-indexed Treasuries, and helps you decide which is right for you.

The Treasury Market

The U.S. Treasury raises money to finance government operations by selling bills, notes, and bonds. Like corporate and municipal bonds, these securities are debt obligations promising to pay periodic interest and the full principal at maturity. All these IOUs are backed by the full faith and credit of the U.S. government. All are exempt from state and local income taxes, but not from federal income taxes.

The state and local tax exemption can be worthwhile if you live in a high-tax state. Let's say that you face a state income tax of 8 percent. A $10,000 bond at 6 percent would pay $600 a year; at an 8 percent state income tax, a taxpayer would lose $48 to taxes. If you file an itemized federal income tax return, you can claim a deduction for the state tax. This would save about $17 at a 36 percent tax rate, for a net loss to taxes of $31.

Treasuries have a tax advantage over corporate bonds and, in most cases, a safety advantage as well. Municipal bonds issued by your state are typically not subject to any income tax. But many investors prefer the safety of Treasury obligations backed by Uncle Sam. The following table shows recent comparative yields of corporate, Treasury, and municipal bonds.

In mid-January 2000, financial newspapers reported these comparative yields:

AA-rated utility bonds	7.76 percent (fully taxable)
Long-term Treasuries	7.58 percent (no state tax)
Municipal bonds	6.04 percent (may be fully tax-free)

Like other debt obligations, Treasuries are sensitive to interest rates. In early January 2000, as an example, Treasury prices declined sharply under renewed inflation concerns. As I pointed out in Chapter 17, "Muni Madness," bond prices and yields have an inverse relationship. When prices decline, yields increase. When the prices of Treasuries drop and yields rise, there's a trickle-down effect that pushes up interest rates on consumer debt in general, including mortgages, credit cards, and auto loans.

More serious pressure on the Treasury market may result from successful efforts to curb the federal deficit. In the face of budget surpluses, the government doesn't need to borrow as much money. So, the Treasury Department is issuing less debt and has announced that it will be buying back some outstanding bonds.

Meanwhile, investors worldwide—both individuals and institutions, including the central banks of other countries—continue to invest in U.S. Treasuries. At the end of 1999, even as some foreign investors shifted to stocks and to riskier bonds with higher yields, 40 percent of outstanding government securities were in the hands of overseas investors. Five years earlier, the figure was 20 percent.

Two "B's" and an "N"

Treasury bills, notes, and bonds are sold periodically throughout the year. All are "marketable securities" because they may be purchased when originally issued and then in the secondary market at prevailing market prices. (EE-bonds, also Treasury obligations, are not marketable. There is no secondary market for older bonds, and only new EE-bonds are available.)

Unlike most municipal bonds, most Treasury issues cannot be called before maturity. An exception is certain long-term bonds issued before 1985.

The primary difference among bills, notes, and bonds is maturity. Until recently, there were varying purchase price minimum amounts as well, but all three are now issued with a minimum price of $1,000. This drop in price—it used to take $10,000 to buy a bill, and $5,000 to buy two-year or three-year notes—makes Treasuries accessible to small investors. It means that you can buy Treasuries directly, at no cost (as described later in this chapter, in the section called "Getting on Board"), instead of through a mutual fund.

Tax Tips

Because the interest is subject to federal income tax in the year the bills mature, investors can use T-bills to bounce taxes into the next calendar year. If you buy a 6-month T-bill in July, for example, it will mature in January. Income tax on the interest will be due fully 15 months later, when you file your federal income tax return for the previous year.

Treasury bills (T-bills) are issued in 3-month, 6-month, and 12-month maturities. Unlike notes and bonds, T-bills are sold at a discount, with the interest deducted in advance from the purchase price. This means that the actual yield is higher than the stated yield. As an example, a $1,000 T-bill might sell for $950; the $50 difference is the profit. But because you didn't have to wait for the $50 until the bond's maturity, the actual yield is not 5 percent, but 5.3 percent.

Treasury notes are issued with maturity periods of 2 to 10 years. Interest is payable twice a year.

Treasury bonds are long-term obligations, issued with a term of more than 10 years and as much as 30 years. Interest is payable twice a year.

Treasuries are safe—if you hold to maturity, you will receive the full principal amount. Still, it is possible to lose money on an investment in government bonds if you sell before maturity. The longer the maturity, the greater the volatility. The following table shows the impact of a 1 percent rise in interest rates.

Here's how the value of a $10,000 investment shifts when interest rates move by 1 percent. Values increase when interest rates drop, and decline when interest rates rise.

3-month Treasury bill	$25
1-year Treasury bill	$100
5-year Treasury note	$400
10-year Treasury note	$650
30-year Treasury bond	$1,000
30-year zero-coupon bond	$3,000

Coming Attractions

Because we are erasing the federal deficit and actually moving toward surpluses—a good move, most observers agree—the federal government doesn't need to borrow as much money to fund its operations. As a result, two major steps are underway with some important implications for investors and for capital markets.

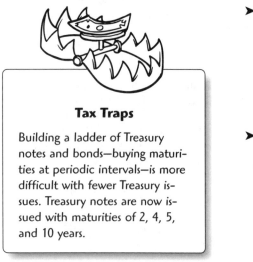

Tax Traps

Building a ladder of Treasury notes and bonds—buying maturities at periodic intervals—is more difficult with fewer Treasury issues. Treasury notes are now issued with maturities of 2, 4, 5, and 10 years.

➤ Fewer new Treasuries will be sold. There have been no seven-year notes since 1993 and no three-year notes since 1998. Also in 1998, the sale of five-year notes was curtailed, shifting from monthly to quarterly auctions. Since 1999, new bonds are being sold only twice a year instead of three times.

➤ Treasury notes and bonds are being retired faster than new ones are being created, and the Treasury has begun buying back outstanding bonds—a move last taken in the early 1970s. Starting in mid-2000, up to $30 billion of outstanding longer-term Treasuries are being bought back from bond dealers. A major result is heightened yields on the issues of federal agencies, discussed later in this chapter.

Inflation-Indexed Treasuries

Since 1997, in addition to regularly issuing bills, notes, and bonds, the Treasury has issued what some observers have called "the ultimate worry-free investment," inflation-indexed securities. (Other government agencies and corporations have jumped on the inflation-adjusted bond bandwagon as well.) Inflation-indexed Treasuries are currently available in 5-year, 10-year, and 30-year maturities.

Inflation has been low in recent years, and investor interest in inflation-indexed notes has been low as well, but they may suit the needs of conservative investors. Here's how they work:

The minimum purchase amount, as with other Treasury issues, is $1,000. The principal is adjusted every six months by the amount of increase in the Consumer Price Index, with any additional amounts paid to investors at maturity. A 3 percent increase in the CPI boosts a $1,000 bond's value to $1,030. Best of all, you can't lose money. If the principal amount has decreased before maturity, the government will make up the difference to keep you whole.

Interest payments are made every six months, based on a predetermined fixed rate applied to a principal that changes with inflation. For example, the interest rate on the 10-year bond maturing January 15, 2010, is 4¼ percent. As the principal goes up, so do the semiannual interest payments. The interest payments are determined by multiplying the inflation-adjusted principal amount by half the stated rate of interest on each interest payment date. Interest payments are automatically deposited into your bank account.

Inflation-indexed securities are clearly a good bet if inflation tops 3 percent—and some economists peg the break-even point at just over 2 percent. In any case, if high inflation returns, these bonds should pay a higher real return than other bonds. If inflation stays low, returns will generally be lower, but you've bought peace of mind.

On the downside, you owe federal income tax on the semiannual inflation adjustment even though you don't receive it in cash. For this reason, as with other investments where you are taxed on phantom income, you may want to own inflation-indexed notes in a tax-sheltered account.

Getting on Board

It's easy to buy Treasury securities. New issues may be purchased directly from the Federal Reserve Bank, at no transaction cost, or through a bank or stockbroker at a nominal fee. Either way, there are no more engraved certificates to safeguard; Treasuries are issued in "book-entry" form with electronic record keeping. You receive a confirmation of your initial purchase, plus periodic statements showing interest credited and amounts reinvested.

As noted previously, however, new issues have limited maturity dates. If you want a Treasury with a specific maturity not available in a new issue, you can turn to the secondary market and buy an earlier issue through a bank or stockbroker. This transaction will be more expensive.

When you buy a Treasury, the key information you need is the interest rate (the bond's "coupon rate"), maturity date, recent price, and current yield. Don't confuse the coupon rate with the current yield. They may occasionally—and coincidentally—be the same, but the coupon rate is fixed at issue, while the current yield is a function of the current price. The current yield reflects both the coupon rate and the capital gain or loss associated with buying the security at a price either above or below its face value.

The following table shows how to glean this information from newspaper listings:

Rate	Maturity	Bid	Ask	Change	Yield
7¾%	Feb. 01	105:12	105:14		5.50
5⅜%	Feb. 01	99:26	99.27		5.44

©1998, The Bond Market Association, investinginbonds.com
The referenced materials and data provided by The Bond Market Association are intended for general information purposes only and are not intended to provide specific investing, tax, business, or legal advice to any individual or entity. The Bond Market Association does not guarantee the accuracy of this information.

The first listing shows a Treasury paying 7¾ percent interest that is due to mature in February 2001. Prices in the Bid and Ask columns are percentages of the bond's face value of $1,000. (Just to confuse us, the numbers after the colons represent 32nds of a dollar; ¹²⁄₃₂nds equals $0.375.) A bid of 105:12 means that a buyer was willing to pay $1053.75, compared to the seller's lowest asking price of 105:14, or $1054.38, a difference of 63 cents per thousand. The bid and ask prices indicate that an investor who bought this bond when it was first issued can make a profit of more than 5 percent by selling it now. The higher interest rate on this older note is offset by the premium in its price, bringing the yield to maturity to 5.50 percent.

The next bond pays a lower interest rate of 5⅜ percent, but it is selling at a discount of $998.44 against its par price of $1,000. Because the security is selling at a discount, its yield to maturity exceeds the coupon rate.

Treasury Direct

The absolutely best way to buy Treasury securities is through Treasury Direct. It's a no fuss, no muss, no cost approach to investing in Treasuries. Once you set up an account, you can buy Treasuries and reinvest the proceeds when they come due.

There is never a cost of any kind to buy. The only time a fee is levied by Treasury Direct is when you have securities worth a total of more than $100,000 in your account; then you will pay a fee of $25 a year. An annual notice is sent, and payment is due each June. Late payments are charged interest and an administrative fee; payments that are really late—more than 120 days—are charged a 6 percent penalty as well.

You can set up a Treasury Direct account by filling out a New Account Request; you can obtain the form online at www.publicdebt.treas.gov or through any Federal Reserve Bank. Once your account is open, you can buy Treasury obligations either online or by calling toll free 1-800-943-6864 between 8 A.M. and 8 P.M. EST, Monday through Friday. You can reinvest the proceeds of maturing securities via the same means, 24 hours a day.

For a free copy of the "Treasury Director Investor Kit," write to the Bureau of the Public Debt, 200 Third St., Parkersburg, WV 26106.

Treasury Direct is meant for investors who want to buy and hold securities until they mature. That's why, until recently, you could not sell securities through the program. Now you can, through Sell Direct, at a charge of $34. Alternatively, you can transfer the securities you wish to sell to a bank or broker and pay a (typically higher) fee to sell through their offices.

To buy a Treasury obligation, you submit a form (called a tender). You no longer have to watch for the schedule of new issues or worry about when to send a check; Treasury Direct will debit your bank account when you buy securities. Once you have a Treasury Direct account, you will be notified when an issue is reaching maturity, and you will have the option of automatic reinvestment.

Banks, Brokers, and Mutual Funds

You can also buy individual Treasury issues through many financial institutions, including commercial banks and stockbrokerage firms. And, if you prefer, you can invest in Treasuries through mutual funds.

Don't expect financial institutions to promote Treasuries. Although they charge a fee for transactions on new issues, it is much less than the typical bond markup or stock commission. Markups on older issues bought in the secondary market will be more substantial. If you maintain a relationship with a broker, however, you may prefer to buy Treasuries as part of your overall account. You should certainly buy Treasuries through a broker if you plan to trade frequently rather than keep securities until they mature.

Although there are dozens of "U.S. Government income funds" listed in the mutual fund directory published by the Investment Company Institute, you really don't need to buy Treasuries through a mutual fund. For one thing, you don't need the diversification. Every Treasury issue is backed by the full faith and credit of the U.S. government and is the safest possible investment. For another, you don't need to pay annual management fees. Even nominal fees reduce your yield, and you can buy Treasuries at absolutely no cost through Treasury Direct.

Treasury STRIPs

Since 1985, investors have been able to hold and trade the individual interest and principal pieces of Treasury securities. STRIPs—the acronym stands for Separate Trading of Registered Interest and Principal of Securities—are not sold directly by the Treasury but are available through banks and brokers. Once purchased, however, a STRIP is a direct obligation of the federal government. As such, it has no risk of default.

When a Treasury is stripped, each piece becomes a separate security with its own identifying number and maturity date. For example, a 10-year Treasury note becomes 21 pieces consisting of a single principal payment at maturity and 20 semiannual interest payments. The individual pieces are usually bundled with comparable stripped pieces of other Treasuries to create a single security with the same maturity date.

The minimum unit that can be purchased is $1,000, with markups typically ranging from less than 1 percent to more than 2 percent, depending on the length of the maturity and the amount of purchase.

Each security has a fixed maturity date that coincides with each of the original interest payment dates, making STRIPs ideal when money will be needed at a specified date in the future. Some state lotteries actually invest the present value of large lottery prizes in STRIPs to be sure that funds are available when needed to meet annual payment obligations to lottery winners.

Because the only payment is made at maturity, STRIPs made up of principal amounts are a form of zero-coupon security. Like other zeros (see Chapter 17, "Muni Madness"), their prices fluctuate more than coupon bonds. If you sell before maturity, you could lose money.

Tax Traps

All strips are not STRIPs. If you buy stripped Treasuries called CATS or TIGRS, you have a different animal. These securities are issued by brokerage firms and are not direct obligations of the federal government.

STRIPs sell at a discount because there are no periodic interest payments. Like other zeroes, the interest earned on STRIPs must be reported as income for federal income tax purposes in the year in which it is earned. As STRIPs approach maturity, compounding produces larger amounts of taxable interest income.

In other words, you must pay income tax on phantom income, income you won't receive until a later date. One way around this is to purchase STRIPs in tax-sheltered retirement plans such as IRAs and 401(k) plans, where no tax is currently due. In these accounts, the difference between the purchase price and the face value is taxable as ordinary income when distributions are made from the account.

The Smart Exchange

Do you have older Treasury securities tucked away in a bank vault, in the form of engraved certificates? If so, you may want to take advantage of what the Treasury calls the Smart Exchange, and trade your certificates for a new book-entry account.

Instead of certificates you have to safeguard, you can choose among safekeeping at the U.S. Treasury or a financial institution such as a bank or brokerage firm. Interest and maturity payments will be automatically credited to the account you select. You won't need to go to a financial institution or a Federal Reserve Bank to cash checks, clip coupons, or redeem matured certificates. You'll have a single master account for all your Treasury holdings, will receive periodic statements of account, and can easily reinvest proceeds when securities mature.

Want more reasons to switch to book-entry? As Uncle Sam puts it, here are six more:

➤ Paper securities cannot be automatically reinvested.

➤ Owners of paper securities cannot receive payments by direct deposit.

➤ Owners of paper securities do not receive regularly scheduled account statements.

➤ Paper securities cannot be traded as fast or efficiently as book-entry securities.

➤ Some financial institutions refuse to accept paper securities unless the owner indemnifies them against loss or theft.

➤ After 2016, U.S. Treasury marketable securities in paper form will no longer exist.

To make an exchange, you first must open a Treasury Direct account. Complete instructions, for opening an account and then delivering your securities, are available online at www.publicdebt.treas.gov/sec/secsestep.htm.

Uncle's Nephews and Nieces

Securities issued by the U.S. Treasury are the safest of the safe. But a wide range of other government agencies also issue notes and bonds to finance their own projects.

Because these securities are not backed by the full faith and credit of the government, their yields are often a bit higher than those on comparable Treasuries. Because the Treasury is cutting back on new offerings, too, these agency offerings are becoming more attractive to investors. Indeed, they are taking on added significance. Fannie Mae, the Federal National Mortgage Association, recently announced its commitment to new offerings that some analysts see as becoming a new fixed-income indicator.

Some of the other agencies raising funds via public offerings include the Farm Credit Bank and the Federal Home Loan Bank. These obligations cannot be purchased directly from the issuing agency; you must buy them from a commercial bank or stockbrokerage and pay a transaction fee. (The Federal Home Loan Banks announced a plan, early in 2000, to auction some notes over the Internet. Watch for further developments along these lines.)

You do not receive a certificate when you invest in agency obligations—instead, there is a computer record of the "book-entry" transaction—but you do receive regular interest payments. The interest is subject to federal income tax and, in some cases, unlike Treasuries, to state and local income tax as well.

If you are interested in agency bonds, check into these considerations:

➤ Ask what markup you will pay to buy. Brokers don't like to disclose the markup, and it can be substantial.

➤ Find out whether the bond is callable. Many are, and while the yield may be higher, make sure that it's high enough to compensate for the risk of early redemption.

➤ Buy if you are reasonably sure that you can hold to maturity. Otherwise, transaction costs will eat up your return.

➤ Find out whether interest will be subject to state income tax. Interest on bonds issued by Fannie Mae and Freddie Mac (the Federal Home Loan Mortgage Corp.) is taxable on the state level. Interest on bonds issued by Sallie Mae (the Student Loan Marketing Association) is not.

Ginnie Maes, obligations issued by the Government National Mortgage Association, are another animal entirely. These are backed by the full faith and credit of the federal government, but they are not bonds with semiannual interest payments and the return of principal at maturity. Instead, they are a pool of mortgage pass throughs. As such, they pay interest and a partial return of principal every month. The interest is taxable (on both federal and state returns); the return of principal is not. You'll get a statement each month showing how much is taxable interest income and how much is nontaxable return of principal.

The minimum purchase price of a new Ginnie Mae is $25,000, but existing certificates may be purchased at sizable discounts. For small investors, the best bet is to buy shares in a Ginnie Mae mutual fund.

Although mortgages typically run 30 years, the average life of a new Ginnie Mae pool is projected to be 12 years. Mortgages are prepaid as individual homeowners move or refinance. Prepayments are accelerated when mortgage rates drop, and homeowners can refinance their mortgages at lower rates. This makes Ginnie Mae income unpredictable; you'll get monthly checks, but the amounts will vary. In addition, because each check includes a partial return of principal, you won't have a lump sum to reinvest at the end.

The Least You Need to Know

➤ Buy Treasuries for safe returns free from state and local income tax.

➤ Treasury bills, with maturities of up to one year, are sold at a discount.

➤ Treasury notes and bonds, with maturities of up to 30 years, pay interest semi-annually.

➤ Inflation-indexed Treasuries let you keep ahead of inflation because the principal increases with rises in the Consumer Price Index.

➤ If you buy Treasuries directly through Treasury Direct, at no cost, you'll earn higher yields than with the least expensive U.S. Treasury mutual fund.

➤ Agency obligations offer slightly higher yields to compensate for the slightly higher risk.

Chapter 20

Ganging Up with Mutual Funds

Mutual funds are enormously popular—and for good reason. Funds offer a way to achieve diversification and professional management while investing relatively small amounts of money.

But there are now more mutual funds than individual securities, so choosing a fund isn't easy. This chapter describes mutual fund options, helps you weigh the costs of investing, and tells you how to get started.

Joining the Crowd

One big advantage of buying individual bonds, as I point out in Chapter 18, "Making the Most of Bonds," is that you can peg the maturity dates to when you will need the money. You can't do that with mutual funds because funds don't mature. Instead, bond funds hold a large number of individual issues with different maturity dates, buying and selling these bonds to achieve the greatest possible return consistent with the fund's objective. Bond funds may be designated as short-term, intermediate-term, or long-term, but the fund as a whole has no maturity date.

The second major plus factor in owning individual bonds is that you can control the tax consequences by deciding when to sell. You can choose between short-term and long-term gains or, if you hold on, incur no taxable gains at all. With a mutual fund, as described in Chapter 22, "There's No Free Lunch," you'll pay taxes on capital gains distributions each and every year even if you hold on to your own shares.

But it takes a lot of money—some advisers say at least $50,000, others at least $200,000—to adequately diversify a portfolio of individual bonds. It also takes a willingness to educate yourself, to seek out the right bonds from among the many offered, and to pay what can be hefty markups. For most investors, therefore, mutual funds have a decided advantage.

With mutual funds, you can get started with very little money. Although some funds are raising their minimum investment requirements, at the end of 1998 more than 60 percent of all funds required $1,000 or less to get started. Nine percent had no minimum amount at all. Even those with sizable minimums often reduce those minimums dramatically if you sign up for automatic investment either by payroll deduction or regular transfers from your checking account. The following table shows the percentage of mutual funds requiring various minimum investment amounts for a lump sum initial investment.

Mutual Fund Minimum Investment Requirements

No minimum	9.4%
$1–$500	13.5%
$501–$1,000	37.9%
$1,001–$5,000	21.1%
$5,001–$25,000	4.5%
$25,001 or more	13.6%

Reprinted with permission of the Investment Company Institute (www.ici.org)

Investing through mutual funds has other advantages. You can easily switch investments within a fund family, often with a simple phone call (although a switch is a taxable event). If you invest through a mutual fund "supermarket," you can switch from one fund group to another and receive a consolidated statement for all your fund investments. Supermarkets have become popular in the last few years, but watch out for transaction fees or, in the absence of transaction fees, higher expense ratios.

With mutual funds, you can reinvest dividends to buy more shares, and you can sell shares whenever you wish, although you may have a capital gain or loss if share prices are up or down from your purchase price. Taxes on mutual funds are discussed in detail in Chapter 22.

Mutual funds are definitely popular. According to the Investment Company Institute, more than 47 percent of all U.S. households owned mutual funds in 1999. When it comes to bond funds, two decades of growth boosted this category from $4.7 billion in assets to $635.6 billion. Municipal bond fund shareholders tend to be slightly older and wealthier than the average mutual fund shareholder—that's not surprising because these funds provide the tax-exempt income that retirees often crave.

The first mutual fund in the United States was the Massachusetts Investor Trust, started in 1924 and still going strong. Just look at what has happened in the mutual fund industry's first 75 years:

➤ More than 7,000 mutual funds now compete for investors' dollars.

➤ More than 65 million Americans own shares in a mutual fund, either directly or through a retirement account.

➤ The value of mutual fund assets is now more than $5 trillion, up from $1 trillion in 1990 and just $47 billion in 1970.

➤ Nearly 38 percent of American households own mutual funds, up from under 6 percent in 1980.

➤ An investment of $10,000 in the first mutual fund in 1924 would be worth more than $13 million today, assuming reinvestment of all dividends and capital gains. Of course, past performance is no guarantee of future results!

A Little at a Time

Another advantage of mutual fund investing lies in the ability to make your investment grow through small additions. There are two ways to do this: The first is by using dividend reinvestment and the second is by dollar cost averaging.

Under the first approach, you reinvest dividends in shares of the mutual fund instead of taking them in cash. If you choose to reinvest dividends, be sure to keep very good records of the cost basis of the additional shares you acquire; you will need these records in order to calculate the taxes due when you sell your shares, as described in Chapter 22.

When you dollar-cost average, you make regular fixed-sum investments and average the price of shares over time. You can arrange regular purchases either through automatic payroll deduction, at many employers, or through automatic transfers from your checking account or money market mutual fund. With many mutual funds, committing to an investment of as little as $50 a month will get you started on a regular investment program.

When you use dollar cost averaging, you buy more shares when prices are down and fewer shares when prices are up. Whether prices rise or fall, however, the process lets you reduce the average cost of your shares over time.

Let's say that you have $600 to invest in a fund whose shares are selling for $10. If you invest it all at once, you'll have 60 shares. As the following table shows, if you invest it in six monthly installments, at a time when the price fluctuates between $5 and $16, you'll wind up with more than 68 shares at an average cost per share ($600 divided by 68.75 shares) of $8.72.

Investment	Share Price	No. of Shares Purchased
$100	$10	10
$100	$8	12.5
$100	$5	20
$100	$10	10
$100	$16	6.25
$100	$10	10

Reprinted with permission of the Investment Company Institute (www.ici.org)

For dollar cost averaging, you have to be disciplined about investing. Instead of getting cold feet when the market goes down, you have to view downturns as an opportunity to acquire more shares.

Different Strokes for Different Folks

When you choose a mutual fund, you want to match the fund's investment objective with your own. That isn't an easy task. First, the name of a particular fund doesn't always accurately identify its investment objective. You have to study the list of holdings in the fund prospectus to see how the fund actually invests. Secondly, the Investment Company Institute classifies mutual funds into 33 categories of investment objectives.

Within the tax-advantaged universe alone, you have a range of choices:

➤ State-specific municipal bond funds invest in municipal bonds issued by a single state, with an average maturity of more than five years. The income from these funds is largely exempt from federal as well as state income tax for residents of that state.

➤ Short-term state-specific municipal bond funds stick to bonds maturing in less than five years. The same tax rules apply.

➤ National municipal bond funds invest in tax-free bonds with an average maturity of more than five years. Income is exempt from federal income tax but may be subject to state income tax for residents of states other than those where the bonds are issued.

➤ Short-term national municipal bond funds invest in munis with maturities of less than five years. The same tax rules apply.

➤ Tax-free money market mutual funds, investing in municipal securities with average maturities of 90 days or less, may be national or state-specific. Money market mutual funds are a place to keep cash reserves; they are discussed in detail in Chapter 16, "Everyone into the (Money Market) Pool."

➤ Government bond funds may be short-term (maturities of 1 to 5 years), intermediate-term (maturities of 5 to 10 years), or general (no stated average maturity). Government bond funds may consist exclusively of U.S. Treasury obligations, in which case they are subject to federal income tax but not to state income tax. Or, they may consist of a blend of Treasuries and other agency obligations. See Chapter 19, "Uncle Sam Treasures You," for more on these securities. If what you really want is Treasuries, consider buying them directly.

Here are some factors to weigh in making your fund choices:

➤ Are you in a tax bracket where it makes sense to have tax-free income? In general, only taxpayers in the highest federal income tax brackets can be certain that tax-free is best. See Chapters 2, "Pay Now, Pay Later, Pay Not at All," and 22 for more discussion.

➤ If you do want tax-free income, should you seek a state-specific municipal bond fund or stick to a national fund? The answer depends on whether you live in a high-tax state—and on whether there is a sufficient supply of good-quality municipal bonds in your state to produce attractive yields.

➤ Should you go long-term? While the answer depends on your individual situation, most investors are better off sticking to short-term and intermediate-term funds. Long-term funds are simply too volatile—and the added yield rarely makes up for the added risk of loss.

➤ Are you subject to the alternative minimum tax? If you are, steer clear of municipal bond funds holding bonds subject to the AMT. See Chapter 22 for more information.

Tax Tips

A move to another state is a good time to review your investment portfolio—especially if you own state-specific municipal bonds or bond funds pegged to your prior residence. Chances are that the income from those investments will become taxable in your new state, and you may want to make a switch.

Money off the Top

Mutual fund investing can cost a little or a lot. You can buy mutual funds directly from many fund companies, at little or no cost. You also can buy mutual funds from a financial intermediary, such as a stockbroker or financial planner. How much you'll pay depends on how much advice you want and the particular funds you choose.

Fees do matter because they are a drag on performance. That's not to say that you shouldn't pay for advice, or that an expensive fund can't do better than an inexpensive fund. Unless you are willing to do your own research and make your own decisions as to which funds to buy and sell, and when, you should seek advice.

Performance is more important than fees. But the more you spend on fees, the less of your money goes directly to work for you. So it pays to pay attention to the costs associated with investing. Costs are particularly important to investors in fixed-income securities such as municipal bonds and Treasuries because these securities typically generate lower returns than equity funds.

Mutual fund costs fall into two broad categories: sales commissions (known quaintly as loads) and ongoing operating expenses. Some funds may also assess other administrative fees.

Loading the Dice

There used to be a simple distinction between load and no-load funds. Load funds were sold by stockbrokers and came with an up-front commission, typically 8.5 percent. No-load funds were sold directly by mutual funds, through direct marketing, and had no sales charge. That distinction has blurred, if not evaporated, in light of today's multiple fees. No-load funds still exist, but there are now several varieties of sales charges:

➤ Front-end loads are still attached to broker-sold funds. They can legally run as high as 8.5 percent of your investment but, because of competitive pressures on broker-sold funds, they typically range today from 3 to 5.5 percent. Some funds drop the front-end load at a specific break point or level of investment; in other words, the more you invest, the less you may pay in loads. Some funds, although not many, also apply the front-end load to reinvested dividends. Being able to reinvest dividends is one of the big bonuses of mutual fund investing; stay away from funds that charge you a load to do so.

➤ So-called "low-load" funds charge up-front loads of no more than 3 percent. Low-load funds are sold through both sales channels, by brokers and directly by fund companies.

➤ Back-end loads (also sometimes called contingent deferred sales charges) are assessed when you sell shares of a broker-sold mutual fund. Back-end loads can start at 5 to 6 percent of the amount sold, declining to zero over a period of six to seven years from the initial purchase.

➤ No-load funds do not carry a sales charge but may have 12(b)1 fees (see below). So-called "pure" no-load funds do not have either a load or a 12(b)1 fee.

Just to complicate matters, many broker-sold mutual funds now offer investors a choice of loads in the form of shares sold as different classes in the same fund.

➤ Class A shares have a front-end load, charged at the time you buy, that usually tops out at 5.5 percent but can legally go as high as 8.5 percent. Class A shares may also charge 0.25 percent as an annual fee.

➤ Class B shares have a back-end load imposed when you sell shares, typically starting at 5 percent and gradually declining to zero after six years. If you hold your shares at least six years, you won't pay a load.

➤ Class C shares may have no front-end or back-end sales charge, but they charge a fee (typically about 1 percent) each and every year that you own shares.

Which is best? According to one study, there's not much difference over the long term between Class A and Class B shares. Class C shares put you ahead if you'll sell your shares within eight years, but they cost the most if you hold for 20 years.

You should also bear in mind that fees are not tax deductible, although loads can be added to the cost basis and reduce any profit—and hence any capital gains tax—when you sell.

Year After Year After Year

Every mutual fund, whether it charges a load or not, has ongoing operating expenses. These expenses always include advisory fees paid to investment managers and the administrative costs of operating the fund. They may also include other fees. Taken together, these costs are expressed as an *expense ratio,* which must be set forth in the fund's prospectus.

In addition to advisory and administrative fees, many funds now charge a 12(b)1 fee, named after the regulatory section permitting its imposition and designed to pay for marketing and distribution costs. Because the 12(b)1 fee is imposed year after year, at 0.25 percent to 1 percent of the fund's assets, it can be a significant drag on performance.

Tax Talk

The **expense ratio** is the amount paid for mutual fund operating expenses and management fees, expressed as a percentage of each shareholder's total investment. The average expense ratio for all bond funds is 1.08 percent, while the average expense ratio for municipal bond funds is 1.05 percent. Steer clear of funds with expense ratios that are much higher than these averages.

12(b)1 fees, sometimes called level loads, are sometimes combined with front-end or back-end loads. Even standing alone, they are often the worst of all worlds. While a front-end load of 5 percent diminishes the amount of money initially working for you—a $1,000 investment minus 5 percent leaves $950 to invest—an annual fee of 1 percent, on a fund you hold for 20 years, will be the equivalent of a 20 percent load. (A fund cannot call itself a no-load fund if it imposes a 12(b)1 fee of more than 0.25 percent.)

Coming Out Ahead

All things being equal, funds with lower expense ratios generally are a better choice. In an example provided by the Investment Company Institute, a $10,000 investment is made in two funds. The first fund has an expense ratio of 1.10 percent, while the second fund has an expense ratio of 1.74 percent. If both funds have annual returns of 10 percent, before taking fees into account, the fund with the lower expense ratio would grow to $302,771 in 40 years. The fund with the higher expense ratio would grow to $239,177.

Tax Tips

By law, 12(b)1 fees used to pay marketing and distribution expenses cannot exceed 0.75 percent of the fund's average net assets per year. But the Investment Company Institute points out that a fund may also pay a service fee of up to 0.25 percent each year to compensate sales professionals for their services. So, the true maximum is 1 percent a year, an amount that can be a real drag on performance over time.

But all things are rarely equal, and a fund with a higher expense ratio but a higher yield may outdistance a lower-cost fund. Similarly, a fund with a front-end load of 5 percent but a low expense ratio may perform better than a no-load fund with a high expense ratio.

In another ICI example, two funds return 10 percent annually before fees. One is a no-load fund with an expense ratio of 1.74 percent, and the other has a front-end load of 5 percent but an expense ratio of 0.94 percent. A $10,000 investment in the load fund would grow to $305,030 over 40 years, $65,853 more than in the no-load fund with the higher expense ratio.

The message is clear: Focusing on fees rather than real return can be a big mistake. Be aware of the cost of investing, but look at costs as part of the big picture.

One-Time Charges

Some funds, but not all, charge a variety of other fees. These other fees may include the following:

➤ Transaction fees of 1 to 2 percent imposed on either purchases or redemptions

➤ Account maintenance fees of $10 to $25 a year, typically assessed only on accounts below a specified minimum level

➤ Exchange fees of $5 to $25, imposed when you switch funds within a fund family

Open and Above Board

The nice thing about mutual funds is that fees are completely disclosed—or almost completely. The one cost of owning fund shares that does not show up in fee tables is the brokerage costs incurred when the fund buys and sells securities within its portfolio. Brokerage costs are included in advertised performance calculations, but you won't know their precise impact.

To find out what it will cost you to own shares of a particular mutual fund, see the fee table in the front of the fund prospectus. The fee table has two sections. The first describes sales commissions and transaction fees imposed when you buy, sell, or exchange shares. The second lists all the ongoing fees paid year after year, grouped as operating expenses. The bottom line for each fee table is an example showing how much, in dollars, it will cost to own shares in this fund for periods of time ranging from 1 year to 10 years.

The following table shows a sample fee schedule as it might appear in a mutual fund prospectus.

Shareholder Transaction Expenses	
Maximum sales charge on purchase (as a percent of the offering price)	4.5%
Maximum deferred sales charge	None
Maximum sales charge on reinvested dividends	None
Redemption fee	None
Exchange fee	None
Annual account maintenance fee	None

Annual Fund Operating Expenses	
Management fee	0.47%
Distribution (12(b)1) fee	0.21%
Other expenses	0.36%
Total fund operating expenses (expense ratio):	1.04%

The following example illustrates the hypothetical expenses that you would incur over various periods if you invest $10,000 in this fund. This example assumes that the fund's annual return is 5 percent and that your shareholder transaction expenses and each fund's annual operating expenses remain the same. The results apply whether or not you redeem your investment at the end of each period:

1 year	3 years	5 years	10 years
$552	$771	$1,013	$1,730

Reprinted with permission of the Investment Company Institute (www.ici.org)

Prospectus Pointers

Fees and expenses are just one vital piece of information you can glean from a mutual fund prospectus. Here are some others:

➤ **Investment objectives**—The prospectus will describe the fund's objectives. As an example, the prospectus for a short-term Treasury fund might say, "The Fund is a bond fund that seeks to provide a high level of current income and preserve investors' principal."

➤ **Investment strategies**—Here the prospectus should be specific about the types of securities the fund purchases, including any limits on specific types of investments. Here the same short-term Treasury fund might say, "The fund invests at least 85 percent of its total assets in short-term bonds whose interest and principal payments are backed by the full faith and credit of the U.S. government."

➤ **Risks**—In describing how an investor might lose money, a short-term Treasury fund might point to two factors: The first is income risk, the chance that falling interest rates will cause the fund's income to decline; this is typically a high risk for short-term bonds. The second is interest rate risk, the chance that bond prices overall will decline due to rising interest rates; this is typically a low risk for short-term bonds.

➤ **Performance**—The prospectus will show annual returns over a period of years, often compared to a broad market index. This information is often provided in a bar chart.

You might want to look for two other things in the prospectus. The first is the turnover rate, a measure of transaction frequency; a higher turnover rate produces higher commission costs. The second is information about the fund's investment portfolio managers. Some mutual funds are run by committee; where a fund has individual managers, look for longevity. Someone who has been managing a specific fund for a long period of time has a track record you can evaluate.

Every mutual fund must provide the same information to investors, making it easy (more or less) to compare funds and decide which investment is right for you.

Prospectuses can be formidable legal documents filled with small print, but two recent rulings by the Securities and Exchange Commission make them easier to read and understand.

First, mutual funds now have the option of providing a simplified profile prospectus (in addition to the full-length prospectus, not in its place), summarizing the key information in the prospectus. These prospectuses are available from some of the funds that sell directly to the public. Don't expect to receive a profile prospectus if you buy from a broker. Second—and this should help every investor—all prospectuses are to be written in plain English instead of legalese.

Measuring Performance

"Past performance is no guarantee of future results." That's the line that jumps out at you from every mutual fund advertisement. And it's true, so true. It's important to read the performance information in the mutual fund prospectus, but chasing performance by buying last year's top-producing fund is a ticket to nowhere. There is simply no guarantee that performance can be sustained from year to year. The only sure thing is that excessive expenses will detract from performance.

Tax Tips

The prospectus won't list the securities held by the mutual fund. Instead, you'll find this vital piece of information in the fund's semiannual and annual reports. Use it to get a sense of how the fund meets its investment objectives, but don't take the list as gospel. In an actively managed fund that buys and sells securities regularly, the list will be out of date almost as soon as it is published.

Still, it's a good idea to evaluate the performance of a mutual fund you're considering buying, as well as the performance of funds you already own. To do so, you need to look not just at yield but also at a fund's total return over a period of several years. You also need to be sure that you're comparing apples with apples, like fund to like fund, and a particular fund to the appropriate benchmark.

Yield measures net income (dividends and interest minus fund expenses) during a specified period of time. Yield is expressed as a percentage of the fund's net asset value. But be careful here. Advertised yields may be simple yields, showing a return based on dividing all the dividends paid out during the year by the current share price. The SEC has a more stringent definition of yield, adjusted for sales loads, and you'll want to get this number as well.

Too many bond fund investors focus on yield, but total return is a far more accurate measure of a fund's performance. It assumes that dividend and capital gain distributions were reinvested in the fund, and it represents those reinvestments along with gains or declines in the fund's share price. Expressed as a percentage of an initial investment in the fund, total return represents the net change in value over the given time period.

Duration is another key element in evaluating mutual funds. Duration is not the same thing as maturity; remember, bond funds don't mature. Instead, duration computes both weighted average maturities and the value of periodic interest payments to come up with a number that is a rough measure of the fund's sensitivity to shifts in interest rates. As an example, a bond fund with a duration of four years would lose about 4 percent of its value if interest rates were to rise by 1 percent.

Duration relies on a very complex formula, but all you need to know—once you get the duration of a particular fund from its representative—is that the higher the number, the more dramatically the fund will fluctuate in response to changes in interest rates.

Standard and Poor's assigns credit quality and volatility ratings to bond funds. Credit quality ratings indicate how much protection from credit defaults is built into the portfolio; the highest level of protection has the rating AAAf, while the lowest is CCCf. Volatility ratings indicate the overall level of risk in the portfolio, with ratings ranging from S1 (the lowest volatility and hence the most stable) to S6 (the highest volatility). Both sets of ratings can be found on the S&P Web site, at www.standardandpoors.com/ratings/criteria/managedfunds.

The Least You Need to Know

➤ In choosing a mutual fund, look at its investment objectives and investment strategy.

➤ Investors seeking tax-free income have a choice of national or state-specific municipal bond funds.

➤ Short-term funds are generally less volatile and therefore less risky than long-term funds.

➤ Check out both loads and ongoing fund expenses before deciding which fund to buy.

➤ Bond fund ratings can help you narrow the field.

Chapter 21

Blue Plate Specials

In This Chapter

➤ Entering the mutual fund marketplace with closed-end funds

➤ Understanding that unit investment trusts come at a high cost

➤ Investing in real estate investment trusts to receive income while maintaining liquidity

➤ Finding opportunities for tax shelter plus possible appreciation with limited partnerships in low-income housing

Municipal bonds, Treasury obligations, and mutual funds may be the way most investors approach tax-free investing—as indeed they should be. But there's more than one way to shelter income in the investment world.

This chapter introduces four more investment vehicles with distinctive tax characteristics. We'll look at closed-end mutual funds, unit investment trusts, real estate investment trusts (REITs), and limited partnerships. Of the four, REITs are most worth considering, but you should understand them all in case you are presented with buying "opportunities" that are better skipped.

The Door Is Closed

A mutual fund is a mutual fund is a mutual fund—unless it is a closed-end fund. Closed-end funds, just like other mutual funds, are professionally managed investment companies with diversified portfolios. But they differ from the more familiar open-end funds in two distinct ways:

Tax Tips

Want to learn more about closed-end funds? Check out the Web site of the Closed-End Fund Association, at www.closed-endfunds.com. Or, write for a free booklet, to Brochure, Closed-End Fund Association, Inc., P.O. Box 28037, Kansas City, MO 64188.

➤ First, they have a fixed investment portfolio and a fixed number of shares.

➤ Second, following the initial public offering, those shares are traded on stock exchanges and bought and sold in the open market.

Where an open-end mutual fund can issue an unlimited number of shares and continue to issue shares as new investors arrive on the scene, closed-end funds have a fixed number of shares from the start. The share price of an open-end fund, called the net asset value, is the value of total holdings divided by the number of shares outstanding at any one time. The share price of a closed-end fund, like the share price of common stock, is largely determined by supply and demand.

Net asset value and share price are not the same thing in closed-end funds. In fact, toward the end of 1999, the NAV of closed-end funds was down 5 percent, while share prices were down almost 16 percent. To some analysts, this spread created a buying opportunity.

Open-end funds are available either through stockbrokers or direct purchase, with or without commissions ("loads"). Closed-end funds may be purchased only from a broker and only by paying a commission.

Closed-end funds may be stock or bond, domestic or international. They are particularly attractive to investors interested in volatile emerging markets and single-country funds. But by far the largest category, making up more than 40 percent of all closed-end funds, is municipal bond closed-end funds. Like open-end muni funds, these funds seek tax-free income for their investors. But some of these closed-end funds aren't all that they seem; yields may be kept high by including lower-rated bonds and other higher-risk ingredients in the portfolio.

Closed-end funds offer some advantages to investors in addition to professional management and diversification:

➤ Managers work with a stable pool of capital and can implement long-term strategy without concerns about inflows or outflows of money. Managers of open-end funds must be ready to meet redemptions by shareholders and must be able to invest inflows of cash.

➤ Because managers of closed-end funds can stay fully invested, yields are often a bit higher than on comparable open-end funds.

➤ Closed-end funds are sold by stockbrokers and can be integrated with investors' brokerage accounts.

➤ In contrast to open-end mutual funds, there is no minimum purchase amount.

Buying a new closed-end fund is generally not a good idea for most small investors. Here's why:

➤ Transaction fees tend to be considerably higher than on open-end funds, with commissions of 6 to 8 percent on new offerings. Some closed-end funds also charge the 12(b)1 fees meant to cover marketing costs—even though they are closed and are not trying to attract new investors.

➤ After the initial public offering, closed-end funds generally trade at less than the value of their holdings. Sophisticated investors seek the higher yield produced by this discount and hope for a narrowing of the discount before they sell, to produce a capital gain. But the discount may never be made up, leaving early investors at a disadvantage when they sell their shares.

In Units We Trust

There's another type of pooled investment, the unit investment trust (UIT). These trusts have fixed portfolios. Unlike closed-end funds, which also have fixed capital, unit investment trusts are unmanaged; the portfolio is fixed at the time of purchase and then runs its course until maturity.

UITs can contain almost anything, but popular ingredients are municipal bonds (there are both national and single-state municipal bond UITs) and Treasury securities. With a UIT made up of municipal bonds, the maturities, quality ratings, and call dates of the bonds are known in advance. You receive monthly interest checks instead of the semiannual interest on bonds held directly. You also receive distributions of capital as individual bonds within the trust mature. Of course, as bonds mature or are called, the amount of regular interest you receive declines.

The "unit" in a unit investment trust is typically $1,000, although a minimum purchase amount may be $5,000. UITs are sold by stockbrokers, and there is always a commission on the sale, typically 4 to 5 percent of the purchase amount. There is also an annual fee to cover operating expenses. There is no management fee, however, because the portfolio is not managed.

Most UITs are held to maturity. If you need to sell early, the sponsor is required by law to redeem outstanding units at the current market value. As a practical matter, however, if you sell, you will lose money.

Tax Traps

Your stockbroker may tell you about a hot new investment: a unit investment trust made up of closed-end muni bond funds. Don't bite. The combination produces high expenses and erratic income—in short, the worst of both worlds.

The REIT Stuff

Real estate investment trusts (REITs), may be the most reasonable investment option presented in this chapter. Placing a small proportion of your investable cash in one or more REITs may be a good way to diversify your portfolio.

Investing in real estate directly can achieve diversification. But most individual investors don't want to get involved in the day-to-day hassle of maintaining buildings and managing tenants. Investing in real estate through a REIT (pronounced "reet") provides the same income flow and hedge against inflation as direct investing in real estate. Investing in REITs offers additional advantages, too.

Investing in REITs lends liquidity to an investment that is otherwise very illiquid. Buying and selling shares of a REIT is easily accomplished; buying and selling actual pieces of property can be a lengthy process.

An individual REIT is itself like a mutual fund in that it is a portfolio of professionally managed properties. But REITs are publicly traded securities; like closed-end mutual funds, their shares are traded on the stock exchanges. That means that you can buy as many or as few shares as suits your pocketbook. It also means that you can track performance in the stock tables of most daily newspapers.

Tax Tips

You can invest in REITs directly or by buying shares in a mutual fund that holds REITs in its portfolio. A "real estate" mutual fund provides additional diversification by holding a number of REITs along with other real estate–related investments such as property management companies. It also offers the expertise of a professional manager in selecting REITs to buy and sell. The trade-off is an additional layer of management fees incurred by investing through a fund instead of directly.

REITs were created by special federal legislation in the 1960s to encourage individuals to invest in the real estate market, but they didn't become particularly popular until the early 1990s. It took the Tax Reform Act of 1986 to propel REITs into the investment limelight. First, this landmark law dimmed the luster of limited partnerships (see the next section of this chapter); second, it permitted REITs not only to own but also to operate and manage most types of income-producing commercial properties.

Even then, and despite some years of outstanding returns, REITs maintained a fairly low profile—until legendary investor Warren Buffett bought some REIT stocks in 1999. His actions may have helped to pull REITs out of a free-fall in prices—a loss of almost 28 percent—from December 1997 until early 1999. REITs have staged a comeback since then. Now, with the REIT Modernization Act of 1999 (effective January 1, 2001), REITs may become even more popular.

REITs qualify for special tax treatment as long as the following criteria are met:

➤ At least 75 percent of the company's assets is in real estate held for the long term.

➤ At least 75 percent of the company's income is derived from real estate.

➤ The company pays out at least 95 percent (90 percent after January 1, 2001) of its taxable income to shareholders.

REIT Basics

There are two types of REITs. Mortgage REITs are in the business of financing real estate. Because they hold significant interest rate risk and don't own actual properties, they are not as popular today as equity REITs, which invest directly in the development, acquisition, and renovation of real estate and often manage the properties as well. There are also some hybrid REITs that hold both mortgages and property.

Equity REITs can hold almost anything. Most common, perhaps, are REITs that own office buildings, apartment houses, and shopping malls. But you'll also find REITs holding hotels, nursing homes, industrial parks, warehouses, and even prisons.

REITs are corporations, but they offer investors a unique tax advantage. Most corporate profits are taxed twice, first to the corporation and then to the individual investor who receives them in the form of dividends. But REITs enjoy special tax status. As long as 95 percent of a REIT's income (90 percent after January 1, 2001) is paid out as dividends, there is no federal tax (and, in many states, no state tax) at the corporate level. That means more profits and, hence, more dividends for shareholders. It also means that REITs can't plow earnings back into the business and must continually expand in order to generate profits.

Because almost all the income is passed through to shareholders, REITs typically generate high yields. Like other investments, however, total return is made up of both current income and capital appreciation. Unlike the limited partnerships that were popular before REITs gained the limelight (see next section), losses are not passed through to shareholders. Unlike common stock, where much of the return is in the form of appreciation taxed at lower capital gains rates, REIT dividend income—a large part of the return—is generally taxed at the higher rates applied to ordinary income.

REITs are often compared to utility stocks because they can provide a steady stream of relatively high income, along with some potential for growth. (With the deregulation of electric and gas companies, however, utility stocks may be entering a whole new world.) REITs are also similar to bonds because they are very sensitive to interest rate trends. Although the prices of REIT shares are related to trends in both real estate and the stock market as a whole, interest rates play the definitive role.

When it comes to REITs, high yield isn't the only goal. In fact, it's wise to be careful about yields out of line with the competition. As with any other investment, unusually high yields often mean higher risk. Income isn't guaranteed, either. Although REITs are required by law to distribute most of their income to shareholders each year, distributions will be cut if a REIT runs into cash flow problems.

Tax Treats

The downside of REITs is that dividends are generally taxable as ordinary income—unless you hold them in a tax-sheltered account such as an Individual Retirement Account or a variable annuity. However, even in a regular taxable account, a portion of your annual dividends may be treated as a return of capital; when this is the case, the tax is deferred until the shares are sold. At that time, the return of capital reduces the cost basis of your shares. Then, if you've held the shares for at least one year, the lower long-term capital gains rate may apply. In addition, when a REIT disposes of property in its portfolio, your share of the distribution may be taxed as a long-term capital gains distribution.

Tax Traps

You may want to be cautious when it comes to REITs concentrated in the healthcare arena. Although demand is high, with an aging population, political considerations can dictate the fortunes of hospitals and nursing homes. As a result, some analysts believe this form of real estate investment to be potentially riskier than other forms. In fact, healthcare REITs lagged all other REITs in performance during 1999. The best performers were in apartments, industrial complexes, and office buildings.

Shares of REITs trade like shares of any stock. But REITs are different. For example, instead of earnings per share, you'll want to evaluate funds from operations (FFO) as a measure of growth. FFO is net income after subtracting gains or losses from debt restructuring and property sales, and adding back depreciation of real estate.

Buying Tips

In buying REITs, consider the following:

➤ **Location**—Look for properties in fast-growing regions rather than saturated markets. Also think about whether a REIT holding properties across the United States may be less risky in the long run than one invested only in a specific locale.

➤ **Type of property**—Office complexes may be hot, but what happens when office buildings are overbuilt in a given area? A REIT that invests in a combination of shopping centers, apartment houses, and office buildings may not be as vulnerable to economic shifts as a REIT that invests in a single type of property.

➤ **Management**—Look for REITs with managers who are experienced in real estate, not just finance, and who have weathered several real estate cycles.

➤ **Ownership stake**—Look for REITs where management owns a sizable number of shares. Stay away from REITs where management is selling its stake.

REIT accounting can be hard to understand, but here are two key figures:

➤ **Yield as a proportion of operating funds**—If most of the yield consists of projected funds from operations, your dividends could be sharply cut if the REIT loses one key tenant.

➤ **Too much debt**—If debt is too high—some analysts peg 35 to 40 percent of capitalization as a benchmark—the safety of dividend payments may be threatened. Higher debt levels increase risk but may lead to potentially higher returns.

The General Is In

Remember *tax shelters?* In the boom years for limited partnerships—before the savings and loan crisis, before the Tax Reform Act of 1986, and before the resulting crumbling of real estate values—lots of individual investors poured thousands of dollars into these arrangements that were supposed to shelter money from taxes.

The key element is that partnerships are not taxable entities. All profit and loss flows through to the individual partners, who report on their individual income tax returns. Until the Tax Reform Act of 1986 made it impossible and forced partnerships to stand on their own merits as investments, people with sizable incomes from other sources could invest in partnerships and offset their taxable income from other sources with tax losses passed through to them from the partnership.

Although real estate was probably the most popular tax shelter, limited partnerships also invested in oil drilling, gas leasing, and equipment. In each case, the structure was the same: A general partner made the business decisions and assumed the responsibility. Limited partners—ordinary investors, like you—put up most of the money. In exchange, you got shelter from taxes and a share of any profits. If the investment soured, your liability was limited—hence the term "limited" partner.

Liability may have been limited, but costs were not. Large chunks of a limited partner's

Tax Talk

A **tax shelter** is an investment designed to legally avoid or minimize the amount of income tax owed by an investor. Many tax shelters are organized as limited partnerships. Taxes can often be reduced through depreciation of assets such as real estate, although the Tax Reform Act of 1986 severely curtailed most shelters.

investment—often more than 20 percent—were typically eaten up by sales commissions, property acquisition costs, administrative charges, and fees paid to the general partner.

Unlike REITs, with shares actively traded on the stock exchanges, units of limited partnerships were and are extremely illiquid. In fact, as many investors have discovered, they are virtually impossible to dispose of before the entire partnership is liquidated by the general partner. Many partnerships were sold with expectations of a specific payoff date, typically within 7 to 12 years. Many partnerships lingered for years longer, dying a slow death when real estate values plummeted in the late 1980s. In the end, investments promoted as conservative proved to be enormously risky.

Limited partnerships have two flavors:

➤ Public offerings are registered with the Securities and Exchange Commission and often in the states in which they are sold. The registration doesn't imply endorsement or approval, but it does mean that the partnerships meet certain standards. Public offerings, described in a prospectus, could usually be purchased in $5,000 units.

➤ Private offerings, unregistered and unregulated, are described in an offering statement. They take fewer partners and usually require a much larger investment, upwards of $50,000. Potential rewards may be greater; so is the risk.

Limited Partnerships Today

Needless to say, limited partnerships have lost a lot of their popularity. Few new partnerships are offered. However, one type of limited partnership may still merit attention as an investment. That's the partnership designed to provide low-income-housing.

The Federal Housing Tax Credit Program offers tax credits as an incentive to invest in the construction or rehabilitation of affordable housing for low-income families and the elderly.

As an example, under a program offered by Boston Capital, investors receive a predetermined stream of tax credits (although not necessarily a steady amount each year) for a 10-year period. Note that these are tax credits—a dollar-for-dollar reduction in your tax bill—and not tax deductions. The credits are limited to an amount that will offset taxes paid on the last $25,000 of taxable income. For someone in the 31 percent tax bracket, the maximum credit each year is $7,750. For a taxpayer in the 39.6 percent bracket, the maximum credit is $9,900.

The minimum investment is $5,000. The tax credits are guaranteed. Investors may also receive the benefit of partnership losses that can offset passive gains from other partnership investments. There is also the possibility of capital appreciation if the properties are sold at a profit.

If you're interested in a low-income housing partnership, look for a sponsor with a successful track record and ask to see how projections have matched performance in the past. Be aware that limited partnerships are long-term illiquid investments; be prepared to stay the course for 12 to 15 years.

Gone but Not Forgotten

Many investors are still stuck holding units of illiquid partnerships that should have been distributed years ago. Is there anything you can do with old units that you may hold or wind up inheriting after a parent dies? (If you inherit partnership units, some tax advisers suggest disclaiming the inheritance. That means turning it down, just to avoid the potential tax headaches.)

Don't count on selling. A small secondary market exists for limited partnership units, but the only units anyone is buying are those with some potential for providing income or actually generating a profit. If that is the case with your units, you might as well hold on.

It's very hard to put a value on old partnership units. In fact, if you do get an offer, you can expect it to be well below the supposed value. Fifty cents on the dollar would be generous; 5 cents is not unheard of. If you get an offer out of the blue, call the company that sold you the partnership and ask what's going on. You may find that the partnership is in the midst of winding down and that you will eventually receive a check wrapping up the deal.

If you get a call and might be interested in selling, find out if the caller is acting as an agent (who will try to match you up with a buyer) or as a principal (buying for his or her own account). An agent will suggest a possible price; a broker will tell you how much he or she is willing to pay. Ask how long it will take to settle the sale and how much will come off the top for fees and commissions. Don't be surprised if the amount you'll end up with looks like a joke—especially because you may wind up owing more in taxes than you gain.

Tax Consequences

Limited partnerships were sold as tax shelters, but many investors didn't realize that the tax was merely postponed, not eliminated. (That's the advantage of today's low-income housing partnerships; tax credits are immediate.) When the paper losses of tax shelters were used to offset other income, they actually reduced the cost basis of your investment. As you'll recall, cost basis is the purchase price of an asset for tax purposes. The lower your cost basis, the higher the eventual tax on any gain in the investment.

To add insult to injury, you may receive a sizable tax bill on phantom income—income generated by the partnership when it disposes of its assets even if the reported amount far exceeds anything you actually receive. It's a way the government makes good on all those tax deductions you claimed in the gravy years of a partnership.

If you still hold any limited partnership units, you will receive an annual end-of-year tax reporting form called the Schedule K-1. The partnership actually files the K-1 directly with the Internal Revenue Service; you get a copy and must enter the information on Schedule E of your Federal Income Tax Form 1040.

There are two problems with K-1 forms. First, they usually arrive late, so you may have to get used to filing for an extension on your federal income tax. Second, the forms may report income that you never actually received but that will nonetheless be taxable. What to do? Grin and bear it. And think about the deductions you claimed in earlier years.

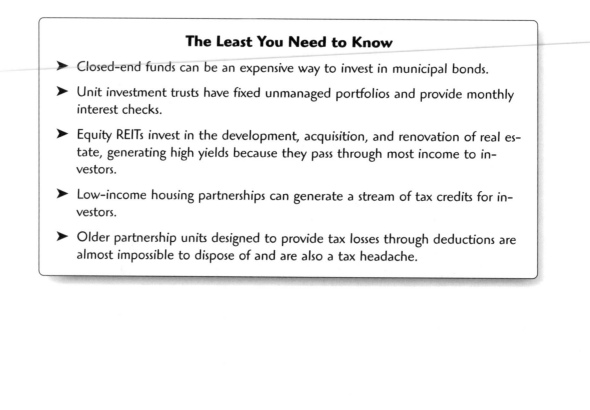

The Least You Need to Know

➤ Closed-end funds can be an expensive way to invest in municipal bonds.

➤ Unit investment trusts have fixed unmanaged portfolios and provide monthly interest checks.

➤ Equity REITs invest in the development, acquisition, and renovation of real estate, generating high yields because they pass through most income to investors.

➤ Low-income housing partnerships can generate a stream of tax credits for investors.

➤ Older partnership units designed to provide tax losses through deductions are almost impossible to dispose of and are also a tax headache.

Chapter 22

There's No Free Lunch

In This Chapter

➤ Discovering that tax-free investments can and do have tax consequences

➤ Paying lower capital gains taxes as a long-term investor

➤ Owning individual securities to give you control over tax timing

➤ Understanding that mutual funds pass through capital gains distributions to shareholders

➤ Understanding how the Alternative Minimum Tax can affect investors

You've chosen tax-free and tax-sheltered investments to minimize your tax bill. But you've probably realized by now that minimizing taxes and avoiding them altogether are two different things.

Even the best of tax-free investments generally come with some tax consequences attached—if not while you own the investments, then when you sell. With some investments, you can bypass state income tax but must pay federal tax. With every investment, even if interest and dividends are income tax-free, profits are taxable.

This chapter explains the tax ramifications of investing in individual securities and mutual funds. It also provides a description of the Alternative Minimum Tax and when tax-free investments become taxable.

The Short and the Long of It

Interest and dividends on tax-free investments are, by definition, generally tax-free—although you do have to report the amounts on your federal income tax return. Interest and dividends on taxable investments are taxed as ordinary income. A profit made on the sale of an asset is defined as a capital gain. Depending on how long you've owned the asset, the gain may be subject to preferential tax treatment.

The history of capital gains taxation is as complicated as the history of ordinary income taxes; the up-and-down rates and variations in holding periods over the decades reflect ongoing disagreement among policymakers about the social and economic impact of taxing capital gains. If rates on profits are low, one theory goes, the rich benefit. If rates on profits are high, according to another camp, investors don't take profits, assets are frozen, and economic growth is curtailed.

As various theories gain proponents, capital gains rates bounce around. From 1913 to 1921, there was a maximum tax of 7 percent on capital gains. From 1922 to 1933, the maximum rate was 12.5 percent. From 1972 to 1978, the rate hit its high point at 35 percent. From 1991 through early May 1997, the rate for long-term gains stayed at 28 percent, thereby offering a rate reduction only for taxpayers in brackets above 28 percent. Then the rates came down again, but with the added complexity of three different rates for three different holding periods. The resulting complexity in tax reporting led to the repeal of the interim holding period after just one year. Today we are back to the relatively simple situation of two holding periods and two tax rates.

For now, at least, these are the rules:

➤ Gains on assets held for 12 months or less are considered short-term gains and are taxed as ordinary income.

➤ Gains on assets held for more than 12 months are considered long-term gains and are subject to a maximum tax rate of 20 percent.

Tax Tips

Taxpayers in the 15 percent tax bracket—the lowest federal income tax bracket—pay capital gains tax of 10 percent on long-term gains.

To encourage long-term investment, a new rule goes into effect for assets purchased after December 31, 2000. On these assets, as long as they are held for more than five years (and as long as Congress doesn't change the rules again), the maximum capital gains tax rate will be 18 percent. Taxpayers in the 15 percent tax bracket get a special break. If they sell an investment that has been held for five years, no matter when it was bought, the maximum capital gains rate is 8 percent.

Not every investment, unfortunately, results in a profit. But losses aren't a total loss. If you sell an asset for less than you paid for it, you can deduct the losses dollar for dollar against capital gains (both short-term and long-term) for the same year. If you have more losses than gains, you can deduct up to $3,000 of the losses against ordinary income. Beyond $3,000, losses can be carried forward indefinitely to offset future capital gains or used against ordinary income up to the limit of $3,000 a year.

Although taxes shouldn't be the sole determining factor when it comes to selling securities, when you do have a profit, it can make good tax sense to hold out for a long-term gain—especially if you are in one of the high-end federal income tax brackets. The following table shows the difference between short-term capital gains at ordinary income tax rates and long-term capital gains taxes.

Short-Term Gains/Ordinary Income Rates	Long-Term Gains
15%	10%
28%	20%
31%	20%
36%	20%
39.6%	20%

The Lone Ranger

One of the big advantages of owning individual securities instead of investing through mutual funds is that you control the timing of sales, and hence the timing of tax consequences. Taxes should be just one part of the buy-and-sell calculation when it comes to investing—put another way, taxes should never be the tail that wags the investment dog. You should buy a security because it deserves a place in your portfolio and sell it when it no longer deserves that place—either because it has reached the target price you set at purchase, is doing badly with little hope of improvement, or has exceeded its designated allocation.

Nevertheless, if you plan to sell a security, you may want to think about the timing in terms of taxes. In other words, will it be more beneficial in terms of your overall tax picture to sell in the current year or the next? Can you wait a little longer to make a sale, in order to qualify for long-term capital gains treatment? Would it make sense to sell one security at a loss and then buy a similar security to maintain your asset allocation?

You probably bought individual municipal bonds because the interest is tax-free. Even where interest is tax-free, however, gains and losses on sales are subject to the same tax rules as gains and losses on other investments. If you buy a municipal bond for $10,000 and hold it to maturity, it will pay $10,000. If you sell the same bond for $10,500 before it matures, you will have a capital gain of $500. If you held the bond for more than one year, you will have a long-term gain, subject to a maximum tax of 20 percent. Otherwise, it will be a short-term gain, and you will pay tax at the same rate you pay on ordinary income.

However, many municipal bonds are bought not at face value, but at a discount or a premium. The discount or premium can complicate your tax calculations if you must sell before maturity. The best bet with munis is to buy and hold to maturity, but things do happen. If you have to sell early, consult a tax adviser.

In brief, however, you may face one of these three situations:

➤ Tax-exempt bonds originally issued at a price below face value are considered "original issue discount" (OID). For tax purposes, OID is additional interest paid at maturity; when a bond is tax-exempt, so is the OID. But OID does increase your cost basis for purposes of calculating gain or loss if you sell before maturity.

➤ Market discount arises on tax-exempt bonds originally issued at face value or at a premium and then sold at a lower price in the secondary market. Unlike OID, market discount is not treated as tax-exempt interest. Instead, part or all of any gain on the sale of the bond will be treated as ordinary income.

➤ When tax-exempt bonds are purchased at a premium (at more than the face amount of the bond), whether when first issued or in the secondary market, the premium reduces your cost basis.

More information is available on the Bond Market Association's Web site, at www.investinginbonds.com/taxarticle.htm. Again, consult your tax adviser.

Pack Mentality

There are many advantages to investing through mutual funds—but tax isn't necessarily one of them.

You'll face tax consequences—even on a municipal bond fund—while you own shares in the fund and when you sell.

Mutual funds are considered pass-through entities. That means that the funds themselves are not taxed if they pass through income and capital gains to shareholders. In turn, this means that capital gains distributions may produce taxable income while you own shares in a tax-exempt fund. When you sell, even if the fund is completely invested in tax-exempt securities, you are subject to tax on any gain.

As a Shareholder

On a taxable fund, of course, dividends are entirely subject to income tax. Dividends on a state-specific tax-free fund are generally tax-free to residents of the state issuing the bonds. Dividends on a national municipal bond fund may be free from federal income tax but subject to state income tax on bonds not issued in the state where you live. At year-end, your fund should issue a statement showing the percentage breakdown of your fund's earnings by state. Note: Dividends must be reported even if you reinvest them rather than taking them in cash.

Funds also make capital gains distributions to shareholders. The net capital gains generated by securities sales throughout the year must be distributed to shareholders. These gains are always taxable on the federal level, although some states may not tax gains earned on bonds issued within the state.

Gains are taxable even if the fund is a tax-free fund, even if you don't sell any of your own shares, and even if you reinvest the distributions to purchase additional shares. Whether they are long-term or short-term gains depends on how long the fund held the securities before the sale, not on how long you have owned shares in the fund. Short-term gains distributed by mutual funds are reported on Form 1099-DIV as ordinary income and cannot be used to offset long-term capital losses. Long-term gains within the fund are offset by losses before the distribution.

However, there is also a special distribution category called return of capital. This is an occasional distribution that does not come from earnings or profits, but instead represents a return of your investment in the fund. Because it is a return of your own capital, the distribution is not taxable but does reduce your cost basis in the shares. If the distribution is greater than your cost basis, you will have a taxable gain on the amount in excess of the cost basis.

When You Sell

The real headaches hit when you sell shares in a mutual fund—especially when you sell only part of your holdings in a fund and when you have participated in a dividend reinvestment plan.

Dividend reinvestment is a neat idea. It lets you acquire more shares painlessly by investing your periodic dividends instead of taking them in cash. The big problem comes when you sell: Each purchase of shares will have been made at a different

Tax Traps

If you invest in a mutual fund shortly before the fund makes a year-end capital gains distribution, you will owe tax on that distribution even though you just stepped aboard and the gains were made earlier. Don't invest in a mutual fund late in the year without inquiring about the date of a distribution. If the payout will give you a tax headache, wait until after the record date to invest.

Tax Tips

Bonds pay interest, not dividends. Distributions to shareholders of mutual funds, however, are termed dividends and must be reported as dividends on your income tax form, even if they originate as interest on bonds held by the fund.

Tax Traps

You may face taxable year-end capital gains distributions even if your fund lost money for the year. Hard to believe? Well, if the fund manager sells a stock that is down 10 percent for the year but up 50 percent since its original purchase, the fund will have a taxable gain. Significant distributions often occur if a fund overhauls its investment strategy or takes on a new portfolio manager; either move may generate massive sales—and resulting taxes.

price. Unless you have kept very good records along the way, it will be extremely difficult to figure out the cost basis of each share. Unless you know the cost basis, you're likely to pay more tax than you actually owe.

Let's say that you put $10,000 into the XYZ fund. Two years later, you sell half your shares for $12,000. That's a taxable profit of $7,000, you think. Wait a minute. Before you pay capital gains tax on the full $7,000, think about the $1,200 in dividends and the $800 in capital gains distributions that you reinvested. You've already paid taxes on the dividends and the capitals gains distributions, and you don't want to pay the tax twice. Because you sold half your shares, you should subtract half of the dividends and half of the capital gains distributions. Doing so brings your taxable profit down to $6,000.

This is a simple example, but it should make the point: Keep records of every fund purchase, whether that purchase is made with cash, dividends, or capital gains distributions.

If you sell out of a mutual fund and redeem all your shares, you can figure the tax by subtracting your cost basis (don't forget those reinvested dividends and returns of capital) from the sale price. If you sell only a portion of your holdings, your calculations are more complicated.

In fact, you have a choice to make. You can choose to identify the specific shares being sold, or you can figure gain or loss using the average price paid for all the shares you own. Your mutual fund may provide you with the average price, but this may or may not be the most advantageous method to use. Note, though, that if you've already sold some shares from a fund and used the average cost method, you must continue to use the same method for subsequent sales from the same fund.

An informed choice can reduce the tax you must pay. In an example provided by the Investment Company Institute, let's say that you bought 100 shares of the XYZ Fund in January 1994 at $20 a share, 100 shares in January 1995 at $30 a share, and 100 shares in November 1998 at $46 a share. You sold 50 shares in June 2000 for $50 a share. Taxable gains on this sale could range from $200 to $1,500, as described below, depending on which method you use. The methods are described in the following two sections, "Be Specific" and "The Law of Averages."

Be Specific

Identifying the shares you're selling can be done either through identifying specific shares or on the basis of "first in, first out."

Specific identification gives you the greatest control because you can sell the shares with the highest cost basis and thereby reduce the tax hit. In our example, you sell the shares purchased in November 1998 because they have the highest purchase price. With a cost basis of $46 a share, your capital gain is $4 a share, or $200. In order to use specific identification, however, you must have precise records of every purchase. You must then identify the shares you're selling, in a letter to the mutual fund or broker, by their purchase date and price. The fund or broker must provide written confirmation of your instructions.

With the first in, first out (FIFO) method, you sell the first shares you bought. This isn't necessarily the best bet when you've owned a fund for a long time because the earliest purchases were probably the least expensive, and your tax bill will therefore be higher. That's probably why this is the method the Internal Revenue Service will assume that you used if you don't make another choice clear. In this example, your cost basis per share is $20 and your capital gain is $1,500. FIFO provides the lowest capital gain only when the fund is a loser and the share value is below your purchase price.

Tax Tips

Some mutual fund distributions are returns of capital. These are nontaxable distributions representing a return of part of your investment. A return of capital reduces your cost basis in the fund shares. But nontaxable distributions cannot reduce your basis below zero. If returns of capital add up to more than your original basis over the years you own shares in a mutual fund, the excess amount is a long-term capital gain.

The Law of Averages

With the average method, you simply divide the total cost of all your shares by the number of shares you own. The cost basis is then the average cost per share multiplied by the number of shares you're selling. Here your cost basis per share is $32, and you have a taxable gain of $900.

A variation on the average method is called double-category averaging because it divides shares into those held one year or less (short-term) and those held longer than one year (long-term). If you want to use the double-category method, you must tell your fund or broker which category of shares you're selling, and the fund or broker must provide written confirmation. In this instance, because you own both long-term and short-term shares, you have a taxable gain on the long-term shares of $1,250 and on the short-term shares of $200. Tax on long-term holdings is at a maximum of 20 percent, you'll recall, while tax on short-term gains is at your ordinary income tax rate, which can be as high as 39.6 percent.

Tax and Consequences

Mutual funds make investing so easy that investors sometimes get confused about the tax implications. Watch out for these common traps:

➤ You reinvested your dividends instead of taking them in cash. Sorry, they're still taxable if the investment is taxable. Keep track of reinvested dividends to add them to your cost basis, or you'll wind up paying taxes on them a second time when you sell your shares.

➤ You made a telephone call and switched funds within the same fund family. Sorry, it may be same family, but the sale of the first fund is a taxable event.

➤ You have owned shares of the XYZ fund for less than a year, so you can't possibly have any long-term gains. Sorry, the holding period for capital gains distributions while you own fund shares is based on the length of time the mutual fund has owned the securities; it has nothing to do with how long you've owned shares in the fund.

Tax-Free? Maybe

As we've seen, tax-free bonds and bond funds still have tax consequences in the form of capital gains or losses when you sell. But there can be other tax ramifications to tax-free investing.

For example, investing in a municipal bond fund that includes private-activity bonds—the kind of bonds issued to finance airports and sports facilities, among other things—can increase your exposure to the alternative minimum tax (AMT). See the discussion of the AMT later in this chapter, in the section called "An Alternative That Isn't."

In another example, Florida has no income tax. However, it does have a tax on intangibles, which includes interest and dividends from municipal bonds and bond funds. If a retiree deriving the bulk of her income from New York municipal bonds moves from New York to Florida, her tax-free income may be taxed. Always consult a tax adviser—and adjust your investment portfolio, if advisable—in a move to another state.

States' Rights

States generally treat mutual fund distributions the same way the federal government does. But it isn't always that simple. If your state has an income tax, consider these points:

➤ Investing in a national tax-free bond fund may mean paying income tax on income from bonds issued in states other than your own. Your fund should provide a year-end statement indicating the proportion of interest that is taxable. This doesn't mean that you should automatically shy away from a national muni fund, however, because it may still produce a higher effective yield than investing in a single-state fund.

➤ Some bonds may be taxable in their own states. The Web site of the Bond Market Association, at www.investinginbonds.com/info/igmunis/Individuals. htm, has a table on state taxation of municipal bonds for individuals.

➤ Dividends on U.S. Treasuries and Treasury funds are generally free from state and local income taxes. But watch out. If your fund puts some but not all of its assets in Treasuries, a portion of the fund income may be subject to state and local taxes. In addition, some states give different tax treatment to Treasuries and other U.S. government obligations. Ask your tax adviser what the story is in your state.

Tax Efficiency

Saving money on taxes when you invest in mutual funds doesn't mean sticking to municipal bond funds. Two other categories of mutual funds can reduce your tax bill year after year.

One of the biggest surprises for many mutual fund investors is the taxability of capital gains distributions made by the fund. Actively managed funds with a high turnover of securities within the portfolio generate more capital gains. Most fund managers don't think about the tax consequences of trades because they are focused on improving returns. In fact, managers have traditionally been compensated on pretax returns.

But two types of funds have lower turnover and, therefore, lower capital gains distributions:

➤ Index funds, designed to mimic a stock market index, are passively managed. A fund containing all the stocks in the Standard & Poor's 500, as an example, doesn't change its portfolio unless one of the stocks in that index changes. The lower turnover rate means fewer capitals gains distributions and a smaller annual tax bite for investors. One cautionary note: Index funds are most tax-efficient in rising markets. Because index funds are fully invested at all times, with no cash reserves, some analysts warn that they would have to sell holdings, thereby generating taxable capital gains, to meet investor demand for redemptions in a market downturn.

➤ Tax-efficient funds are a relatively new breed of funds whose managers are committed to weighing the tax consequences before making trades. Strategies to keep taxes down might include reducing turnover or trying to offset capital gains with losses. A tax-efficient fund will be designated accordingly in its prospectus.

Tax Swaps

Just as you can sell off underperforming individual bonds and buy new ones to capture a tax loss (as described in Chapter 18, "Making the Most of Bonds"), you can do the same with mutual funds. If you realize late in a calendar year that you own shares of funds selling below the price you paid to purchase them, you may want to sell to establish a tax loss.

Selling before your fund makes its year-end capital gains distribution lets you bypass the tax on the income from the distribution. Reinvest the money in a similar fund to keep your asset allocation in balance. Don't buy the same fund or one that is almost identical, though, or you'll trigger IRS "wash-sale" rules on the transaction. Also be careful not to buy into a new fund just before it makes its distribution, or you'll be swapping one tax liability for another.

Tax Traps

When is tax-free interest taxable? When it's counted in determining whether Social Security retirement benefits are taxable. As much as 85 percent of Social Security benefits may be taxable where Social Security recipients have "provisional income" (defined as adjusted gross income plus tax-exempt interest, plus half of Social Security benefits) exceeding $44,000 as a married couple filing jointly or $34,000 as a single taxpayer. Retirees seeking tax-free income from municipal bonds are often dismayed to see a tax bill they didn't expect.

An Alternative That Isn't

Want to fall into a black hole of taxes? Just qualify for the alternative minimum tax (AMT), and tax-free becomes taxable.

The AMT was originally designed to ensure that wealthy people couldn't sidestep taxes altogether by using tax loopholes. The problem for the rest of us is that "loopholes" prove to be plain, ordinary deductions. Simply living in a high-tax state, having high medical expenses, or lots of children can thrust you into the AMT for federal tax.

For purposes of the AMT, income is taxed at 26 percent on the first $175,000 and 28 percent on income over $175,000. On the surface, these are lower brackets than the high-bracket 36 percent and 39.6 percent on ordinary federal income tax.

But there are no personal exemptions or standard deductions under the AMT. Instead, there is a flat exemption of $45,000 for married taxpayers filing jointly and $33,750 for single taxpayers. The exemptions begin to phase out for joint filers earning more than $150,000, and single taxpayers earning more than $112,500. The entire exemption is lost for joint filers earning more than $330,000, and single taxpayers earning more than $247,500.

The impact goes beyond the dry numbers. A well-publicized example brings it to life: A Kansas family with a taxable income of just under $90,000, 13 children, and large medical expenses was slapped with an additional federal income tax bill of more than $3,700. The per-child tax exemption plus large medical deductions—one child suffers from leukemia—exceeded the flat exemption of $45,000 under the AMT.

The family lost an appeal, because the Tax Court ruled that the law clearly treats children as tax preferences.

If you might be subject to the AMT, you must calculate your federal income tax under the regular system and under the AMT, and then pay whichever amount is larger. The calculations alone are mind-numbing and can drive do-it-yourselfers to seek professional tax help.

The AMT calculation starts with adding "tax preference items" to your taxable income to get your AMT income. Tax preference items include normally deductible items that may wind up increasing your tax bill instead. State income taxes and local property taxes combined are enough to kick many taxpayers into the AMT. Having a lot of children can pose a tax problem because personal exemptions are disallowed. Sizable capital gains are a problem, along with investments in some *private-activity municipal bonds*.

Tax Talk

Private-activity municipal bonds are bonds whose proceeds are used to finance facilities used by private business. Examples include many bonds issued to raise money for housing, industrial development, pollution control, airport development, and sports facilities.

The big problem with the AMT is that the exemptions are not indexed for inflation. As a result, the number of taxpayers subject to the AMT has been rapidly increasing—and more of those taxpayers are middle-income rather than wealthy. In 1987, only 140,000 taxpayers were subject to the AMT. By 1998, the total was just over 1 million taxpayers. By 2008, according to an estimate by the Joint Tax Committee of the U.S. Congress, more than 8.8 million taxpayers will be paying the AMT, unless the law is changed. Sentiment in Congress is moving toward changing, if not repealing, the AMT. Meanwhile, in early 2000, President Clinton proposed modifying the law to permit taxpayers to claim the standard deduction as well as exemptions for children. At this writing, however, the law has not been changed.

If you might be subject to the AMT, you may want to rethink your municipal bond investment strategy. It's easy to avoid individual taxable munis. If you invest in municipal bonds through mutual funds, however, it may be a bit more difficult. Many muni bond funds load up on taxable issues to increase yield. If you might be subject to the AMT, bypass the temptation of increased yield; you'll just lose most or all of it to taxes. Also check the fund prospectus to determine the type of muni bonds in its portfolio.

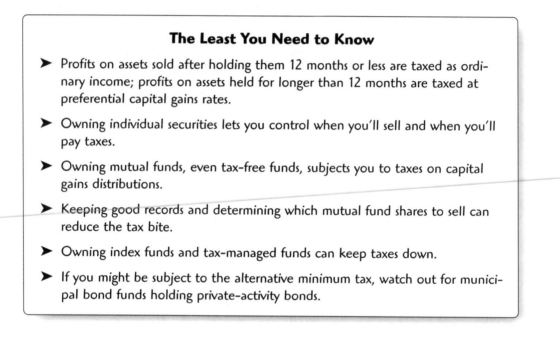

The Least You Need to Know

➤ Profits on assets sold after holding them 12 months or less are taxed as ordinary income; profits on assets held for longer than 12 months are taxed at preferential capital gains rates.

➤ Owning individual securities lets you control when you'll sell and when you'll pay taxes.

➤ Owning mutual funds, even tax-free funds, subjects you to taxes on capital gains distributions.

➤ Keeping good records and determining which mutual fund shares to sell can reduce the tax bite.

➤ Owning index funds and tax-managed funds can keep taxes down.

➤ If you might be subject to the alternative minimum tax, watch out for municipal bond funds holding private-activity bonds.

Part 6
End Game

You can't take it with you, but you can make life a lot easier—and less taxing—for your survivors.

In this part of the book, you'll find guidance on life insurance, estate planning, and writing a will. These may not seem the liveliest of subjects, but ignore them at your peril. This is the place to learn how to make sure that your hard-earned (and, of course, carefully tax-sheltered) dollars go to the people you love. And it's the place to find out how to keep Uncle Sam from dipping into the money along the way.

Chapter 23

Your Money for Your Life

In This Chapter

➤ Understanding that the primary purpose of life insurance is to replace income

➤ Learning that term insurance pays a death benefit if you die while the policy is in force; it has no other features

➤ Discovering that permanent insurance—whether whole life, universal life, or variable universal life—builds tax-sheltered cash value

➤ Finding that life insurance proceeds are not subject to income tax but may be part of a taxable estate

Life insurance isn't a favorite subject for most people. Right up there with estate planning, it summons intimations of mortality.

Yet life insurance can be an important part of your financial planning. It provides a death benefit that can replace income for your family. Along the way, it can shelter dollars from income tax.

Life insurance can also be confusing. This chapter helps you decide whether you need life insurance at all, what kind to buy, and ways to keep taxes down.

Hidden Value

Life insurance is often sold as a financial tool that can serve a variety of purposes—to pay for a college education, as an example, or to fund retirement. There may be other, more efficient ways to accomplish these objectives, but there is only one way to create an "instant estate," to create a pool of money that is immediately available to your family upon your death.

You create an instant estate the minute you pay the first premium on a life insurance policy. At that moment, no matter how small that first premium payment may be, the entire death benefit will be paid if you die.

If you have loved ones who depend on your income, you need life insurance. Later in life, when both your children and your assets have grown, you may not need life insurance to replace income for dependents. You might want to keep life insurance in force until the end of your life, however, if your estate will be subject to federal estate tax.

In 2000, amounts over $675,000 are potentially subject to federal estate tax; the amount rises to $1 million in 2006 and thereafter. (See Chapter 24, "You Can't Take It with You," for a complete discussion of estate taxes.) Life insurance lets you "prepay" estate taxes at the cost of the premiums. Life insurance may be especially valuable if your family would have to sell off illiquid assets such as real estate or a family business to pay estate tax.

The proceeds of life insurance that you own at your death will be included in your estate for the purpose of calculating whether federal estate tax is due. But life insurance proceeds are not subject to income tax. (As you'll recall from Chapter 14, "Hold On to Your Gains," if you leave an Individual Retirement Account at death, the money may be subject to both estate tax and income tax.)

Another reason for owning life insurance until the end of life might be to equalize bequests to your beneficiaries. Let's say that one of your daughters is your business partner. Logically, that daughter should inherit the business upon your death. But if most of your assets are tied up in the business, where does that leave your other daughter? Life insurance can provide cash so that you are fair to both children and, as important, leave them on good terms after you are gone.

Tax Traps

Group life insurance is a nice perk, but it has some potential drawbacks. First, it often disappears when you leave your job or retire. If you anticipate a lifelong need for life insurance, you will want individual coverage as well. Group life insurance may be convertible to an individual whole life insurance policy, but premiums will be high at retirement age. Secondly, the cost of group term life insurance in excess of $50,000 counts as income for tax purposes, so the perk may add to your tax bill.

How Much Is Too Much?

Assuming that you do need life insurance, you have two decisions to make: First, how much do you need? Second, what type should you buy?

A general rule of thumb is that you need life insurance (including any group life insurance you may have) in an amount equal to seven times your annual gross income.

But rules of thumb have definite shortcomings, and this one is no exception. Let's say that you earn $70,000 a year and buy a half-million dollars of life insurance, a bit more than seven times $70,000. Invested at 6 percent, the proceeds would throw off $30,000 a year. If inflation averages 3 percent a year, the buying power of $30,000 will be a bit more than $22,000 in 10 years. Will this be enough to support your family?

> **Tax Tips**
>
> Inflation has been fairly low for several years, so we don't give it much thought. But over time, even at low inflation, it costs more to buy most things even as the dollar is worth less. Want a graphic example? A first-class stamp cost 6 cents in 1967 and 33 cents—more than five times as much—in 1999.

Furthermore, you may earn $70,000 a year and be part of a two-income couple with no dependents. Your neighbor may earn the same $70,000 a year and be a single parent supporting two young children and an aging mother. Your life insurance needs are clearly quite different.

Instead of blindly following a general guideline, take a little time and try to estimate how much your family will actually need after you are gone and what assets they can draw on to produce income. Don't forget the impact of inflation as you do your calculations.

In determining how much money will be required, consider both immediate and ongoing needs.

Immediate needs include ready cash for funeral and other final expenses (such as uninsured medical expenses and probate fees), and money to pay any debts you may leave behind.

Ongoing needs may include these:

➤ Income to cover a readjustment period of two or three years, during which the family reshapes its financial affairs

➤ Income during the years when young children are still at home, when Social Security survivor benefits may take up part of the slack

➤ Money for college, at a time when Social Security has probably ended and expenses are heavier

➤ Income to provide a comfortable lifestyle for a surviving spouse, either entirely or to supplement his or her own income

When you've pinpointed your family's potential need, identify your existing income-producing assets. Make a list of bank accounts, money market funds, securities, pensions, Social Security survivor benefits, and life insurance that you may have on the job. Any gap between your family's needs and available income can then be made up with life insurance.

Life insurance may be either short-term or permanent.

Meeting Short-Term Needs

Insurance for the short haul is best bought as term insurance. Term insurance is pure insurance, with no bells and whistles. It will pay a death benefit if you die during the term. Period. You can't borrow against term insurance because it has no cash value.

Tax Tips

If you're tempted to take up your mortgage lender's offer of insurance to pay off your mortgage if you die, consider buying an individual term insurance policy tied to the term of your mortgage instead. Buying on your own will probably be much cheaper, and it will let your survivors choose what to do with the money. They may have a more pressing need than paying off the mortgage.

But because many life insurance needs last for a specific length of time—paying off a mortgage or providing a college education are prime examples—many people do very well with term insurance. If you buy a 20-year term policy when your first child is born, or a five-year policy when your first-born is entering high school, your family should have the money to pay for college even if you aren't here when the time comes.

Because term insurance is pure insurance, without the "extras" in permanent insurance, it's possible to buy a much larger death benefit at lower cost. The premium does go up at each renewal, based on your age. But where the standard term insurance policy is annual renewable term, with the premium rising each year, many insurers are now issuing level-term policies running up to 20 years (sometimes 30 years), letting you lock in level premiums for that stretch of time. On a level-term policy, premiums will start a bit higher, but the policy will probably cost less over the entire period.

Because you can't be sure what your future insurance needs may be, buy a term policy that is convertible to permanent insurance without evidence of insurability.

Tax Treats

Term insurance rates are falling so dramatically that you should compare policy costs every few years. You may lock in a low rate on a 10-year, level-term policy and then find—just two or three years later—that you can save money by switching to a new 10-year level-term policy with another company. Just be sure to fill out the application accurately; if you die within two years of taking any insurance policy, the insurer can deny a claim for a material misrepresentation. Don't terminate the old policy until the new one is in force.

To Have and to Hold

If you are certain that you will need life insurance throughout your life, then you'll want to consider permanent insurance. For maximum protection, take a combination of term insurance and permanent insurance.

Permanent insurance comes in several flavors. All have an investment feature in the form of cash value that builds tax-free inside the policy. This "investment" can bring widely varying rates of return. A study by the Consumer Federation of America a couple of years ago found that the rate of return on many policies becomes attractive only after the policy is held for at least 15 years. That's all the more reason to buy life insurance not as an investment, but as replacement income for your family.

On the plus side, the cash value is not subject to income tax either during your life or when the policy proceeds are paid after your death. There is one exception; if you take out more than you paid in, the difference will be taxable.

Little cash value accrues in the early years of a permanent policy but, once it has built up, cash value provides you with several options:

➤ If you stop paying premiums, the cash value can be used to continue your current insurance protection for a specific period of time or, if you so choose, to provide a smaller death benefit no matter how long you may live.

➤ If you cancel ("surrender") the policy, in whole or in part, you can receive the cash value as a lump sum of money. If this lump sum exceeds the premiums you paid for the policy, the difference will be taxable.

Tax Tips

The cash value in permanent insurance is not the same thing as the face value of the policy. The face amount is the death benefit, while the cash value is the amount available to borrow against or to receive in cash when you surrender a policy early. The cash value is not guaranteed and may be affected by the insurance company's financial results.

➤ If you surrender the policy, instead of taking the cash value, it can be used to convert the policy into an annuity. An annuity is an insurance product that is the reverse of life insurance; instead of paying its benefits at death, it is designed to provide income during life.

➤ You may borrow against your life insurance policy, using the cash value as collateral. You don't have to repay the loan but, if you don't repay the principal and interest, the amount will be subtracted from the death benefit when you die. At the very least, you should always pay the interest on a life insurance loan so that you don't wind up paying interest on interest and diminishing the value of your life insurance.

If you are interested in permanent insurance, you can choose among three basic types: whole life, universal life, and variable universal life.

Whole Life

In this plain-vanilla variety of permanent insurance, the premiums are generally level, based on your age at the time of purchase. In essence, you pay more than necessary when you're young and less when you're older (compared to the cost of a term insurance policy); in exchange, you receive a guarantee that you will always be covered and that the price will never go up.

In some varieties of whole life insurance, you may choose to pay larger premiums in the early years so that the policy will be fully paid-up with policy dividends and so that further premiums may not be due after you reach a specified age. But so-called "vanishing premium" policies have been sold based on unsustainable interest rates, leaving unsuspecting policyholders owing premiums for many more years than planned. The term "vanishing premium" isn't often used any more, but the concept is still being sold. If you are interested in this arrangement, find out what interest projections are being used and what guarantees, if any, you will have.

Annual dividends on whole life policies may be taken in cash, applied to premiums, or used to purchase additional insurance. Note, though, that dividends are not guaranteed.

Universal Life

This flexible variation of life insurance offers coverage with an ongoing choice of premium and death benefit. After the initial premium, you can raise and lower premiums, and even skip a payment without causing the policy to lapse. You can withdraw part of the cash value without paying interest.

Universal life insurance, a form of interest-sensitive life insurance, was very popular in the high-interest days of the 1980s. It became considerably less popular as interest rates dropped and policyholders had to pay more in premiums to keep their policies in force.

Universal life insurance offers the advantage of visible pricing. On an ordinary life insurance policy, it can be almost impossible to find out what portion of your premium goes for administrative costs, commissions, and the actual cost of the insurance. On the other hand, in an effort to be competitive in the marketplace, some insurers offer a much better deal to new universal life customers while shortchanging existing customers on costs.

If you're interested in a universal life policy, independent insurance agent Richard Mayer suggests that you request the minimum level premium and maximum death benefit based on the current interest assumptions of the insurer. Otherwise, you may be sold a more expensive policy than necessary.

Tax Tips

You don't lose your life insurance as soon as you miss a premium due date. Life insurance policies typically have a 30- or 31-day grace period during which you can pay the premium, without interest, and keep the policy in force. There is an additional 30 days in which you can pay the back premiums and reinstate the policy without evidence of insurability. An Automatic Premium Loan rider also can prevent policy lapse by automatically deducting the next premium payment from the cash value and keeping your policy in force.

Variable Universal Life

This form of permanent insurance provides cash values and death benefits pegged to the performance of an underlying portfolio of investments. As with universal life insurance, premiums may be increased, decreased, or stopped. Unlike a universal life policy, where the insurance company decides how to invest the assets, with variable universal life you get to choose among investments with varying degrees of risk and reward. Because fees associated with these policies tend to be high, however, you'll want to choose investments with potentially higher returns.

If you choose wisely and your investments do well, both the cash value and the death benefit can grow. Conversely, they can also decrease, although the death benefit usually has a minimum guarantee. In other words, the investment risk is concentrated in the cash value. If there is not enough cash value, one of three things may occur: The policy may end, the death benefit may be reduced, or higher premiums will have to be paid.

Tax Tips

Because policyholders assume the investment risk, variable life policies are regulated as securities. Agents who sell them must be licensed to sell securities and life insurance in the state where the insurance is issued.

Variable life insurance has some attractive tax benefits. Dividends in the underlying funds are reinvested tax-free. There is no capital gains tax when you buy and sell funds within the insurance policy. But—and it's a *big* but—the tax advantages disappear if you surrender the policy. At that time, anything you get over what you put in is taxable. If you borrow against the cash value, however, it is not taxable.

Variable life insurance is popular in an era when stocks are doing well. But it can take 15 to 20 years to pay off, and you may want to think twice about pegging life insurance protection to stock market performance for the long term. You may also want to think twice if you won't have the time or inclination to monitor performance carefully.

The following highlights the features of various types of life insurance.

Term insurance:

➤ Provides maximum protection at minimum cost

➤ Provides protection for a specified period of time

➤ May be renewable each year, at an increasing premium, or issued at a level premium for periods of up to 30 years

➤ Has no cash value

➤ May be convertible to permanent insurance

Whole life insurance:

➤ Provides lifelong protection as long as premiums are paid

➤ Has a fixed premium and death benefit

➤ Has tax-free growth of earnings within the policy

Universal life insurance:

➤ Offers permanent protection

➤ Has flexible premiums and death benefit

➤ Has cash value that reflects premiums paid, the company's investment results, and prevailing interest rates

➤ Has tax-free growth of earnings within the policy

Variable universal life insurance:

➤ Offers permanent protection

➤ Has flexible premiums

➤ Gives the policyholder a choice of underlying investment options

➤ Involves fluctuating death benefit and cash value in relation to investment performance

➤ Has tax-free growth of earnings within the policy

Policy Riders

Even though permanent life insurance policies come with a bunch of bells and whistles built in to the basic policy, you may be offered a choice of "riders" with additional special provisions. Evaluate your choices carefully because some riders, offered at additional cost, are not worthwhile.

A rider doubling the death benefit if death is caused by an accident rather than an illness (so-called "double indemnity") is one you may want to skip. Why should your family need more money if you die in an accident than if you die in bed? Buy the amount of insurance your family will actually need, and forget about paying an extra premium for this rider.

A rider waiving premiums if you are disabled may be worth considering, although it should not take the place of disability income insurance that will replace income if you are ill or disabled and unable to work.

Some companies offer "accelerated benefits" either within the policy or as a rider. Accelerated (sometimes called "living") benefits let you receive the proceeds of your life insurance during life under certain circumstances. Typically the policies will pay if you suffer a catastrophic or terminal illness or are confined to a nursing home.

But there is an optional rider that you should definitely accept if you have cash value insurance. That's the rider providing an automatic premium loan from the cash value. With an APL rider, you will never lose your life insurance because you forget to make a premium payment.

Tax Tips

Name a beneficiary and a secondary (contingent) beneficiary to your life insurance policy. Then be sure to review beneficiary designations and change them as appropriate if you marry, divorce, remarry, or become a parent or a grandparent.

Special Coverage

Other variations on the life insurance theme may be attractive. A popular policy among affluent older couples, for example, is the second-to-die policy. Such a policy, which may take any of the permanent life forms, insures two lives but pays only upon the second death. As a result, it is less expensive than it would be to insure two people with separate policies, and can actually make life insurance affordable when one spouse is healthy but the other has a serious medical condition.

Second-to-die policies are most often used where the surviving spouse won't need the money but the beneficiaries will need cash to pay estate taxes.

Money on the Line

Life insurance has traditionally been purchased from life insurance agents. (To be honest, life insurance has been sold by agents rather than bought by eager customers.) Today, however, you have several choices.

You can still buy from an agent, and this may be your best bet if you need advice, as most people do. Life insurance can be confusing, and a reputable agent can be your best ally.

If you know what you want, you can buy direct from some companies, often at considerable savings. To buy direct, look to the handful of well-respected companies that sell policies directly to consumers. Work with a fee-only insurance adviser. For term insurance, scout the online sites. Or, if you live in a state with savings bank life insurance (New York, Massachusetts, and Connecticut), get a quote from your local savings bank.

Tax Tips

Toll-free and online sources for insurance information—especially term insurance—are proliferating. Here are just a few: Quotesmith, at www.quotesmith.com or 1-800-431-1147; SelectQuote, at 1-800-343-1985; and TermQuote, at 1-800-444-8376.

Agents

Many competent life insurance agents will do their best to find the coverage you need at the right price. However, this is also a field with very high turnover; if you're not careful, you may wind up with, at best, an inexperienced agent, and, at worst, an unscrupulous one.

Because agent-sold cash value policies pay very high commissions to the agent—anywhere from 50 percent to 100 percent of the premium in the first year—there can be a strong incentive for some agents to sell you the highest-priced policy without regard to your real needs.

If you decide to work with an agent, ask for recommendations from friends, family, and other professional advisers. Look for an independent agent representing several companies rather than an agent under contract to a single life insurance company; no one company has the best product for everyone. Find out what training and professional credentials he or she has. The initials "CLU" after the person's name, as an example, means Chartered Life Underwriter. CFP means Certified Financial Planner. People who have gone to the trouble of earning these professional designations tend to have more experience.

One warning: It can be extraordinarily difficult to compare permanent life insurance policies. You'll want to take "illustrations," the mind-numbing charts full of projections shown by insurance agents, with a large grain of salt. Regulators have tightened guidelines, but illustrations may still convey unrealistic expectations.

In reviewing an illustration, ask which numbers are actually guaranteed as you review annual premiums, cash values, accumulation values, and the death benefit. Remember that interest rates and dividends are never fixed; projections based on current interest rates can't be fixed either. Also bear in mind that an illustration is not a legal document. The insurer's legal obligations are spelled out in the policy itself.

Because cash value insurance comes in so many variations, it is a form of insurance that is often best purchased through an agent. Term insurance is a simpler matter, and you may want to secure quotes and possibly buy the insurance through a toll-free telephone call or online.

Whether you make your purchase through an agent or on your own, compare rates from several companies. The differences can be surprising. Also be sure to buy from a solid well-rated insurance company. Life insurance won't pay up for many years—you hope—and you want your insurer to be solvent when the time comes. A good way to check financial stability is to consult one of the rating agency reports at your local library; ask your research librarian how to find the reports from A.M. Best Co., Standard & Poor's, Moody's, and Duff & Phelps.

Tax Tips

Your occupation, health, finances, and even your driving record will determine whether you can buy life insurance and what the cost of that insurance will be. But different companies take different attitudes toward specific risk factors. If you have a serious medical condition such as heart disease or diabetes, ask an agent to find a company willing to write policies for people in your situation.

Tax Tips

Most states have guaranty programs that will come to your rescue if an insurer bites the dust. But it can still be a long drawn-out hassle to get your money back. It's better, if possible, to choose a stable insurance company in the first place.

Swaps

An old life insurance policy may serve the purpose, but a new one may be better. What should you do if an agent suggests that you trade in your old policy for a new one with a better rate of return, superior features, or a larger death benefit?

You should periodically review and update your life insurance, especially if your needs change dramatically or if a much better policy is introduced. But be extra careful if an agent suggests an exchange.

You won't owe any income tax on an exchange as long as you actually trade one policy for another rather than surrendering the old policy and then using the cash to buy the new policy. (If you surrender a policy, you'll owe income tax on any excess of cash value over the premiums you've paid.) A direct exchange between two life insurance policies, or from a life insurance policy to an annuity, is tax-free if it is a "Section 1035 exchange," named after the applicable section of the tax code.

But remember what I said earlier about hefty commissions in the early years of a permanent policy. Commissions can be an irresistible lure to some agents to urge swaps on their policyholders. Commissions also eat away at cash value for the first few years, so it can take quite a while for a new policy to catch up to an old one.

Before you agree to a swap, be sure that the agent gives you a detailed written comparison of the old and new policies. Also insist on the following information:

➤ How soon the new policy will provide the same amount of cash value that you currently have in the existing policy, and how soon that cash value will be accessible. Many policies issued under an exchange arrangement have a one-year waiting period before either policy loans or cash surrenders are allowed.

➤ The difference in guaranteed values between the two policies, and what will happen if interest rates go down.

Remember that dying within two years of taking out an insurance policy opens the door for the claim to be challenged. If you need more insurance, you might want to keep your old policy in force and add additional coverage through a new permanent or term policy.

Burying the Wealth

Life insurance proceeds can be used to pay federal estate taxes, leaving the rest of the estate intact for your beneficiaries. But life insurance proceeds themselves are included in your taxable estate—unless you don't own the policy at the time of death.

For this reason, people who expect their estates to be subject to federal estate tax— the excluded amount at this writing is $675,000, going up to $1 million by 2006— often arrange to have their life insurance policies owned by an adult child or by an irrevocable life insurance trust. The owner—the child or the trust—should also be the beneficiary. If you, the insured, can control the policy in any way, the proceeds will be right back in your taxable estate. And if three parties are involved, watch out. If a trust owns a policy on your life with your child as beneficiary, for example, gift tax will come into play. If a trust owns the policy, the trust should be the beneficiary; the trust documents can then govern distribution of the proceeds.

Even if you don't own the policy, you can still provide the money to pay the premiums, using the annual gift tax exclusion of $10,000 to provide the cash to your child or the trust.

The simplest approach is to have your child purchase a new policy on your life. A slightly more complicated but sometimes preferable approach is to set up an irrevocable trust and have the trust purchase the policy.

You also can transfer ownership of an existing policy, but this approach has inherent problems. First, if there is sizable cash value, the transfer may be subject to gift tax. Secondly, if you die within three years of the transfer, the policy proceeds will be counted in your taxable estate. It's even possible that the IRS could charge the estate with interest on any gift tax that should have been paid when the transfer was made.

Tax Tips

If your spouse owns your life insurance, it will also be out of your estate, but the proceeds will eventually wind up in his or her taxable estate. It's preferable to have a child own your life insurance—if that child is mature, if you have just one child (so there won't be sibling conflict), and if your surviving spouse won't be dependent on the insurance proceeds and hence on the child. Otherwise, an irrevocable trust is a better choice.

A solution to this potential problem, if you own a low-cost policy you would like to transfer, is to buy an inexpensive three-year term insurance policy to cover the estate tax liability during the period of exposure. Once the three-year window is closed, you will no longer need the term insurance.

The Least You Need to Know

➤ You need life insurance if your survivors will suffer financial hardship at your death.

➤ Cash needs for the short term can be met with term insurance; lifelong needs should be met with permanent insurance.

➤ Permanent insurance varieties include whole life, universal life, and variable universal life.

➤ A tax-free exchange of life insurance policies can be arranged if you need more or different coverage, but be wary of exchanges arranged primarily to generate agent commissions.

➤ If your estate will be subject to federal estate tax, you can keep life insurance proceeds out of your taxable estate by not owning the policy.

Chapter 24

You Can't Take It with You

In This Chapter

➤ Federal estate tax is currently levied on estates in excess of $675,000, rising gradually to $1 million by 2006

➤ Planning your estate well can minimize the tax your heirs must pay

➤ Giving assets to your family during life can be a wiser move than letting them inherit the same assets after you are gone

➤ Giving charitable gifts to also reduce your taxable estate

What, me? Worry about estate tax? You must be kidding! I'm not rich.

To some extent, you're right. The federal estate tax is assessed only on estates over $675,000 and is paid by a mere 1 percent of all estates each year. But you're probably richer than you think you are, and you're almost definitely richer dead than alive. A lot of the money in your name—just think life insurance and the assets locked in retirement plans—becomes available only after you die. If you want your family to receive the money and not have a large chunk go in taxes, you've got to do some serious estate planning.

This chapter explains how the estate tax works and then shows you how to minimize its impact on you and your loved ones. Read it, even if you know that your estate won't be subject to the tax, because good financial planning at any level of income and net worth requires paying attention to what happens after you are gone.

Uncle Sam Collects

You have an estate. Yes, you, because I don't mean a mansion on extensive acreage. An estate, in the legal sense, is everything you own at the time of your death. That includes cash and securities, of course, but also your house, automobiles, jewelry, life insurance, retirement benefits, coin collection, and the classic car you've spent hours lovingly restoring.

When you die, Uncle Sam wants a piece of the action. There's historic precedent for the claim. Hundreds of years ago in England (the source of much American law), all property reverted back to the king upon death; the estate tax was the price one's heirs paid to get it back.

Federal estate tax has been collected since 1916, but the size of affected estates has changed from time to time. In 1976, as an example, you could give away up to $30,000 during life and leave up to $60,000 at death without federal tax. By 1987, there was a *unified credit,* applied to both gifts and estates, of $600,000. Today the unified credit is $675,000, but it is going up, as shown in the following table. Listed are the amounts that can pass to your heirs free of federal gift and estate tax:

Year	Amount
1999	$650,000
2000	$675,000
2001	$675,000
2002	$700,000
2003	$700,000
2004	$850,000
2005	$950,000
2006	$1,000,000

The increase may not be as magnanimous a gift as it appears on the surface. The $600,000 exclusion that went into effect in 1987 would be more than $900,000 by now, if it had been adjusted for inflation, and probably would be well over $1 million by 2006. But let's not look a gift horse in the mouth. This particular tinkering with the tax code has actually helped many middle-class families.

You can actually own more than the exclusion amounts and still escape federal estate tax because your taxable estate is your gross estate reduced by funeral expenses, outstanding debts (including income taxes that may be due after you die), attorney's fees, and some other items.

If your taxable estate exceeds the amount excluded from federal estate tax, your heirs can expect to be hit hard. The tax is paid by the estate itself, not by the heirs, but it diminishes the amount available for distribution.

The tax starts at 37 percent and rises steeply to 55 percent. Due to a phaseout of the unified credit on estates over $10 million, the actual marginal rate on these super-size estates is 60 percent. Fortunately or not, this doesn't affect too many people. It wouldn't be pleasant to owe the tax, but it sure would be nice to have that much money!

Tax Talk

The **unified credit** is a federal tax credit applied to money transferred by an individual through a combination of certain lifetime gifts and the estate left at death. Amounts up to the unified credit are free from tax.

Business Before Pleasure

Family businesses have long complained that they are too often forced out of business by the need to liquidate assets to pay federal estate taxes. The "Letters" column in *The Wall Street Journal* in August 1999 bore the headline "Death Tax Is the American Nightmare." Two letters described the havoc wrought on family-owned construction companies by the estate tax and preparations to pay the estate tax.

Yet the same 1997 tax measure that increased the amounts exempt from federal estate tax attempted to ease the burden on small business. It granted a full $1.3 million tax exemption for family businesses starting January 1, 1998. Unfortunately, the exemption proved to be more glitter than gold.

For one thing, the exemption started out at twice what was then the $650,000 exclusion for any estate, but it included that exemption. So it declines in value as the standard exemption increases. By 2006, when the standard exemption reaches $1 million, the special exemption will give business owners only an additional $300,000.

To make matters worse, it's not all that easy to qualify for the extra exemption. Three tests must be met:

➤ First, the business must be at least half the value of the taxable estate.

➤ Second, family members must actively participate in the business in five out of the eight years preceding your death.

➤ Third, the family members who are your heirs must similarly participate for 5 out of any 8 years in the 10 years following your death.

The catch is in the third provision. A lot can happen in the 10 years following your death. The business might be sold or go into bankruptcy, or one of the heirs might die. If heirs aren't participating, for any reason, the family will have to pay the estate tax that would otherwise have been due at your death. So, you may want to plan your estate as if there is no extra exemption; your family can regard it as a bonus if it happens.

Greedy States of Affairs

Uncle Sam isn't the only one who wants a piece of the pie. States have death taxes, too. Every state gets a piece of the federal estate tax collected on its residents, but some states have their own *estate tax* and *inheritance tax* as well.

Inheritance taxes are often based on the level of relationship. In many states, for example, a surviving spouse and children pay no inheritance tax. Distant relatives and people outside the family are most likely to have to pay an inheritance tax. Every state has different laws; you should consult a professional adviser in your state.

If you're considering a move to another state, you may want to consider estate and inheritance taxes as well as income and property taxes before you make your decision. Once you've chosen, if you're moving from a high-tax to a low-tax state, be sure to firmly establish your new legal domicile—and spend at least six months a year there—or the former state may come after your estate for taxes.

You can establish legal domicile in these ways:

Tax Talk

An **estate tax** is a tax on the right to dispose of property; it is assessed on the estate before assets are distributed. An **inheritance tax** is a tax on the right to receive property and is paid by the recipient.

➤ Closing former bank accounts and opening new ones in the new location

➤ Transferring brokerage accounts

➤ Getting a new driver's license

➤ Registering to vote

➤ Giving up religious, civic, and social memberships in the former state and forming new attachments

➤ Living in the new state for more than half the year (and don't forget visits to your old neighborhood in calculating the total time spent)

Bypassing the Tax Man

It often has been said that the richest people pay the least tax. To the extent that this is true, it's because they (or their advisers) know how to take advantage of provisions in the law to lessen the tax bite. You can take advantage of many of these provisions, too.

You have several tactics to consider: splitting ownership of assets between husband and wife (see the section in this chapter, "The Merry Widow(er)"), taking maximum advantage of the *step-up in basis* at death (see the section "Step Up to Tax-Free Gains") and giving assets away during life (see "Gaining by Giving"). One or more trusts can also serve to reduce estate taxes; wills and trusts are discussed in Chapter 25, "You Must Be Willing."

The Merry Widow(er)

Jointly owned property automatically belongs to the survivor when the first partner dies. Any amount of individually owned property may also be left to a surviving spouse without estate tax (as long as your spouse is a citizen of the United States; see the "Tax Traps" note). But this doesn't mean that you should own everything jointly, if you're married, just to escape the estate tax when the first one dies. Doing so will simply subject the estate to estate tax when it's the survivor's turn to go—on the original inherited amount plus all of the added growth in the intervening years.

Good estate planning involves deciding who owns what today, as well as who should inherit what tomorrow. If you and your spouse own substantial assets, you should consider splitting ownership so that you each own approximately half—or, at least, up to the excluded amount. You may want to keep the family home in joint ownership for sentimental reasons, but ownership of cash and securities is often best split between husband and wife.

Common ownership forms include these:

➤ Individual ownership is property held by a single person.

➤ Joint tenancy with right of survivorship means that each partner automatically inherits from the other—but it also allows either owner to sell his or her interest and force a division of the property.

➤ Tenancy in common does not have the right of survivorship and is more often used by business partners than by spouses.

Tax Talk

Capital gains tax is assessed on profits, on the difference between the price you pay for an asset and the price you sell it for. A **step-up in basis** means that the price you paid is automatically bumped up to the value of the asset at the date of your death. When your heirs then sell the asset, capital gains tax will be due only on the appreciation from the date of death to the date of sale.

Tax Traps

The unlimited marital deduction—the provision that lets you pass unlimited property to a spouse without estate tax—does not apply when your spouse is not a citizen of the United States. Instead, the standard exclusion (currently $675,000) applies. Many noncitizen spouses choose to become citizens when faced with this financial reality. If your spouse is not so inclined, be sure that the attorney drafting your will is informed.

➤ Tenancy by the entirety, permitted only between spouses, has the right of survivorship and also requires joint action. Neither of you can force a sale; both of you are protected. Tenancy by the entirety is the assumed form of ownership by husband and wife in some states, unless the ownership papers spell out a different arrangement.

Review Chapter 14, "Hold On to Your Gains," for a refresher course on inheriting retirement plans. Read both this chapter and Chapter 25 to get an overview of estate planning. Then, if your estate might wind up over the taxable threshold, consult a knowledgeable trusts and estates attorney about what to do.

Step Up to Tax-Free Gains

Property is valued at the time of death for estate tax purposes. That means that your heirs can start fresh, keeping their records on assets with potential capital gains consequences based on the market value at the time of your death. The blue chip stock that you bought at $50 in the 1950s may be worth $200 a share at the time you die; your heirs take over the stepped-up cost basis of $200.

Ascertaining value is easy when it comes to cash. It's a tad more complicated for securities. You can't just look at the newspaper stock market tables the day after the death. The value for estate tax purposes is the mean between high and low prices, and includes accrued interest and dividends. Estate attorneys often use specialized computer services to calculate the value of securities.

Tax Traps

One big problem for many folks in separating ownership of assets for estate planning is that retirement benefits in the form of a 401(k) or rollover IRA make up a sizable portion of their assets. Ownership of retirement benefits belongs to the person who socked away the money and can't be split.

Yet securities are a cinch when compared to real estate or a family business. To satisfy the IRS, your executor may have to secure appraisals to fix the value for the estate tax return. Chapter 25 describes the duties of the executor.

Although estate tax may be due, the step-up helps your heirs because they won't owe capital gains tax on the appreciation between the time you bought the asset and the time of your death.

But step-up in basis also plays a direct role in estate planning. On jointly held property, in most states, the survivor gets a step up of half the cost basis. The exception is in community property states. In the nine states that currently use some variation of community property law, a surviving spouse generally receives a step-up of the entire value.

The following are states with community property laws:

➤ Arizona ➤ New Mexico

➤ California ➤ Texas

➤ Idaho ➤ Washington

➤ Louisiana ➤ Wisconsin

➤ Nevada

Property acquired while you live in a community property state is generally considered community property, even if you later move away. Separately owned property brought into a community property state remains separate property, unless you mingle it with other assets; then it becomes community property. If you have moved or plan to move between a community property state and another state, consult a professional adviser about property ownership and estate planning.

Gaining by Giving

Want a good way to reduce your taxable estate? Give it away before you die.

Not if you need it, of course. But if you have enough to live on and expect to have enough to see you through a lengthy retirement, you may want to start removing assets from your estate by making gifts to your nearest and dearest.

The gift tax rules, as you'll remember, are integrated with the estate tax rules. But you still can come out ahead by giving money away. Start with annual gifts that are free of gift tax, consider additional gifts that are direct payments to medical or educational institutions, and then think about more sizable gifts. The sizable gifts may be taxable, but you and your family can still end up with more money by giving some away today.

No Gift Tax Here

Every individual can give away up to $10,000 each year to as many people, related or unrelated, as they please. There is no tax and no need to file a gift tax return. A married couple, if they agree to

Tax Traps

If you're giving gifts to young children, you'll probably want to establish a custodial account under the Uniform Transfers to Minors Act (sometimes the Uniform Gifts to Minors Act). But be careful. If you give the money and name yourself custodian, the money will go right back into your taxable estate if you die while the child is still a minor. Solution: Name a trusted relative—perhaps the child's parent, if you're the grandparent—as custodian.

do so, can give up to $20,000 per recipient. These amounts have been indexed to inflation since a law was passed in 1997. However, inflation has been low in recent years, and, because the threshold increases only in multiples of $1,000, it hasn't budged.

This annual exclusion can be a good way to reduce the size of your taxable estate. If you have two children and they each have two children, you and your spouse could jointly give as much as $120,000 in a single year—and that's without giving anything to your son-in-law or daughter-in-law.

Here's a tip: Keep your annual gifts well under the allowable $10,000 or $20,000. Then you can also give a birthday or holiday gift without running into gift tax complications.

In addition to the gifts that come under the annual exclusion from gift tax, you may make gifts of any amount as long as they are paid directly to a medical or educational institution. This can be a good way to pay for a grandchild's braces or college education—if you can afford to do so and want to do so.

Want more good reasons for giving money to your family while you're alive? Appreciation on their part—and knowledge, on your part, of making a difference in their lives.

Tax Tips

Don't wait until the very end of December to write gift checks for the year. If the recipient does not deposit the check before year-end, the IRS may claim that the gift doesn't qualify for the gift tax exclusion in the current year. In fact, a federal district court recently ruled that gift checks that did not clear the bank before the donor's death wound up back in the donor's taxable estate.

Giving Big Bucks

If you make gifts of more than $10,000 (or $20,000, if you're married), other than the medical and educational gifts mentioned previously, the amount counts toward your total lifetime exemption from gift and estate tax. In 2000, that exemption is $675,000, but as you'll recall, it is going up over the next few years.

Gift tax doesn't have to be paid at the time the gift is made, but a gift tax return (Form 709) must be filed. Uncle Sam keeps the return on file and subtracts the amounts you've given during life when estate tax is calculated after your death. If you give $100,000 to your daughter in one year, as an example, $10,000 comes under the annual tax-free gift rule and $90,000 counts toward your lifetime credit of $675,000.

Even so, if you can afford to do so, it's much better taxwise to give during life. That's because even though the gift and estate tax is unified, there is a big difference in the way the two are calculated. In tax jargon, the gift tax is "exclusive," while the estate tax is "inclusive." In practical terms, the gift tax is paid out of the sum given, while the estate tax is paid on top of the sum.

Let's say that you leave your children $1 million (just to use nice round numbers) in your will. At a 50 percent estate tax rate, the government gets $500,000, so your heirs actually receive $500,000. If you give away the same $1 million during life and the tax comes out of the amount the children actually get, the children receive about $667,000 because a 50 percent tax is $333,000. So, your children get more, while the amount of the gift itself reduces your taxable estate.

Doing Good

Charitable gifts are not subject to either gift or estate tax. You can reduce your taxable estate by giving money to charity either during life or after death. But why wait? If you have the money and the inclination, there's enormous satisfaction—as well as tax benefits—to be gained by giving.

I'm not talking here about the $25 or $50 checks you write each year to a bunch of charities in response to their annual appeals. I'm talking about sizable gifts to help causes that matter to you.

You don't have to be a millionaire or take advantage of fancy trust vehicles (trusts, fancy and otherwise, are discussed in Chapter 25) to give a meaningful gift. A gift of $1,000 will earn you a great deal of gratitude. Think in terms of $5,000 or more, and you might consider a gift annuity or a contribution to a donor-advised fund.

A gift annuity produces both a tax deduction and lifelong income, starting either right away or at a designated future date. A gift of $5,000 won't produce much income, although actual returns are based on your age. Rates recently ranged from about 5.5 percent for a single 20-year-old (not likely to buy an annuity!) to 12 percent for a single 90-year-old.

Also, because you will receive income, the gift itself has a discounted value for tax purposes. The older you are—and the less likely you are to receive income for an extended period—the more you can deduct. A gift annuity is worth considering if you have a favorite charity you'd like to support but you still need income from your donation. Just be sure that you understand all the details, including the tax ramifications, before you sign on the dotted line.

Tax Tips

If you give gifts to your family (other than cash), the best bet is an asset, such as a growth stock, expected to appreciate in value. The worst bet is an asset that has already appreciated significantly because the recipient of your gift will take over your tax basis for capital gains purposes instead of the stepped-up basis that would be available in your estate. The opposite is true if you are making the gift to charity. If you give appreciated securities, you bypass the capital gains tax while getting a tax deduction for the full current market value.

Another alternative is a donor-advised fund. Here you donate money or other assets, taking an immediate tax deduction, to an organization that will manage the money and pass it on to charity later. The fund is "donor-advised" because you can recommend (but not dictate) the charity or charities to receive the money.

The original donor-advised funds were community foundations such as the New York Community Trust, local groups set up to channel contributions to worthy local causes. These still exist, but there are also donor-advised funds at specific institutions (Harvard University has one) and run by financial institutions (including Fidelity Investments).

The donor-advised approach has distinct advantages. You can make contributions over time, and you can recommend distributions over time. You can involve your children in selecting causes to support.

But investigate carefully first. Ask about minimum requirements for initial and subsequent contributions. Inquire about administrative and investment fees. Find out how the fund invests its money. Also ask how often you can request that distributions be made, and whether those distributions must be in a minimum amount.

The Least You Need to Know

➤ You're richer than you think you are, and you should plan your estate so that as much as possible goes to your loved ones, not to Uncle Sam.

➤ Federal estate taxes are levied on estates over $675,000, going up to $1 million by 2006. States may also collect estate and/or inheritance taxes on the assets that you leave behind.

➤ Estate and gift taxes are imposed at the same rate but are calculated differently, so you can save money by making gifts during life.

➤ Charitable giving during life and at death can also reduce estate taxes.

Chapter 25

You Must Be Willing

In This Chapter

➤ Learning that everyone needs a will

➤ Helping to reduce the tax bite on your estate with one or more trusts

➤ Carefully choosing the executor of your will and the trustees of any trusts you establish: They will represent you after you are gone

➤ Planning well by setting up a durable power of attorney, a living will, and a healthcare proxy

---

You need a will. Yes, you. Whether you're young or old, married or single, poor or rich, you need a will. A will—more formally, a last will and testament—is the only way to direct the disposition of everything you've worked so hard to acquire. It's the only way to protect your family. And it's an important step toward saving money and possibly minimizing taxes on the assets you leave behind.

There are other steps to take as well. You may want to establish one or more trusts. You should execute advance directives, the documents that spell out the kind of care you want if you are unable to speak for yourself. And you should definitely have a durable power of attorney so that someone you trust can handle your financial affairs if you cannot.

This chapter takes you through the documents and procedures needed to wrap things up tidily at the end of life. It should be read together with Chapter 24, "You Can't Take It with You."

Where There's a Will

A will is a legal document directing the disposition of property. If you care at all about what happens to your property and, more important, to your family, you should write a will.

As some attorneys point out, everyone dies with a will. It can be one you write yourself; or it can be one that your state will write for you if you die *intestate,* without leaving a will of your own.

Tax Talk

Intestate means dying without leaving a valid will ("last will and testament"). When someone dies intestate, state laws govern the disposition of property.

Tax Traps

A husband and wife should each have a will, even when one spouse does not work outside the home or have independent income. Unless it is very carefully drafted, a joint will may be treated as a legally binding document on the surviving partner— no matter what happens in his or her life that would warrant a change in the distribution of assets.

By some estimates, two out of three Americans die without a will. Some people think they don't have enough money to bother. Some don't want to confront their own mortality. Some just never get around to the chore.

Dying without a will is a big mistake because it means that the laws of your state will determine who gets what, without regard to what you might have wanted—or even, sometimes, what makes sense. For example, most states divide assets between a surviving spouse and the children, even when the children are young. So, your children may receive funds that the surviving parent needs to raise them. Worse yet, the state will very likely authorize payment, out of your estate, to someone it appoints to supervise the children's money.

Only with a will can you leave everything to your spouse, knowing that he or she will care for the children. Only with a will can you name a guardian to raise minor children if you are a single parent or if you and your spouse die in a common accident. Only with a will can you be sure that your dearly beloved partner, to whom you are not married, will get a proper share of your property.

The list goes on. Only with a will can you spread the distribution of your assets over a period of years, or delay a child's receipt of a large sum beyond the age of legal adulthood. Only with a will can you leave property to a favorite charity or a close friend. And only with a will can you make provisions to help an aging parent, or skip a generation with bequests for your grandchildren.

Have I made my point? Good.

Are You Prepared?

A will doesn't have to be complicated or expensive to prepare. If your affairs are uncomplicated and your assets are below the level where federal estate tax is an issue (under $675,000 in 2000), you may be able to prepare your own will using a self-help book or software.

If you decide to go it alone, type the document or prepare it on a computer; handwritten wills are valid in some places, but why take a chance? Appoint an executor, the person who will carry out the instructions you leave in your will (more on executors later in this chapter). Have at least two witnesses (some states require three), and don't name a beneficiary under the will as a witness.

The will does not have to be notarized, but it helps to have a "self-proving affidavit" notarized and attached to the will. This sworn statement by your witnesses, that they have indeed witnessed the signing of your will, means that they won't have to be located to swear to this fact after your death.

However, you should consult an attorney under the following circumstances:

➤ You are in a "blended" family, with his-and-hers children.

➤ You want to leave more money to one child than to another, perhaps because one has special needs.

➤ You want to set up a trust.

➤ You own real estate (other than the family home) or a business.

➤ Your estate might be subject to estate tax.

When you have your will signed and witnessed, be sure that the original document is kept where it can be found when it is needed. If you used an attorney, he or she can put it in safekeeping. If not, keep it at home in a secure location, and tell someone where it is. A safe deposit box in a bank is not

Tax Traps

Do you live together without benefit of matrimony? Don't count on your partner inheriting anything from you—unless you write a will. A spouse has protection under the law and cannot be disinherited; if a married person dies without a will, the surviving spouse automatically receives at least a portion of the estate. When an unmarried person dies without a will, the closest blood relatives will inherit. Write a will.

Tax Tips

A good source for do-it-yourselfers is Nolo Press, a publisher dedicated to self-help law. You'll find several Nolo books listed in Appendix A, "Resources," or visit them online at www.nolo.com. Nolo's WillMaker is a good software program for creating a simple will; Microsoft Lawyer is another.

generally a good place to stash a will because the box may be temporarily sealed at the death of the box-holder.

But don't put your will away and totally forget it. You should review it every few years, to make sure that it still fulfills your wishes. You should definitely review your will if one of the following takes place:

➤ You get married, divorced, or remarried.

➤ You acquire children or grandchildren, by birth or adoption.

➤ You move to another state.

➤ Tax laws are changed.

Provisions in a will may be changed by a "codicil," a signed and witnessed amendment that is a separate document to be kept with the will. If changes are extensive, however, it's best to prepare a new will. Then destroy the original and all copies of the old one to eliminate any confusion from conflicting documents at your death.

When Wills Don't Count

While it's vitally important to have a will, it's also important to know that your will won't govern the disposition of all your property. Some assets pass directly outside of your will, although they may still be included in your estate for purposes of calculating whether estate tax is due.

Tax Tips

Your will may not be read right away, so you may want to write a separate letter to your family. The letter might include your wishes about the funeral service, tell your survivors where to find important documents, and perhaps confirm that you want your granddaughter to have a particular piece of jewelry. File the letter with a list of your advisers and their phone numbers, and tell your family where it can be found.

First, anything you own jointly with the right of survivorship automatically belongs to your joint owner when you die. If you own your house with your husband or wife, he or she will own it after your death. If you have a joint checking account with a spouse or a child, that person will own the account when you are gone.

The other large category of assets that is not governed by the terms of your will is anything with a named beneficiary or beneficiaries. The proceeds of your life insurance policy will go directly to the beneficiary of that policy. Similarly, an Individual Retirement Account goes to the person designated as its beneficiary. If you fail to designate an IRA beneficiary on the account, the money may wind up in your estate. As noted in Chapter 14, "Hold On to Your Gains," this is the worst possible outcome because taxes will have to be paid almost immediately instead of deferred over a beneficiary's life expectancy.

Just Say "No"

Believe it or not, there can be times when it makes sense to turn down a bequest. Let's say that your rich uncle dies, leaving you his money with your children as backup beneficiaries in case you die first. You're still around when Uncle Moe dies, but you really don't need the money. If you accept it anyway, it will simply add to the size of your own estate—and, eventually, to the estate tax bill you pass on to your children.

If you turn down the bequest, in the eyes of the law, it's as if you did die first; the money goes directly to your children.

Disclaiming an inheritance may also make sense when a spouse has left a sizable estate directly to the other spouse, so that the estate tax exclusion described in Chapter 24 is lost. If the inheriting spouse disclaims the amount of the exclusion ($675,000 in 2000), it will go directly to the secondary beneficiaries.

If you want to turn down a bequest, first be sure that a secondary beneficiary is named in the appropriate document (the will or the beneficiary form) and that you want the property to go to that beneficiary. If you want your beneficiaries to be able to disclaim a bequest from you, be sure that you have named secondary beneficiaries. Logically, in the appropriate circumstances, your spouse is the primary beneficiary and your children are secondary beneficiaries.

A disclaimer is irrevocable and must be made within nine months of the date of death.

Tax Tips

Until recently, beneficiaries could be designated on life insurance policies, retirement accounts, and bank accounts, but that was about all. Now a majority of the states have adopted legislation letting you name beneficiaries for stocks, bonds, and mutual funds. Ask your stockbroker or mutual fund if beneficiaries can be designated in your state; if the answer is yes, request a beneficiary form, fill it out, and return it. Then these assets will automatically be transferred to your named beneficiary at your death.

Telling It Like It Is

Okay, you've set down in black and white your wishes about who gets what after you die. But you should prepare other documents so that you'll get the care you want while you're still alive and kicking. In fact, a good estate plan consists of a will plus all of the following documents:

Tax Talk

Disclaiming an inheritance is legal jargon for turning it down. It's a voluntary rejection of a specified right to inherit, and it may apply to all or part of a bequest.

➤ A durable power of attorney

➤ A living will

➤ A healthcare proxy

The durable power of attorney deals with financial matters; the living will and healthcare proxy (also called a durable power of attorney for health) focus on medical issues. They are very different but they are each important to prepare—and to keep where your loved ones can find them when the need arises.

Tax Treats

Good financial planning is "what if" planning. What would happen if you were in an accident and someone needed access to your checking account to pay your hospital bills? Or what if, late in life, a family member wanted to help because you became confused and paid some bills twice and others not at all? What if you fell into a coma and were being kept alive on a ventilator? Unless you plan today, no one will be able to act for you in this kind of situation tomorrow. Planning begins with preparing "advance directives" consisting of a durable power of attorney, a living will, and a healthcare proxy. You can name the same person to act for you in each document, or you can choose different people.

Managing the Money

A power of attorney designates someone to act for you to manage your money if you cannot. It is a legal document in which you name someone as your agent and give that person authorization to perform one or more specific tasks—or, in its broadest form, to do everything with your money that you can do.

You might grant a limited power of attorney, as an example, if you were going to be out of town and needed someone to act for you at the closing on a house. You might grant a limited power to someone who could pay bills for you while you took a trip around the world (wouldn't that be nice?).

In terms of estate planning, however, you want to do two things:

➤ Give a trusted relative or friend the right to manage all or most of your financial affairs.

➤ Make that right *durable* so that it remains legally valid if you become incapacitated and unable to act for yourself. An ordinary power of attorney becomes effective when it is signed and ends if the giver becomes incapacitated—exactly when it is most needed.

Without a durable power of attorney, your family cannot tap your assets to pay your bills. Your spouse can write checks on a joint checking account. But even your spouse will have no legal authority to sell your individually owned securities if money must be raised to pay a hospital or nursing home. The family may be forced to go to court to prove that you are incompetent to handle your own affairs so that a guardian can be named to act in your behalf. This is an unpleasant experience, one that you can spare your loved ones by signing a durable power of attorney now.

Tax Talk

Durable, in a power of attorney, means that the document remains in effect even if the giver becomes incapacitated and unable to manage his or her affairs.

You can create a durable power of attorney in one of the three following ways. They are not mutually exclusive and you may want to use more than one:

➤ For a few dollars, in most states, you can buy a standard form in a stationery store. This type of form does the job for most people. Fill it out completely, have your signature notarized, and you're all set.

➤ For a few hundred dollars, an attorney can prepare a customized form for you. This is a wise move if you have substantial assets because only a tailor-made form (in some states) will allow your designated agent to make annual gifts for you, determine the best method to distribute money from your IRA, or transfer assets to a trust.

➤ Banks and brokerage firms have their own power of attorney forms. You may want to sign these even if you have one of the other two forms because these institutions are notoriously sticky about using only documents that their own lawyers have approved.

These are some things you should know about the durable power of attorney:

➤ Because your agent can clean out your bank account, you should be sure to choose someone you trust completely. Or, leave the document with your lawyer, with instructions that it is to take effect only when two doctors confirm that you are unable to act independently.

➤ Name a backup or alternate agent in case the first is unavailable or unable to serve.

➤ Update the document periodically. Many financial institutions insist on recent authorization and won't accept old documents.

Healthy Choices

If you become unable to speak for yourself in financial matters, chances are that you will be unable to speak for yourself in making medical decisions. Here there are two documents that you must have:

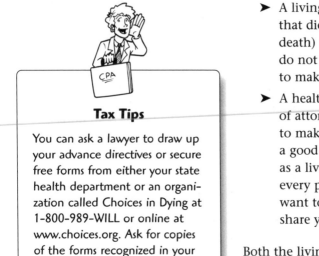

Tax Tips

You can ask a lawyer to draw up your advance directives or secure free forms from either your state health department or an organization called Choices in Dying at 1-800-989-WILL or online at www.choices.org. Ask for copies of the forms recognized in your state.

➤ A living will (not to be confused with the will that dictates the disposition of property after death) spells out exactly what care you do and do not want if you are terminally ill and unable to make your wishes known.

➤ A healthcare proxy (sometimes called a power of attorney for healthcare) designates someone to make decisions for you when you cannot. It's a good idea to have a healthcare proxy as well as a living will because it's difficult to anticipate every possible eventuality. Of course, you'll want to name someone you trust and be sure to share your feelings about end-of-life care.

Both the living will and the healthcare proxy should be in writing, signed, dated, and, in most states, witnessed by two adults. When you've completed the documents, give copies to your family and to your doctors.

Trust in These Documents

A will is the only document most people need when it comes to deciding who gets what. But if you are in a special situation (perhaps with a disabled child) or have assets over the estate tax exclusion amount ($675,000 in 2000), you may also want one or more trusts.

A trust is simply a three-party agreement in which you, as the owner of property (the donor or grantor), transfer ownership to someone else (the trustee) for the benefit of one or more third parties (the beneficiaries). You choose the trustee or trustees, and you name the beneficiary or beneficiaries.

Trusts may be "testamentary," going into effect at the death of the grantor, or "*inter vivos,*" established during the grantor's life. A trust may also be "revocable" (meaning that the grantor can revoke it or change its terms at any time) or "irrevocable" so that it can never be changed.

A testamentary trust is always irrevocable. An *inter vivos* or living trust may be either revocable or irrevocable. If a living trust is still in effect at the death of the donor, it becomes irrevocable. Only irrevocable trusts, whether established during life or at death, can remove assets from a taxable estate.

Trusts can be tailored to meet just about any specific need. Following is a brief rundown of just a few types of trusts; consult an attorney who specializes in estate planning if you think that a trust might be appropriate in your circumstances.

Tax Tips

Jointly owned property cannot be placed in a bypass trust; it passes automatically to the surviving co-owner. Bypass trusts are most effective when each spouse individually owns assets up to the amount of the federal estate tax exclusion.

➤ Bypass or credit shelter trusts let a married couple use the federal estate tax exclusion most effectively by placing up to the exclusion amount in a trust when the first partner dies. The surviving spouse usually receives the income from the trust, but the principal goes to the children, without being subject to estate tax, when the second spouse dies. This trust can be incorporated in a will; it does not need a separate trust document. It is most useful when the assets of a married couple total twice the federal estate tax exclusion (currently $675,000 per person) and when the assets can be separately titled.

➤ A qualified terminable property trust, or QTIP trust, is most often used by people married more than once who want to provide income to the surviving spouse but who then want their property to go to their own children from a prior marriage. Putting assets in a QTIP trust means that the survivor cannot then leave them to his or her own beneficiaries. In this instance, the trust assets are added to the survivor's estate and may be subject to estate taxes.

➤ A special needs trust can provide support for people who are unable to care for themselves. Parents with a disabled child, as an example, might want to put assets in trust and name a trustee to manage the assets on

Tax Tips

If you have minor children, you will name a guardian to raise them in your will. But what if that guardian shares your values and is wonderful with kids, but isn't very good with money? You can name a separate "guardian of the property" to manage the money you leave for your children until they are adults. Or, if you leave the money in trust, the trustee will fulfill that role.

behalf of the child after they are gone. But be careful to get expert advice so as not to jeopardize the dependent's eligibility for government benefits.

Generation-skipping trusts are discussed in Chapter 9, "For Grandparents Only"; life insurance trusts are described in Chapter 23, "Your Money for Your Life."

Who Represents You?

As you've noticed by now, specific people must be named to represent your interests after you are gone. One is your executor, the person who will carry out the terms of your will. The other, if you have established any trusts, is the trustee or trustees designated to administer the trust in accordance with your wishes. Both jobs are vitally important when it comes to your family's well being, so choose your agents carefully.

Your executor will be in charge of your estate until it is closed, a period that can run from about a year for the simplest estates up to three years for more complicated ones. During this time, the executor's responsibilities include the following tasks:

➤ Preparing a complete inventory of your assets, with their value at the date of your death. Appraisals may be needed to ascertain the value of real estate, partnership interests, or a family business.

➤ Collecting any money owed you in the form of salary, pension, profit-sharing, veterans' benefits, Social Security, outstanding loans, and so on.

➤ Paying any debts you leave behind, including taxes, the expenses of your last illness, and the funeral (these expenses are deducted from the value of your estate in calculating your taxable estate).

➤ Filing tax returns, including a federal estate tax return for an estate over the excluded amount, any state estate or inheritance returns that may be required, your final income tax returns, and income tax returns for each year the estate itself is in existence.

➤ Managing assets wisely, liquidating them as necessary to pay taxes.

➤ Distributing assets to the beneficiaries when the estate is closed.

Clearly, this is a time-consuming job that carries real responsibility. Although your executor should hire an accountant and a lawyer if the estate is substantial or at all complicated, he or she will be held responsible if anything goes wrong.

In making your choice, then, choose a trusted relative or friend who is knowledgeable, meticulous, and willing to serve.

Unlike executors, trustees make a long-term commitment. A trust can go on for decades, during which the trustee must supervise investments, maintain financial records, and file tax returns. Because this is so, you should be sure to name successor trustees if you rely on individuals. You also may want to select an institutional trustee, either as co-trustee with named individuals or to act alone. You may also want to include a provision permitting your beneficiaries to change trustees in the future.

Trusts for the Living

You may have noticed that I didn't mention *living trusts* in the section on trusts. Because they are heavily promoted, they need a section of their own.

Two claims frequently are made for living trusts: first, that they avoid *probate* and, second, that they let you avoid estate taxes. The first is true. The second is not. When assets are transferred to a living trust, they are outside your probate estate but are still subject to estate tax if that tax is due.

A living trust can be a very useful tool for managing assets. At the same time, the hyping of living trusts by aggressive salespeople has become so outrageous that some states have taken action. Florida has brought a lawsuit against some firms, for example, and Colorado has started a consumer education campaign against what the attorney general of that state has termed "living trust scams."

Here's the deal. Assets in a living trust do avoid probate. But probate, in most states, has been streamlined so that it costs very little. Estate administration takes just as long and is just as expensive, whether assets are owned by a living trust or transferred through a will. You could even wind up losing money for your family when the costs of setting up and funding the trust are factored in.

More important, living trusts don't save a penny in taxes. The only way to get assets out of your taxable estate is to relinquish control, to give them away irrevocably. Because living trusts are often revocable, thereby letting you continue to control the assets you've placed in the trust, they don't escape taxation.

Tax Tips

Never designate an executor in your will without consulting that person in advance. It's a time-consuming job, one that carries real responsibility. Not everyone is either willing or able to do the job. Even if your first choice as executor says "Yes," you should name a successor executor in case the first is unable to serve when the time comes.

Tax Talk

A **living trust,** as the term is most often used, is a revocable trust established during life. In legal terms **probate** is the act of proving that a will is valid.

That said, you may want to transfer assets to a living trust under these circumstances:

➤ You live in a state that does have high probate fees.

➤ You own a business and want to avoid what might be costly probate delays.

➤ You own property in two states and want to eliminate the necessity of going through probate in both states. You don't need a living trust if you own the property jointly because it will automatically belong to the survivor. But you may want to put it in trust when one of you dies.

➤ You want a contingency plan in place in case you become incapacitated and cannot handle your own affairs. A durable power of attorney is all most people need for this purpose, but people with substantial assets or more complicated affairs may do better with a living trust.

Tax Traps

If you establish a living trust, it will be totally useless unless you take the next step and transfer title to your assets so that they are owned by the trust. You must execute new deeds on real estate and change ownership of securities and bank accounts, or your living trust will be an empty shell. Even so, you still need a will to cover property that won't be owned by the trust when you die. Such property could include jewelry and other personal items, or a settlement if you die in an accident.

The neat thing about a living trust is that you can be your own trustee and continue managing your assets as you always have. Just be sure to name as successor trustee the person you want to take over when you are no longer either able or willing to continue.

The Least You Need to Know

➤ Your estate planning should include a will, a durable power of attorney, and advance directives for healthcare.

➤ A will can't direct the disposition of assets with designated beneficiaries; life insurance, as an example, goes directly to the named beneficiary.

➤ You may want to establish one or more trusts to minimize estate taxes, protect a minor child, or provide for both a current spouse and children from a previous marriage.

➤ A living trust can help you manage your money but will not reduce taxes on your estate.

➤ Choose executors and trustees who will carry out your wishes after you are gone.

Resources

Reading Materials

The following is a list of books and pamphlets you can read for more information:

Block, Ralph L. *Investing in REITs*. Princeton, NJ, Bloomberg Press, 1998.

Bochner, Arthur Berg, and Adriene Berg. *Totally Awesome Money Book for Kids and Their Parents*. New York, Newmarket Press, 1993.

Bogle, John C. *Common Sense on Mutual Funds*. New York, John Wiley & Sons, 1999.

Bogosian, Wayne G., and Dee Lee. *The Complete Idiot's Guide to 401(k) Plans*. New York, Alpha Books, 1998.

Bove, Alexander Jr. *The Complete Book of Wills, Estates, and Trusts*. New York, Owl Books, 2000.

Brenner, George D., Stephen Abramson, Barry L. Rabinovich, Stanfield Hill, and Steven K. Rabinaw. *Plan Smart, Retire Rich*. New York, McGraw-Hill, 1999.

Brenner, Lynn. *Building Your Nest Egg With Your 401(k)*. Washington Depot, CT, Investor's Press, 1995.

Chany, Kalman A. *Paying for College Without Going Broke*. Princeton, NJ, Princeton Review, 1999.

Clifford, Denis. *Nolo's Will Book*. Berkeley, CA, Nolo Press, 1997.

DeJong, David S., and Ann Gray Jakabcin. *J.K. Lasser's Year-Round Tax Strategies*. New York, Macmillan, 1998.

Downing, Neil. *Maximize Your IRA*. Chicago, IL, Dearborn Financial Publishing, 1998.

Eldred, Gary. *The Complete Guide to Second Homes*. New York, Wiley, 1999.

The Ernst & Young Tax Guide 2000. (A new edition is published each year by John Wiley & Sons.)

Fredman, Albert J., and Russ Wiles. *How Mutual Funds Work*. Paramus, NJ, Prentice Hall, 1997.

Friedman, Jack P., and Jack C. Harris. *Keys to Mortgage Financing and Refinancing*. Hauppauge, NY, Barron's Educational Series, 1993.

Garner, Robert J., et al. *Ernst & Young's Retirement Planning Guide*. New York, John Wiley & Sons, 1997.

GeRue, Gene. *How to Find Your Ideal Country Home*. New York, Warner Books, 1999.

Goldberg, Seymour. *J.K. Lasser's How to Protect Your Retirement Savings From the IRS*. New York, John Wiley & Sons, 1999.

Goldinger, Jay. *Keys to Investing in Government Securities*. Hauppauge, NY, Barron's Educational Series, 1995.

J.K. Lasser's Your Income Tax 2000. (A new edition is published each year by Macmillan USA.)

Jacobs, Sheldon. *The Handbook for No-Load Fund Investors*. Published annually by The No-Load Fund Investor, Inc., P.O. Box 318, Irvington-on-Hudson, NY 10533.

Lank, Edith. *The Home Buyer's Kit*. Chicago, IL, Dearborn Financial Publishing, 1997.

Lavine, Alan. *Your Life Insurance Options*. New York, John Wiley & Sons, 1993.

Lavine, Alan, and Gail Liberman. *The Complete Idiot's Guide to Making Money with Mutual Funds*. New York, Alpha Books, 1995.

Leider, Anna & Robert. *Don't Miss Out: The Ambitious Student's Guide to Financial Aid*. Octameron Associates, 1999. (For information on a series of useful college planning guides, write to Octameron Associates, P.O. Box 2748, Alexandria, VA 22301, or go online at www.octameron.com.)

Leimberg, Stephan R., Charles K. Plotnick, Daniel B. Evans, and Russel E. Miller. *The New Book of Trusts*. Bryn Mawr, PA, Leimberg Associates, 1997.

Lemke, Thomas P., and Gerald T. Lins. *How to Read a Mutual Fund Prospectus*. Great Falls, VA, Mercer Point Press, 1999.

Maple, Steve. *The Complete Idiot's Guide to Wills and Estates*. New York, Alpha Books, 1997.

McCormally, Kevin. *Kiplinger's Cut Your Taxes*. Washington, D.C., Kiplinger Books, 1998.

Morris, Virginia B. *Creating Retirement Income*. New York, Lightbulb Press, 1998.

O'Hara, Shelley. *The Complete Idiot's Guide to Buying and Selling a Home, Third Edition*. New York, Alpha Books, 2000.

Pearl, Jayne A. *Kids and Money*. Princeton, NJ, Bloomberg Press, 1999.

Pederson, Daniel. *Savings Bonds: When to Hold, When to Fold, and Everything in Between*. Traverse City, MI, Sage Creek Press, 1999.

Peterson's College Money Handbook. Princeton, NJ, Peterson's Guides, updated regularly.

Randolph, Mary, and Denis Clifford. *9 Ways to Avoid Estate Taxes.* Berkeley, CA, Nolo Press, 1999.

Rejnis, Ruth. *The Everything Homebuyers Book.* Holbrook, MA, Adams Media Corp., 1999.

Renberg, Werner. *All About Bond Funds.* New York, John Wiley & Sons, 1995.

Rottenberg, Dan. *The Inheritor's Handbook.* Princeton, NJ, Bloomberg Press, 1999.

Rowland, Mary. *A Commonsense Guide to Your 401(k).* Princeton, NJ, Bloomberg Press, 1997.

————. *The New Commonsense Guide to Mutual Funds.* Princeton, NJ, Bloomberg, 1998.

Sasanow, Richard. *The 401(k) Book.* New York, Henry Holt, 1996.

Sheldon Jacobs' Guide to Successful No-Load Fund Investing. Irvington-on-Hudson, NY, The No-Load Fund Investor, 1998.

Shenkman, Martin M. *The Beneficiary Workbook.* New York, John Wiley & Sons, 1998.

————. *The Complete Book of Trusts.* New York, John Wiley & Sons, 1997.

————. *Estate Planning Step by Step.* Hauppauge, NY, Barron's Educational Series, 1997.

Slesnick, Twila, and John C. Suttle. *IRAs, 401(k)s, & Other Retirement Plans: Taking Your Money Out.* Berkeley, CA, Nolo Press, 1998.

Slott, Ed. *Your Tax Questions Answered.* Plymouth, MI, Plymouth Press, 1998.

Smith, Marguerite. *Paying for Your Child's College Education.* New York, Warner Books, 1996.

Walker, David M. *Retirement Security.* New York, John Wiley & Sons, 1997.

Williamson, Gordon K. *All About Annuities.* New York, John Wiley & Sons, 1993.

Winton, E.B.B. *International Encyclopedia of Mutual Funds, Closed-End Funds and REITs.* New York, AMACOM, 1999.

Zabel, William D. *The Rich Die Richer, and You Can Too.* New York, John Wiley & Sons, 1995.

Web Sites

Here is a sampling of financial Web sites:

Finance.yahoo.com

www.bankrate.com

www.financenterinc.com/products/funds.html

www.moneycentral.com

www.morningstar.com

www.personalfund.com

www.quicken.com

AARP:

www.aarp.org/programs/retire/reaarp.html

Annuities:

www.insure.com/life/annuity

www.annuitynet.com

www.annuitiesonline.com

Bond Market Association:

www.investinginbonds.com

Consumer Information Center:

www.pueblo.gsa.gov

Employee Benefit Research Institute:

www.ebri.org

Insurance:

www.insweb.com

www.quickeninsurance.com

www.insure.com

Money market mutual funds:

www.ibcdata.com

National Association for Real Estate Investment Trusts:

www.nareit.com

Social Security:

www.ssa.gov

U.S. Department of Education, for college cost charts and financial aid information (can also be reached at 1-800-872-5327):

www.ed.gov/pubs/parents.html

www.finaid.org

www.collegeboard.org

U.S. Department of the Treasury, on savings bonds:

www.publicdebt.treas.gov/sav/savinvst.htm

Reverse Mortgages

The National Center for Home Equity Conversion, an independent nonprofit authority on reverse mortgages has information at this Web site:

www.reverse.org

The same information is available in print:

"Reverse Mortgages for Beginners: A Consumer Guide to Every Homeowner's Retirement Nest Egg." Published by NCHEC.

For the print version, mail a check for $14.95 to NCHEC, 7373 147th Street, #115, Apple Valley, MN 55124.

Call NCHEC at 1-800-732-6643 for information on reverse mortgages and a list of reverse mortgage lenders.

Securities and Exchange Commission

The Securities and Exchange Commission has the following publications that can be obtained by calling 1-800-732-0330:

"What Every Investor Should Know"

"Invest Wisely—An Introduction to Mutual Funds"

In addition, the SEC maintains many Web sites:

www.sec.gov/mfcc/mfcc-int.htm (to calculate fund·fees)

www.sec.gov/consumer/online.htm (for mutual fund information)

www.sec.gov/invkhome.htm (for investor assistance and complaints)

IRS Publications

Publications from the Internal Revenue Service are available by calling 1-800-829-3676 or by accessing this Web site:

www.irs.ustreas.gov

For a full list of IRS publications, get Publication 910, "Guide to Free Tax Services." Here are a few you may find useful, listed by publication number:

17: "Your Federal Income Tax"

525: "Taxable and Nontaxable Income"

550: "Investment Income and Expenses"

552: "Record Keeping for Individuals"

564: "Mutual Fund Distributions"

575: "Pension and Annuity Income"

590: "Individual Retirement Arrangements"

950: "Introduction to Estate and Gift Taxes"

Additional Publications

For these publications available from the Pension and Welfare Benefits Administration, call 1-800-998-7542:

"Protect Your Pension: A Quick Reference Guide"

"What You Should Know About Your Pension Rights"

To obtain the following publication, free from the Pension Benefit Guaranty Corporation, call the Consumer Information Center at 1-888-878-3256:

"A Predictable, Secure Pension for Life "

From tax publishers CCH Incorporated, you can obtain these materials at moderate cost; call 1-800-248-3248:

"New IRA Opportunities," a booklet by Jeffrey A. Hackney and Linda M. Johnson (1998)

"Social Security Benefits Including Medicare" (updated annually)

Glossary

12(b)1 fee   A fee that may be deducted from mutual fund earnings to cover distribution and marketing expenses.

401(k) plan   A defined contribution plan under which employees contribute pretax dollars and choose their investment vehicles, with the tax on investment earnings deferred until the employee takes a distribution at retirement or upon leaving the company.

403(b) plan   Similar to the 401(k) plan, but available to employees of some nonprofit organizations.

adjusted gross income (AGI)   Your gross income, minus "adjustments" for such things as contributions to a retirement plan. AGI is calculated before subtracting deductions.

annuity   A stream of regular payments, typically from a retirement plan or an annuity policy issued by a life insurance company.

ask price   The price at which a bond is offered to investors.

asset allocation   An investment strategy involving a balance among different types of investments. A simple asset allocation strategy might divide investment dollars among stocks, bonds, and cash reserves.

assets   Possessions with monetary value, including investments in securities and real estate.

back-end load   A fee charged when you sell shares in a mutual fund. Sometimes called a redemption fee or deferred sales charge.

basis point   A measure used in quoting yields on stocks and bonds. One percentage point is divided into 100 basis points; 100 basis points equal 1 percent.

bear market   An extended period during which the stock market loses more than 10 percent of its value.

beneficiary   The person named to receive the proceeds from a financial instrument such as a retirement plan or life insurance contract.

bid price   The amount a bond dealer will pay to buy a bond.

bond   An IOU, or debt instrument, representing a loan from you to the issuing corporation or agency. The issuer typically promises to pay periodic interest and to return the principal at maturity.

bull market   An extended period of sustained upward movement for the stock market.

call feature   Provision permitting the issuer of a bond to pay it off early.

capital gain/loss   Profits or losses from the sale of invested assets, based on the difference between the cost basis and the sales price.

closed-end funds   Mutual funds with a fixed number of shares, traded (like shares of stock) on an exchange.

codicil   A document making a change to a will.

collateral   Anything of value—such as your house—pledged by a borrower to secure a loan.

commercial paper   Very short-term corporate IOUs.

corporate bond   A debt instrument issued by a corporation, with taxable interest payments.

cost basis   The original price of an asset, taking into account both the transaction cost and any additions such as reinvested dividends.

coupon bond   A bond carrying detachable coupons to be submitted in exchange for periodic interest payments. Bonds are no longer issued in this form, although older coupon bonds may still exist.

credit risk   The risk that a bond issuer will not meet regularly scheduled interest payments and/or be able to repay the principal amount at maturity.

current yield   The interest income on a bond divided by the bond's current market price.

default   A bond issuer's failure to make promised payments.

deferred annuity   An annuity under which payments will begin at a future date, typically at a specified age or in a specified number of years.

defined benefit plan   A retirement plan that promises benefits based on a formula of earnings and years on the job. Traditional pension plans are defined benefit plans.

defined contribution plan   A retirement plan that spells out contributions that may be made, usually expressed as a percentage of the employee's salary. Matching contributions may be made by the employer, but the responsibility rests on the employee.

depreciation   Allocating tax deductions for income-producing property over the useful life of the property; for rental residential real estate, depreciation is calculated over 27.5 years.

discount broker   A stockbroker who arranges the purchase and sale of securities, at a lower cost than a full-service stockbroker but typically without services such as research and recommendations.

diversification   The strategy of investing in a variety of asset classes in order to reduce risk.

dollar cost averaging   Strategy of making regular fixed-dollar investments, buying more shares when prices are lower and fewer when prices are higher, thereby reducing the average cost of shares over time.

dynasty trust   A trust, permitted under the laws of several states, allowing assets to be held in trust for several generations.

estate tax   A tax on the transfer of property at death, paid from the estate before assets are distributed.

executor   The person responsible for carrying out the provisions of a will.

expense ratio   The amount paid for mutual fund operating expenses and management fees, expressed as a percentage of each shareholder's total investment.

face value   Principal amount, noted on the face of the bond, of a corporate or municipal bond.

first in, first out (FIFO)   A method for calculating tax on the sale of mutual fund shares, based on the first shares purchased being the first shares sold.

fixed-income fund   Another term for a bond mutual fund.

front-end load   A sales commission paid when shares of a mutual fund are purchased.

general obligation bond   A municipal bond backed by the full taxing power of its issuer.

gifting   The tax-free transfer of assets to another person under unified federal gift and estate tax laws.

global fund   A mutual fund that invests both overseas and at home.

guaranteed investment contract (GIC)   An investment backed by an insurance company and available through a defined contribution plan, where the return is guaranteed for a fixed period of time.

high-yield bond funds   Often called "junk bond funds," these mutual funds invest in high-yield bonds issued by companies with poor credit ratings. Investors assume a greater risk of loss in exchange for potentially greater return.

index   A measure of market performance, such as the Dow Jones Industrial Average and the Standard & Poor's 500 Index.

index fund   A mutual fund that holds the securities in a particular market index, thereby mirroring the performance of the index.

immediate annuity   A contract sold by an insurance company, offering guaranteed lifetime income starting right away.

inheritance tax   A tax, usually levied by states, on the right to inherit property; an inheritance tax is paid by the recipient of a bequest.

intermediate-term bond funds   Mutual funds that invest in bonds maturing in 5 to 10 years.

international bond funds   Mutual funds investing exclusively in debt securities issued by foreign governments or corporations.

intestate   Dying without leaving a will.

irrevocable trust   A trust that cannot be changed or canceled.

joint and survivor benefits   A pension that provides a reduced benefit to a retiree with the guarantee that the surviving spouse will receive lifetime income based on some percentage of the retiree's benefit.

junk bond funds   Sometimes called high-yield bond funds, these mutual funds invest in debt obligations of governments and corporations with poor credit ratings.

liquidity   The ease with which you can convert investments into cash with no loss of value.

living trust   A trust established during life; living trusts are usually but not always revocable.

load   A fee (commission) paid when buying or selling shares in a mutual fund.

long-term bond funds   Mutual funds investing in bonds maturing in more than 10 years.

low-load fund   A mutual fund with an up-front charge of no more than 3 percent.

lump sum distribution   A single payment from a retirement plan, based on the actuarial equivalent of making lifetime payments. A lump sum distribution may be made when an employee leaves the company or retires.

management fee   Charge paid to an investment adviser for running a mutual fund.

market correction   A sharp drop in price, typically 20 percent or more.

market value   The prevailing market price of an asset, such as real estate or securities.

markup   The profit on a bond transaction.

maturity date   The date on which the principal amount of a bond is repaid to investors.

money market mutual fund   Mutual funds that invest in short-term securities such as U.S. Treasury bills, commercial paper, and certificates of deposit.

Morningstar   A research company that rates the relative performance of mutual funds.

municipal bonds   Debt obligations issued by state or local government entities, often—but not always—free of federal and state income tax.

net asset value   The NAV, reported in newspaper mutual fund columns, is the price per share determined by dividing the fund's assets (after liabilities are subtracted) by the number of shares.

net worth   The extent to which your assets (what you own) exceed your liabilities (what you owe).

nonqualified plans   These plans do not receive favorable tax treatment because they do not meet the requirements of the Internal Revenue Service.

par   The face value—not the market value—of a security at the time it is issued.

passive loss   For tax purposes, a passive loss is from investments, such as real estate, in which taxpayers don't actively participate. Passive losses may be written off only against income from other passive investments.

phantom amount/income   Money you do not actually receive but which is nonetheless subject to income tax. An example is the interest on taxable zero-coupon bonds.

points   Additional fees on a mortgage, with each point representing 1 percent of the amount of the mortgage loan.

portfolio manager   The individual responsible for making mutual fund investment decisions.

premium   The amount that a bond sells for above par (over 100).

pre-refunded bonds   Municipal bonds backed by an escrow fund consisting of U.S. Treasuries.

principal   The original dollar amount of a fixed-income investment such as a bond. This is the amount returned to the investor at maturity.

principal residence   Your home for tax purposes. If you own just one home, it's where you live. If you own more than one home, it's where you spend most of your time.

probate   The process of having a will approved by the court.

prospectus   Official document describing a mutual fund's holdings, objectives, and fees.

qualified plans   These plans receive favorable tax treatment, including the deferral of income tax on investment earnings until the money is distributed.

redemption   The process of liquidating an investor's holdings in a mutual fund.

return of capital   Mutual fund distributions that are not taxable because they represent a return of part of your investment.

revenue bond   A bond issued by a city, county, or state for a specific purpose. A revenue bond issued for the construction of a toll bridge will pay interest on the bond from the tolls.

revocable trust   A trust that can be changed or revoked.

rollover   Movement of investments from one tax-sheltered plan to another, with favorable tax treatment if the money is moved directly from plan to plan.

Schedule D   The tax form, attached to your federal income tax return, on which capital gains and losses are reported to the Internal Revenue Service.

secondary market   Where securities can be bought and sold after their original issue date.

Section 529 plans   State-sponsored plans allowing tax-deferred savings for college; these may be either prepaid tuition plans or college savings plans.

single-state municipal bond funds   Mutual funds investing in the bonds of a single state. Residents of that state typically enjoy exemption from both federal and state taxes on interest income.

spread   The difference between what a broker/dealer pays for a bond and the price at which it is sold to an investor.

stripped treasuries   An investment created when a brokerage firm separates a Treasury bond into a series of certificates representing either interest or principal.

tax credit   A dollar-for-dollar reduction in taxes.

tax deduction   An allowable expense (such as mortgage interest and property taxes) subtracted from adjusted gross income to arrive at taxable income.

tax shelter   Partnerships designed to shelter income from taxation.

taxable bond funds   Bond mutual funds in which interest is subject to income tax.

taxable income   The amount of income, after subtracting deductions and exemptions, that is subject to income tax.

tax-deferred   Income that is earned but not taxed until a later date. Tax-deferred assets include Individual Retirement Accounts, life insurance policies, EE-bonds, and annuities.

tender   An offer to buy.

total return   The total change in value of an investment, including reinvestment of all dividends and capital appreciation.

Treasury obligations   Bills, notes, and bonds issued by Uncle Sam. The interest is exempt from state and local income taxes, but not from federal income tax.

trust   A legal document by which assets are managed for the benefit of a third party (the beneficiary).

trustee   The person who carries out the provisions of a trust.

turnover rate   The rate at which a mutual fund buys and sells securities.

Uniform Gift to Minors Act and **Uniform Transfers to Minors Act**   Both are vehicles for custodial accounts for children; assets transferred to an UGMA or an UTMA belong to the child.

variable annuity   An annuity with benefits pegged to the performance of underlying investments chosen by the insured.

vested   Entitled to retirement plan contributions made by an employer.

volatility   Fluctuations in market value; a security or mutual fund with great volatility has wide fluctuations between high and low prices.

yield   Dividend and/or interest earnings on an investment, typically expressed as a percentage.

yield to maturity   The amount earned on a bond over its lifetime, with each interest payment reinvested at the same interest rate.

zero coupon bonds and **bond funds**   Debt obligations that do not pay regular interest but that pay both accumulated interest and principal at maturity.

Index

J